EROS
——plus——
Massacre

EROS
—— plus ——

Massacre

AN INTRODUCTION TO THE
JAPANESE NEW WAVE CINEMA

David Desser

Indiana University Press

BLOOMINGTON AND INDIANAPOLIS

Manufactured in the United States of America

Library of Congress Cataloging-in-Publication Data
Desser, David.
  Eros plus massacre.

  Filmography: p.
  Bibliography: p.
  Includes index.
  1. Motion-pictures—Japan.   I. Title.
PN1993.5.J3D47   1988   791.43'0952   87–45245
ISBN   0–253–31961–7
ISBN   0–253–20469–0 (pbk.)
1 2 3 4 5 92 91 90 89 88

Contents

Illustrations of Scenes from . . .

Acknowledgments

A project like this, which relies so strongly on primary research into films not readily available, naturally proved quite challenging. For their aid in helping me meet that challenge, to the extent that I was able, I would like to thank the following people.

In Japan I would like to thank Mr. Maruo Sadama and his helpful staff at the National Film Center; Mr. Shimizu Akira of the Japan Film Library Council/Kawakita Archives; the Audio-Visual Department of the Japan Foundation in Tokyo, especially Mr. Ishida Takashi; Ms. Tomiyama Katsue and her extremely kind staff at Image Forum; and Mr. Mizuno Katsuhiro of Shochiku Studios. I would also like very much to thank the staff of the International House of Japan (*Kokusai bunka kaikan*). Some of my fellow scholars at the International House helped me in ways they might not realize: Ted Hoffman, Alvin Coox, and Jill Kleinberg. I would also like to thank Lisa Spalding for her extraordinary kindness and help in the last stages of this project—I wish we had met sooner!

For their time and effort on my behalf I would like to thank film directors Yoshida Yoshishige, Shinoda Masahiro, Oshima Nagisa, Kinoshita Keisuke, Ogawa Shinsuke and Tsuchimoto Noriaki. Their brilliance as filmmakers is equalled by their extraordinary kindness and generosity.

I would like to acknowledge the help and encouragement of Donald Richie, whose expertise in Japanese Cinema is matched by his knowledge of Tokyo's finest Indian restaurants. I would especially like to thank two people without whom this project might simply have run aground: Ms. Hirano Kyoko, an emerging important Japanese film scholar in her own right, who gave of herself to help this book come to life; and Mr. Yokobori Koji, who showed me genuine friendship and warmth, who made a *gaijin* feel at home.

In the U.S. I would like to thank Ms. Nancy Goldman of the Pacific Film Archive for her willingness to work with me under trying circumstances. I would also like to thank New Yorker Films for lending me some prints for close study; and Films Inc. for reducing their prices on some films to aid the cause of scholarship.

For their considerable expertise and willingness to share some of it with me, I would like to thank David Goodman, Kazuko Fujimoto Goodman, Keiko McDonald (an extra-special thank you), and David Owens. I can also not neglect to thank Ruth Hottell for her help with French sources and Hiroyo Demers for her invaluable aid in some of the Japanese materials. Robert Carringer made some extremely helpful suggestions while Arthur Nolletti and Dana Polan provided encouragement as did, most crucially, my wife Cathleen.

This project was immensely aided by a grant from the National Endowment for the Humanities Summer Stipend, and by grants from the University of Illinois Research Board, Center for Asian Studies, the College of LAS Fund; and the Unit for Cinema Studies—a heartfelt thanks is owed to Edwin Jahiel, Director and Richard Leskosky, Assistant Director.

Stills reprinted by permission of Shochiku Studios and the Japan Film Library Council.

A note on Japanese names: Japanese names are presented in the Japanese style, last name first, given name second. This reflects a basic respect for Japanese language and culture. For ease of printing, I have eliminated the system of macrons used in transliterating Japanese into English (macrons are used in Asian studies scholarly journals, but are not typically used in film studies publications).

A note on Film titles: The Japanese title of a film is typically given first followed in parentheses by the most commonly used American title, if there is one. In the case of a film never released in the U.S. I have provided a translation title. In some instances, there are films which have had no real U.S. release but which do have an English-language title. In these instances, I typically provide a translation of the Japanese title and, if the English title differs, I indicate this with "aka" (also known as). Such is the case, too, with films that are known by more than one title which have similarly had no major U.S. release or distribution by which one title or another has entered into common usage. In the filmography section, I indicate whether the English title is the American release title or a translation title provided by me.

E R O S
—— plus ——
Massacre

Introduction

In 1959, Jean-Luc Godard released *A bout de souffle* (*Breathless*), a film which inaugurated a "New Wave" of filmmaking in France and which also gave cinematic form to a new kind of film hero. Alienated, disaffected, violent, a product of the media (especially cinema), this new hero was an accurate harbinger of the youthful rebellions and protests that rocked France and the Western world a little later, in the '60s.

In 1959, Oshima Nagisa released *Ai to kibo no machi* (*A Town of Love and Hope*), the story of a slum youth who commits crimes with the same remorselessness as Godard's protagonist. A new wave of filmmaking struck Japan, too, issuing challenges to established social and cinematic practice. The rebelliousness manifest in the West's young could be attributed to the natural proclivities of youth, to adolescent high spirits among the "baby boom" generation. In Japan, however, such stirrings were both more shocking and significant. In a society which prizes group identity, stability, respect for elders and their traditions, and a certain reluctance to express one's feelings publicly, the events of the 1960s, presaged by Oshima's film, indicated a potentially radical rethinking of Japanese society.

Whereas the French *nouvelle vague* has been somewhat scrupulously examined from a variety of viewpoints, there as yet has existed no full-length treatment in English (and precious little in Japanese) of the Japanese New Wave of the 1960s. Part of this is due to American insularity as well as our continuing puzzlement about Japan and the Orient. Part of this is also due, undeniably and tragically, to the unavailability of so many of the Japanese New Wave films for nontheatrical rental or study. But the main reason, perhaps, that the Japanese New Wave cinema has remained unexamined is that few film specialists seem willing to investigate the full range of the phenomenon. The Japanese New Wave films are not simply political tracts or historical records; nor, on the other hand, are they merely aesthetic texts which intersect with currently fashionable areas of film theory and criticism. Like the French New Wave, the Japanese cinema of the period bears a relationship to its cultural/political context and to the cinematic past from which it arises and rebels.

The most facile analyses of the Japanese New Wave cinema of the 1960s attribute its origins to a reaction against the previous generations of Japanese filmmakers. Oshima Nagisa, Shinoda Masahiro, and Imamaura Shohei (probably the best known of the New Wave directors in the U.S.) are thus understood to be rebelling against the styles of Ozu Yasujiro and Mizoguchi Kenji, and the themes of Kurosawa Akira and Kinoshita Keisuke. This kind of closed dialectic of film history, while it has a modicum of merit, will not suffice to explain the rigorous, insightful, insistent, and often angry challenges the best of the New Wave films and filmmakers issued to Japanese society.

While few film scholars read the New Wave in such overly reductive terms, those who have dealt in passing with the New Wave simply acknowledge the sociocultural context and then proceed to examine the films from their more preferred, narrow viewpoint. Noel Burch, for instance, in his essay, "Nagisa Oshima and Japanese Cinema in the 60s," notes the manner in which the New Wave tried to radicalize the salient features of the previous generations in terms of both form and content. He then goes on to acknowledge the difficulty a Westerner has in understanding radical Japanese politics for the way in which traditional Japanese values underlie its ideologies. With that caveat in place, Burch feels free to discuss the films (mostly Oshima's) in purely formal terms.[1] Implicit in Burch's statement is the need to understand and come to terms with Japanese politics of the period in order to understand the films produced. Implicit as well, is the concomitant need to recognize and come to terms with the scope of Japanese film history, and to recognize the links between this film history and its place within Japan's cultural evolution.

The ideological purpose of this volume, then, as I have conceived and written it, is to try and bring historical specificity to the Japanese New Wave cinema and to place it within the wider discourses of historical, political, social, and cultural studies. I am by no means claiming that the kind of "historical-cultural" approach utilized here is the best and only way to study the Japanese New Wave movement. Not only would that be wildly pretentious, it would be wrong. Any perspective which sheds genuine light on the movement or its components is a welcome and valuable one. I am not one of those who feels the need to disparage approaches to film that I do not find appealing; I do not need to try and negate the works of others to justify my own. I maintain only that the manner in which I have chosen to examine and explain aspects of the Japanese New Wave cinema fills a certain gap in the critical literature. Many individual critical works have demonstrated, for instance, the importance of individual New Wave directors in terms of the challenge they pose to dominant Film theory and practice. Other critics have demonstrated the particular manner in which certain filmic structures have been uniquely handled in particular films. Still other writings have taken a "psychoanalytical" approach and demonstrated the significance of certain films for an understanding of how the self is constructed in culture and cinema. This study simply seeks to situate the New Wave within a particular historical, political, and cultural context—something that has not yet been attempted.

One particular manner in which I would like to try and approach the Japanese New Wave is to attempt to return to its origins, to return to its immediacy. Too many approaches to the Japanese cinema in general have tended to dehistoricize it. Studies which show Japanese cinema's continuity with traditional Japanese culture, studies which attempt to prove Oshima's continuity with Ozu, studies which seek to claim that the Japanese cinema is a unified field (against which it may be opposed to another unified field) deny individual films and filmmakers any political importance, any sense of cultural *engagement* with a historical moment. The purpose of this study is, above all else, to return us to an era, the 1960s primarily, and show how certain Japanese filmmakers used cinema as a tool, a weapon in a cultural struggle.

This notion of a cultural struggle has implications beyond the scope of this book, for we must recognize that if filmmakers on and of the Left can, and have, used cinema as a weapon, so too, the Right has made use of this medium for ideological ends. Thus to return, as it were, to the 1960s in Japan is also to reinvigorate the decade in the West. The 1960s has come in for a significant rewriting by the culture of Reaganism, a rewriting aided in no small measure by theatrical films which have, for instance, rewritten the Vietnam War. In this sense, to look at the Japanese cinema is to ask for a look again at the decade in the U.S.

This study, then, is about the films of the 1960s as expressions of cultural concerns in the 1960s. Thus, an appreciation of the films, as aesthetic or political texts, can only come about through an understanding of their place within this particular moment. This is not a radical claim. Few in the U.S. would deny that a full appreciation of many films of the 1930s would require a little contextualizing. John Ford's *Young Mr. Lincoln* may not be as directly applicable to 1939 as the famous *Cahiers du Cinema* essay on it would like to try and insist, but some knowledge of the '30s, and certainly a good deal of knowledge about Abraham Lincoln go a long way toward a full appreciation of the film, even if it still emerges as a "timeless masterpiece." (In this case, it emerges as *also* a timeless work of American film art.) A knowledge of the events of May-June 1960 is fundamental to any appreciation of the emergence of the Japanese New Wave; a film like Yoshida's *Kaigenrei* (*Martial Law*, 1973; aka *Coup d'etat*) not only grows out of the New Wave, but requires a quite significant amount of knowledge about Japan in the 1930s in telling a fanciful story about the famous *ni-ni-roku* (February 26) Incident of 1936. It is perhaps this sort of unfamiliarity, to be sure, with Japanese history and culture which prevents many from fully appreciating the films. I feel, therefore, that this study is, among other things, an *annotation* of the New Wave.

Historicizing and contextualizing the New Wave cinema in Japan also returns to Japanese cinema its own identity. Judging the Japanese cinema in terms of Hollywood, even to isolate its divergences, still puts it in an inferior position (the position of difference) and thus consigns it to the half-light of the imaginary (to adopt Laura Mulvey's memorable phrase). Superficial comparisons between the Japanese New Wave cinema and the French New Wave, typically to imply greater integrity to the latter, have served the cultural cliché that the Japanese are merely great imitators, that they do nothing original. Comparisons of Oshima to Godard, of Yoshida to Antonioni, while they have some justification (masterfully deflated by Oshima who responded to the question, "Which are the subjects you have in common with Godard?" with the Zen-like answer, "One is politics and the other is cinema"[2]), deny Oshima and Yoshida not necessarily originality (a questionable value, in any case) but specificity. To see the Japanese New Wave as an imitation of the French New Wave (an impossibility since they arose simultaneously) fails to see the Japanese context out of which the movement arose. Few make the claim that the British New Wave, the "Angry Young Men Movement" in film, was a response to or an imitation of the French New Wave, for it is clear that films like *Look Back in Anger* (1958), *Room at the Top* (1959), *Saturday Night and Sunday Morning* (1960), and *A Taste of Honey* (1961), among others, have a specifically British context and grow out of a linked series of historical and cinematic events and movements. While the Japanese New Wave did draw benefits from the French New Wave, mainly in the form of a handy journalistic label which could be applied to it (the *"nuberu bagu"* from the Japanese pronunciation of the French term), it nevertheless possesses a high degree of integrity and specificity. And it is these aspects that this book will constantly elaborate.

The Japanese New Wave is here defined as films produced and/or released in the wake of Oshima's *A Town of Love and Hope*, films which take an overtly political stance in a general way or toward a specific issue, utilizing a deliberately disjunctive form compared to previous filmic norms in Japan. The New Wave is conceived of as an "avant-garde movement," using the terms as defined by Renato Poggioli in *The Theory of the Avant-Garde*. Poggioli believes that "a movement is constituted primarily to obtain a positive result, for a concrete end."[3] In this respect, the Japanese New Wave movement, while it did not necessarily define its concrete ends, may be said to have been concerned with creating a film content and form capable of revealing the contradictions within Japanese society and with isolating the culture's increasingly materialist values and its imperialist alliances. The "avant-garde" component is to be taken in two ways: as being in the vanguard of a new social movement, and as utilizing artistic strategies of a new and challenging nature. Poggioli's realization that "the avant-garde, like any culture, can only flower in a climate where political liberty triumphs, even if it often assumes an hostile pose toward democratic and liberal society,"[4] is appropriate to the Japanese context. The sometimes virulent, satiric, black-comic denunciations of aspects of mainstream Japanese culture and ideology, reminiscent of '60s radicals in the U.S. (with their cries of "Amerika"), arose within the context of a relatively liberal, mostly censorship-free society.

The notion that the New Wave is a movement is important in terms of defining it against the idea that it constituted a school, for the New Wave rejected the "school" ideology implicitly.

> The school notion presupposes a master and a method, the criterion of tradition and the principle of authority. It does not take account of history, only of time (in terms of the possibility and necessity of handing on to posterity a system to work by, a series of technical secrets endowed with a vitality apparently immune to any change or metamorphosis: *ars longa, vita brevis*). The school, then, is preeminently static and classical, while the movement is essentially dynamic and romantic. Where the school presupposes disciples consecrated to a transcendent end, the followers of a movement always work in terms of an end immanent in the movement itself. . . . The movement . . . conceives of culture not as an increment but as creation—or, at least, as a center of activity and energy.[5]

This notion applies most particularly to the Japanese situation. The "school" idea in Japanese cinema was especially apparent in the form of the assistant-director system out of which virtually all film directors arose. As we will see later, the rebellion from, or at least the transformation of, this system was an important component of the New Wave movement.

Another aspect of Poggioli's differentiation between schools and movements also sheds light on the Japanese New Wave movement: " . . . movement is differentiated from schools by that passion and conceit which seek to transcend the limitation of art and reach out to all areas of culture and civilization."[6] The New Wave was part of a clarion call to arms on the part of politically committed artists working in a variety of media; filmmakers perhaps felt themselves especially able to work toward the movement's ends by virtue of film's status as a popular art.

The assumption that an avant-garde artistic movement *already* has a political dimension was as crucial to the Japanese New Wave as it had been to the Russian Revolutionary cinema of the 1920s, the theatrical theories of Bertolt Brecht, and the French *nouvelle vague*, especially after 1968, with Jean-Luc Godard entering into the *"Dziga-Vertov"* collective. Poggioli sees something suspect in the idea of formal radicalism being equal to political radicalism and one should certainly share a basic mistrust of this facile equation.[7] We would thus maintain that the Japanese New Wave cinema moves beyond the merely formally radical, or avant-garde, that many Western critics are fond of claiming is already political. This is a problematic area in regard to the Japanese cinema, which by certain Western standards is already "radical" juxtaposed to the Hollywood classical style. The canonization of Ozu and Mizoguchi in the West is in no small measure a function of this implicit radicalism or "modernism" (I am in this instance equating the two). Paul Willemen has pointed out "that nearly all Japanese films can be said to be modernist in some way or other if tested against the Hollywood norm . . . ," but that within the Japanese context, Ozu's works are seen "as precisely Japanese classics. Japanese readings have always recognized the systematic set of difference [of his cinema], but located them as a form of traditionalism."[8] To be sure, the Russian Formalist idea of *ostranenie* (making strange) has a *potentially* political dimension, but this notion was intended to help define art, to separate the artistic from the prosaic. Avant-garde art, then, merely, if you will, "makes stranger." The concept of ostranenie was extended by Brecht into the political realm. Dana Polan has maintained that "Brecht . . . sees a difference between art and political art. Art, [Brecht] argues, automatically embodies a distancing, a making strange. But there's nothing yet socially distancing about that. Brecht continually emphasizes the way bourgeois theatre has become acceptable to audiences despite its strangeness to them."[9] Thus, political art must do more than make strange the level of its own signification—it must in some ways address the social signified; it must, simply, be about something political.

It should be stressed that the avant-garde/political cinema that constitutes the Japanese New Wave movement occurred within a mainstream context. With the exception of the early features directed by Hani Susumu, all the major films within the initiating moments of the New Wave were produced at a major commercial film studio, Shochiku studios in particular. It means that the movement arose within the confines of one of the world's most rigidly commercial cinemas. It distinguishes the Japanese New Wave from its radical counterparts in France and England, whose New Waves came from the ranks of independent filmmaking or were aided by government subsidies. (The origins of the British Free Cinema and its "Angry Young Men" cycle are greatly owed to the British Film Institute.) Similarly, the Polish radical cinema of the late '50s, which Japanese film historians and New Wave directors themselves have claimed was more immediately influential on the early Japanese New Wave than the French *nouvelle vague*,[10] was entirely produced without commercial restraints. In the case of the United States, whose New Wave (the "Hollywood Renaisance" of 1967–72) could be understood as equally commercial as Japan's, filmmakers were aided by the increasing need for independent productions and, in any case were rarely as overtly political and stylistically radical as the Japanese New Wave directors. And while independent production was indeed the mode chosen by almost all the New Wave directors in Japan, it was only *after* the movement was inaugurated within commercial circumstances.

The commercial, mainstream origins of the New Wave, by which I basically mean the contract-director status of the major filmmakers, has implications for the resultant film practice of the movement. Immediately striking to the viewer is the virtual ubiquity of CinemaScope photography. Yoshida Yoshishige explains this reliance on CinemaScope quite simply: "Shochiku owned the theatres and spent the money equipping them with CinemaScope lenses, making CinemaScope films a virtual requirement."[11] CinemaScope was introduced in Japan, according to J.L. Anderson and Donald Richie, in 1953 for the showing of *The Robe*; by the end of 1955, five hundred theatres were equipped with anamorphic lenses and by the end of 1956, over a thousand theatres had CinemaScope lenses. However, Anderson and Richie note that these theatres "showed nothing but foreign films."[12] The end of 1956 and the beginning of 1957 saw the production of Japanese features in various wide-screen formats, the bulk of which required anamorphic lenses. Shintoho and Toei pioneered in-house CinemaScope productions, with Toei going all out in the format by equipping its own theatres and aiding its contract theatres in the purchase of lenses. Soon after, Toho and Shochiku adopted the format, with Nikkatsu hard on their heels.[13]

Anderson and Richie report that the studios' impetus behind the wholesale adoption of wide screen (CinemaScope and, in the case of Daiei, VistaVision) was "to get the jump on television." Television was just beginning to make inroads into Japanese homes; the studios tried to use wide screen to prevent a precipitous decline when television increased its presence. Anderson and Richie believe, however, that wide screen "was particularly troublesome to Japanese filmmakers because the proportions did not lend themselves well to Japanese sets."[14] This assertion seems suspect. For Kurosawa Akira, the CinemaScope ratio posed no problems; he used the format for the first time in 1958 with *Kakushi toride no san akunin* (*The Hidden Fortress*), an old-fashioned action picture which reveled in the wide-open spaces of the wide screen.[15] Kinoshita Keisuke solved the problem of scope with his first wide-screen effort, *Narayama bushi-ko* (*The Ballad of Narayama*, 1958), by deliberately theatricalizing his sets in Kabuki style, which lends itself well to CinemaScope photography with its primarily horizontal staging of action. And their contention of the troublesomeness of Japanese interiors for CinemaScope is belied by Ichikawa Kon's first wide-screen film, *Enjo* (*Conflagration*, 1958, produced at Daiei in Cinema-Scope, not VistaVision).

By 1960, almost every Japanese film was made in wide screen, typically CinemaScope. While the old master, Ozu, never turned to CinemaScope, that other venerable master, Naruse Mikio, did. Kurosawa worked exclusively in CinemaScope following *The Hidden Fortress* until 1970, while Kobayashi Masaki, something of a Kurosawa protégé, also mastered the wide screen and favored the ratio beginning in the late '50s. It is difficult to say, contrary to Anderson and Richie, whether Japanese directors quickly mastered CinemaScope (and films like *Yojimbo*, *Seppuku*, and *An Actor's Revenge*, among others one could name show this mastery beyond a doubt) or whether mastery was forced upon them by the studios' wholesale adoption of its use. Whatever the case, the New Wave directors found themselves working in CinemaScope. Of course, the particular utilization of Cinema-Scope—hand-held long takes for Oshima, radically decentered compositions for Yoshida, a deceptive classicism for Shinoda—demonstrate the deconstructive intentions and the sometimes radical departures the New Wave would bring to the Japanese cinema. In fact, as the decade of the '60s wore on, many directors, Oshima and Shinoda included, abandoned CinemaScope as a way of going against the mainstream.

The question of color cinematography seems to have been less determined by the studios across the board. While almost everything at Nikkatsu, for instance, was produced in color, other studios permitted both color and black-and-white films to flourish. Oshima's early films at Shochiku were all in color; he did not turn primarily to black and white until the late '60s. Yoshida, on the other hand, preferred black and white during his entire career (at least through 1973)—only four of his sixteen films of the period through '73 utilized color photography. All the independently produced films of Hani were black and white, but his choice, perhaps, was a budgetary consideration.

Hani's independent status, it should be noted, was rather anomalous. The lack of independent production in the late '50s-early '60s was a function of the structure of the Japanese motion picture industry. Unlike their American counterparts following the Second World War, Japanese studios maintained control of the major phases of the industry—production, distribution, and exhibition. The most successful companies of the postwar era controlled the largest number of theatres, either through outright ownership or exclusivity contracts. Even into the 1980s, despite the severe decline in the quality of film production, Shochiku, Toho, and Toei retain a very high visibility and status on the strength of their prestigious theatres. It would seem that a radical film movement was unlikely to arise from within such a rigidly commercial context.

In a sense, the New Wave arose from within the commercial sphere only out of sheer luck. Despite the turn to wide-screen productions, the motion picture audience began to drop off in numbers in the late '50s; the increasing encroachment of television was the major factor in this decline. In 1960, television had begun to make its presence felt in a significant manner; by 1965, it had penetrated approximately 60 percent of all Japanese homes; by 1970, 95 percent of all Japanese homes had television.[16] Attendance at movies peaked in 1958 at 1,127,000,000; in 1960, the figure was down to a still massive 1,014,000,000. By 1963, however, attendance had been cut almost in half to 511,000,000; in 1965, it dropped off to 373,000,000, and by 1970, the depressing statistic was a mere 253,000,000 moviegoers per year. (Unfortunately, the bad news for moviemakers did not end in 1970. In 1975, attendance stabilized at only 170,000,000 per year.) As might be predicted, the number of movie theatres fell right along with attendance: from 7,457 cinemas in 1960 to 3,246 in 1970.[17] (By 1975, the number of theatres stabilized at 2,400.[18]) As attendance fell and theatres closed, film production declined from 547 films in 1960 to 423 films in 1970;[19] by 1978, this number stabilized at 340, the bulk of which were "pink movies, *roman poruno*, and other marginal sex exploitation pictures."[20] To try and counter this grim tide, studios tried a number of things besides wide screen, and among them was the promotion of younger assistants to the ranks of directors. This is the beginning of the New Wave. Unfortunately, as the figures indicate, it is clear that the New Wave, whatever else it did or did not do, did not save the movies from the onslaught of television.

Kinoshita Keisuke, one of Shochiku's most important directors at the start of the 1960s, attributes the precipitous decline in moviegoing, in large measure, to the New Wave itself. Kinoshita feels that movie audiences became dispirited by the attitudes and films of these younger directors; that the New Wave filmmakers shirked their responsibility to society by making films critical of the culture and highly challenging in their style.[21] While the temptation might be to reject this comment out of hand, in Kinoshita's defense, it is certainly the case that even in a highly literate, artistically vital country like Japan, no avant-garde movement is going to achieve the kind of massive popularity that movies require to maintain a successful and profitable industry. On the other hand, it is also the case that the New Wave never achieved anything like a majority in terms of numbers of films produced. Only 10 percent (and even that is a generous figure) of the films in any given year in the 1960's could be linked to the New Wave. It is therefore clear that the decline in attendance was due to an overall disenchantment with the cinema, probably in its competitition with television; and Japan's situation reflects a worldwide decline in movie audiences in nations with television.

The drop in attendance, and the subsequent decline in commercial production, was the major factor enabling the New Wave directors to escape their strictly commercial confines and enter into independent production. By the middle of the 1960s, almost every major New Wave director had formed his own production company, while the major studios were forced to become merely the distributors and/or exhibitors of the films by their former contract workers. (Shochiku, for instance, maintained a relationship with their former directorial employees and distributed a number of New Wave films for independent directors. Ironically, the decline in in-house production at Shochiku was brought about in the 1960s not only by the death of Ozu in 1963, but by the temporary abandonment of feature film-making in favor of television by Kinoshita Keisuke.) The stranglehold on the industry by the major studios eventually lessened to the point that independent distribution and exhibition companies were formed. The most important of these was the Art Theatre Guild which began primarily in exhibition in 1962, and produced one film that year. The ATG experienced a temporary setback in production, but continued in exhibition, showing exclusively foreign films, many of a political nature from France, Poland, Italy, the U.K., and the U.S. While they continued to exhibit in a centrally located Tokyo theatre, they reentered production in 1967. Their typical policy was to put up half the production budget in partnership with a director's own company, which put up the other half. The importance of the ATG in sustaining the New Wave cannot be overestimated. Oshima's films from 1968 through 1972 were ATG co-productions/distributions, while Shinoda's *Double Suicide*, Hani's *The Inferno of First Love*, and Yoshida's *Eros plus Massacre* (three crucial texts of the movement), among others, were similarly ATG partnerships.

That the New Wave did not sustain itself for very long, even with the rise of independent production, distribution, and exhibition, should not come as any great surprise, nor in any way disgrace the movement's artistic vitality. No national New Wave was able to sustain itself; one might say that the very idea of "new" and "wave" implies a short, sudden burst. In the case of the Japanese New Wave, the political goals which gave life to the movement came to seem increasingly out of reach, mirroring the shift in the quality and quantity of political activity at the end of the decade of the '60s. While there is nothing necessarily determinig that the beginning of a new decade would lead to new cinematic and political movements, and that the end of the decade would see a decline in these movements, in Japan it happens that 1960 and 1970 stand at the poles of a rise and fall of an avant-garde wave. As chapters 1 and 7 will show, the New Wave was intimately linked to events in 1960 and 1970, respectively.

The remainder of this study is organized as a survey of the major motifs and concerns of the Japanese New Wave. While studies of many New Wave movements, such as the French and German, have chosen to examine the movements by isolating their major directors, I have avoided that strategy in an effort to show how the New Wave was a *movement* and not just a group of new and different filmmakers who happened to work at the same time. Within each individual chapter, the contributions of particular directors are examined as a way of organizing the chapter, but the intention is to show how different directors handled the same set of issues and motifs.

While directorial organization is eschewed, it is important to recognize that individual filmmakers, represented by a number of their most important works, constitute the New Wave movement as it is here conceived and defined. Oshima Nagisa, by any standard, must be acclaimed as the movement's major figure by virtue of the immediate and extraordinary influence he had at its originating moments, and the international status he has since achieved. The same may be said, to a lesser extent, of Imamura Shohei, whose prestige in the early 1960s was significant, and whose reputation has since solidified in Japan and the U.S. (That he is less well known than Oshima may be attributed to the relatively recent availability of his films in non-theatrical formats). Hani Susumu was of almost equal importance in setting the tone for the New Wave in the early '60s. He was unable to sustain his status into the latter part of the decade, but he remained a central figure of the movement throughout the '60s.

Shinoda Masahiro and Yoshida Yoshishige, along with Oshima, inaugurated what was then called the New Wave (*nuberu bagu*) when they were all young directors at Shochiku studios. Their works of the '60s exemplify what is most politically and formally significant about the movement. Shinoda is fairly well known in the West, mainly by virtue of his films from the middle '60s and after; Yoshida, sad to say, is virtually unknown in the West. A handful of his films seem to me as good as virtually any of the period.

A handful of directors constitute the remaining major figures of the movement and for the most part they are unknown to the West. Suzuki Seijun, whose firing from Nikkatsu studios in 1968 became a *cause célèbre*, is among the most interesting directors of the period. Rarely as deliberately political as his contemporaries in the movement, he was as formally challenging, as *disruptive*, as any of them. Masumura Yasuzo, whose *Kuchizuke* (*Kisses*, 1957) was an important precursor to the New Wave, might be said to stand alongside of the movement in the '60s. While his films are often thematically appropriate, their style is formally closer to the works of Kobayashi and Ichikawa than to Oshima or Yoshida. The style and themes of Wakamatsu Koji, the most genuinely controversial figure of the period, link him centrally to the New Wave, but the enormity of his output prevents a full appreciation of his place within it.[22] The well-known director Teshigahara Hiroshi must be linked to the New Wave, but the sparsity of his output and the singular nature of his films makes him a special case.

The chapter titles of the remainder of this work (as the title of the work itself) are derived from individual films which may be said to be paradigmatic of the specific chapter's main theme. Thus, Chapter 1, "Night and Fog in Japan," owes its title to Oshima's film which deals explicitly with the emerging separation of a new generation in Japan from its predecessors. The chapter outlines a series of narrative strategies which came to dominate a particular period of Japanese cinematic history, and relates these narrative strategies to contemporary modes of literary or theatrical production to show how ideological paradigms are reflected in artistic texts. Chapter 2, "Cruel Stories of Youth" (again taken from a film by Oshima), outlines a fundamental concern of the New Wave, the concern with youth. Chapter

3, "Ruined Maps," derives its title from a novel by Abe Kobo, adapted into a film by Abe and Teshigahara. The chapter, like the novel and film, is concerned with questions of identity, with what it means to be Japanese. The chapter goes on to show how the question of identity became linked with issues of sexuality and violence, and their relationship to politics. Chapter 4, "Insect Women," derives its title from a film by Imamura, and deals, as Imamura's film does, with the problem of women and women's problems. Chapter 5 is inspired by a documentary film by Ogawa Shinsuke, "Forest of Pressure." The chapter looks at the issue of discrimination in Japan—prejudice against ethnic Koreans, *eta*, the working-class, the powerless. Chapter 6, "Shinjuku Thieves," derives its title from Oshima's complex, highly theatricalized film of student-radicals in Tokyo's youth center. The chapter deals with the links between the New Wave Cinema and the Post-Shingeki theatre and tries to show the importance of the "theatrical signifier" to the New Wave cinema.[23] Chapter 7, "Three Men Who Left Their Will on Film" (the title from an Oshima film, again), examines, by way of summary and elegy, three paradigmatic New Wave films.

In the decade and a half since the end of the New Wave, no subsequent cinematic movement has arisen in Japan; the New Wave thus constitutes something (as of this writing) like the last "golden age" of the Japanese cinema. The most important of the younger directors to have emerged in the 1970s and '80s, like Higashi Yoichi, Oguri Kohei, and Yanagimachi Mitsuo, have clearly been influenced by the New Wave, while New Wave directors like Oshima (working mostly outside of Japan), Imamura, and Shinoda still receive the highest critical esteem. Interestingly enough, directors like Suzuki and Yoshida, who "retired" in the late '60s or early '70s, have recently returned to filmmaking. But it may be that the New Wave represents the last time a Japanese film movement reflects a mass upheaval in the Japanese psyche, the last time that Japanese film stands in fascinating relationship to a unique set of historical, social, political, and cultural circumstances.

CHAPTER ONE

Night and Fog in Japan

Ideology and Narrativity

Most knowledgeable critics recognize that over time the Japanese cinema has undergone certain changes; that it has somewhat distinct "periods" into which it may be divided. Noel Burch has said that "there is much to be said for a division of Japanese film history into four broad periods."[1] J.L. Anderson and Donald Richie, in their pioneering, still indispensable history of Japanese cinema, similarly recognize unique periods; Anderson, for instance, claims that Oshima helped bring about a "fourth Golden Age of the Japanese film . . . ."[2] Audie Bock sees "three significant eras . . . ," the "first golden age" of the 1930s; "a second generation . . . (which) emerged from the moral chaos after the war," and a "new mood" which overtook the cinema in the 1960s and created a "new wave."[3]

It might appear, then, that the Japanese cinema has been subjected to historical/critical analyses which have isolated the various forces which shaped this complex artistic and cultural product. Yet a closer examination of the critical literature reveals two overwhelming, if implicit, assumptions which underlie the majority of writing about Japanese cinema. The first assumption enables one to see the Japanese film as a closed system. Aside from admitting major outside events to the world of film (like the Kanto earthquake of 1923, or the Second World War and its aftermath), the Japanese cinema has changed over time due solely to technical innovations (sound, color), audience demands, film-industry upheavals (strikes, financial failures), and the whims and personalities of important filmmakers. The other, more influential assumption, underlies an image of the Japanese cinema as a basically *unified text* (despite some minor, internal shifts) in opposition to the Western cinema. Such critics talk about the "dominant mode" that is Hollywood, and the Japanese cinema's variations from it. This image, best exemplified by Noel Burch and extended in important ways by other critics, has much to recommend it. But there is a foundational linchpin to this approach which needs further examination.

Underlying Burch's general assertion about Japanese cinema is the claim that Japan's films are fundamentally different from Western (Hollywood) cinema due to the differences of Japan's culture. Certainly, Burch is at some pains to make this point in the opening chapters of *To the Distant Observer*. He discusses general semiotic aspects of Japanese traditional artistic practice, and then goes on to state that the Japanese cinema reveals fundamental shared aesthetic principles with this classical art. What Burch actually then goes on to do is claim a certain "classical" status for certain Japanese directors (Ozu, Mizoguchi, Kurosawa in certain films, Oshima) who manifest what he feels are the paradigmatic aspects of Japanese culture in its differences; thus there is a certain tautological character to Burch's thesis. To Burch, the alternative that the Japanese cinema represents to the Hollywood model is thus a function of culture, a function of Japanese classical culture, which, the implication is (must be), has remained unchanged in the intervening millennium since its origins. For, of course, if Japanese culture of the twentieth century differs in fundamental ways from Japanese culture of the twelfth century (or earlier), then to claim cinema's manifestation of the older tradition is certainly to make an anomalous, even bizarre, claim.

We might make explicit the three linked assumptions which underwrite Burch's project: (1) That the Japanese cinema reproduces the essential characteristics of traditional Japanese culture, which began in the middle 600s, refining itself in the twelfth through the seventeenth centuries (Burch says explicitly: "The pertinent traits of Japanese aesthetics were defined almost entirely between the ninth and twelfth centuries");[4] (2) That Japanese culture has undergone no significant changes since its pertinent traits were defined; (3) That the cinema of Japan is a unified text reproducing these pertinent traits in a unified manner (and any deviation from these traits makes such films "unJapanese"—deliberate adoptions of the Hollywood model is the explanation for such un-Japaneseness).

Making explicit these assumptions highlights the problematic nature of some of Burch's thesis. The Japanese cinema may be less unified than Burch is willing to allow without casting such cases out of the pantheon of Japaneseness. It may be that Japanese cinema of a certain period (Burch's Golden Age of the '30s and the films which led up to it) did initially reproduce the essential characteristics of Japanese traditional art, but there were later cinematic reactions against these films, against this traditional culture. And it may be that Japanese culture itself has, in fact, undergone some significant changes over time. To a Westerner, especially an American, it would be strange to conceive of a culture *not* changing over time, especially the eight hundred years since Burch claims the culture's traits were solidified. Such a view of Japan as held by Burch is not uncommon, in fairness to Burch. Ian Buruma, in his *Behind the Mask*, makes the case for cultural continuity in Japan:

Japanese culture has been worked on by history, both native and foreign, by Buddhism, Confucianism, and even at times by Christianity. But underneath the changing surface it has never quite let go of its oldest native roots which are connected to the Shinto cult . . . the whole range of sensual nature worship, folk beliefs, ancient deities and rituals. It is the creed of a nation of born farmers, which Japan in many ways still is.[5]

While there is something to this belief, it is more wishful thinking than solid sociocultural analysis.

It is fundamental to my understanding of the origins and significance of the Japanese New Wave cinema that the Japanese cinema as a whole is less unified than Burch and others would have it; and that Japanese culture has also changed, that it is itself less unified. The real problem with making claims about Japanese culture as a whole, as a basically unchanging national or racial entity, is that it denies integrity to the possibility of deliberate, active, conscious change. This is not to claim that the individual filmmakers who formed the Japanese New Wave could, with complete success, break away from their cultural origins. But it is to claim that within a certain cultural and historical moment, a subcultural group arose in opposition to the dominant cultural ideology of its time. It is to claim that throughout the course of Japan's long history, the culture did experience significant shifts under the impetus of various forces; and that the New Wave movement in cinema, itself part of a larger cultural movement, represents one such shift. To understand the boundaries of this shift it is necessary to see the immediate circumstances out of which it arose. To do this, I would like to return to the idea that the Japanese cinema has undergone certain changes, that it has certain distinct periods, but I would like to bring greater specificity to an understanding of these periods.

One can agree with Audie Bock and see three distinct periods of Japanese film through the early 1970s, corresponding roughly to the 1930s (and the decades leading up to it), the '50s, and the New Wave of the '60s. But chronology does not account for the origins of these periods, nor any understanding of the essential characteristics of the films produced in each period. To account for this phenomenon, I would like to put forth the idea of *dominant paradigms*, or *modes*, of Japanese film style predominantly revolving around narrative technique. And instead of calling each important period a "golden age," or attribute it to decades, I would like to term each paradigm according to its dominant ideological feature. Bock's first period, which she terms "the early masters," I would like to call the "classical" paradigm, Bock's second period is termed "the postwar humanists," and I would like to call this the "modern" paradigm, while the New Wave, her third period, I describe as "modernist."

I am using the term "mode" of narration as it is used by David Bordwell in his *Narration in the Fiction Film*. To Bordwell, "a narrational mode is a historically distinct set of norms of narrational construction and comprehension."[6] Bordwell isolates four major modes of narration: classical, art-cinema, historical-materialist, and parametric. The terminology I have chosen here, classical, modern, and modernist, does not correspond to Bordwell's, but rather to the Japanese cinema as *self-contained*, as narrational modes compared to each other. Bordwell considers modes "to transcend genres, schools, movements, and entire national cinemas."[7] While I do not disagree with this idea, and in fact could find equivalents (to an extent) between the narrational modes he isolates and the modes as I have termed them, I would like, in this study, to put aside Bordwell's paradigms and use the ones I have named to consider the Japanese cinema as part of a system, a system called "Japan," to demonstrate how Japanese cinema reflects, is worked on and works upon, Japanese culture.[8]

The three paradigms isolatable across Japanese film history, at least from the late 1920s through the 1970s, should not prevent us from understanding that one mode does not necessarily replace another—that is the problem with chronological accounts of Japanese film history, and the problem with seeing this history as unified. Paradigms may, and do, co-exist; while Kurosawa and others are "postwar humanists," the early masters Ozu, Mizoguchi, and Naruse continue to work in the '50s (and later) in their same "early-master" style. Thus the notion of paradigms allows for continuity and simultaneity and it allows for the kind of deliberate rebellion that characterizes the New Wave.

The terms classical, modern, and modernist need to be associated with their ideological underpinning, their respective model of ethical thought and social interaction. The classical paradigm subscribes to a "transcendental" schema; the modern to a "psychological" one, and the modernist includes a "metahistorical" model. For each paradigm, we may assign a paradigmatic film or filmmaker and discuss the salient characteristics associated with it, and relate this filmic paradigm to a contemporary literary mode to demonstrate continuity and change across aesthetic boundaries as a way of understanding art as reflective of paradigm shifts in the culture at large.

The salient features of the classical narrative in Japan may be outlined:
    chronological
    episodic
    cyclical
    mythic
    transcendental
The major features of the modern paradigm may be expressed:
    chronological
    causal
    linear

historical
individual
The modernist narrative, then:
  achronological
  arbitrarily episodic
  acausal
  dialectical
  anti-mythic and anti-psychological
  metahistorical

The classical narrative is best exemplified by Ozu. The classical nature of his narrative style may be linked to many of the classical arts of Japan. This is certainly Noel Burch's major contention and it is supported by David Bordwell in his review of Burch's book. Bordwell notes that a typical "characteristic of the Japanese mode of representation is the *disruption of narrative linearity* . . . [Bordwell's italics]. The Western mode saturates every element with story information; the Japanese mode sets narrative apart, designating it as only one function."[9] Elsewhere, Bordwell notes about Ozu that "Narrative causality is relegated to the status of only one 'voice' in a polyphony that gives equal role to purely spatial manipulations."[10] Thus it is easy to see Ozu's narrative strategy as similar to that of the Noh theatre in which the action has typically occurred before the drama is enacted; Ozu's narrational mode may be compared to the Kabuki theatre which, as Burch points out, possesses "a completely free contraction and dilation of narrative time . . . ."[11] We should also note the points of similarity between Ozu's films and the Japanese novel. Masao Miyoshi tells us that "the Japanese writer . . . stops and starts the narrative flow, and uses tension between passages and their crucial placement to propel his story, which will often leap from one episode to another . . . ."[12] Compare this to Bordwell's and Thompson's description of narrative in Ozu's films: "Instead of making narrative events the central organizing principle, Ozu tends to decenter narrative slightly; spatial and temporal structures come forward and create their own interest. Sometimes we learn of important narrative events only indirectly, an ellipsis occurs at a crucial moment."[13] One can say, overall, that Ozu's narrative strategy is best duplicated in the Japanese novel, especially as practiced by authors like Shiga Naoya, Natsume Soseki, Tanizaki Junichiro, and, most particularly, Kawabata Yasunari, Japan's Nobel laureate and arguably its greatest novelist.

Ozu's *Bakushu* (*Early Summer*, 1951) can stand as emblematic of films in the classical narrational mode. The film relies on chronology insofar as there is no sort of chronological uncertainty in terms of past, present, and future. Yet it is also the case that the amount of time which passes is quite vague. The order of the scenes is not dependent on the preceding scene, thus making the structure episodic. An example: Early in the film Ozu shows a shot of the heroine, Noriko, waiting at a train station. Following a short conversation with her neighbor (the man she will eventually marry), Ozu cuts to a long shot of the train pulling out. From there he cuts to Noriko's home, where her father is cutting his grandson's nails. What is expected, of course, in the shot following the train, is to see the *effect* of this shot—Noriko at her office in Tokyo. We do, in fact, see this, but only *after* the scene with grandfather and grandson.

Even such a seemingly minor moment as this demonstrates the way narrative is sacrificed for other concerns. In addition to the elimination of plot-logic and causality, Ozu also eliminates (and "eliminates" is a relative term vis-à-vis dominant film practice—he has not eliminated anything from the Japanese classical point of view) "climactic" moments of the narrative. The "plots" of his films typically revolve around the desire of a parent to see a child, usually a daughter, married. Yet in none of the films which use this basic narrative, do we ever see anything like a wedding ceremony, the culmination of the narrative desire. In *Early Summer*, for instance, the plot uses this basic idea but elides the wedding, along with, moreover, the doubtless tearful departure of Noriko for Akita and her parents move from Kamakura to Yamato. Once Noriko declares her intention to marry, Ozu's use of ellipsis is extreme. After informing her family that she will marry the widowed neighbor, Noriko goes up to her room and cries. Ozu shows three angles of her crying face (a fairly rare display of emotion, actually), then cuts to the following sequence of shots:

(1) long shot of a field in rural Japan
(2) closer shot of field with a village in the background
(3) closeup of a traditional-style rooftop
(4) shot of old Uncle sitting in his house
(5) reverse angle shows Noriko's parents in background of shot

Over the still-life shots we realize that the wedding and departure has occurred.

Ozu's dominant strategy of ellipsis is counterbalanced by the inclusion of the ordinary, by a focus on the "dailiness of daily living." While climactic moments are elided, small moments are included. In *Early Summer*: the nail-cutting scene; the old folks' excursion to the Kabuki-za; the outing by Noriko, her Uncle, and nephews to the Giant Buddha park; Noriko and her sister-in-law enjoying a piece of cake, among others. A number of these "daily" scenes end in moments of quiet reflection on the characters' part. An important scene focuses on Noriko and her friend, Ayako, who have gathered together at Noriko's home for a small party, only to find they have been "shunned" (as they say) by their married friends. This causes them to reflect on changing times, on growing older, on drifting apart. This scene is juxtaposed to an emotionally similar scene involving Noriko's parents at the park as they, too, reflect upon changing times.

This strategy of narrative ellipsis, of the ignoring of the climactic moments in favor of dailiness and the small epiphanies of life, enables Ozu's cinema to bring forth the special Japanese aesthetic concept known as *mono no aware*. For Kawabata, *aware* is at the very core of the Japanese aesthetic essence. The interrelated feelings of love, loneliness, loss, and sadness derive from an intuitive understanding of time, its passing and its inevitability.[14] Yet such feelings do not bring about depression, for *aware* is not simple sadness nor mere nostalgia. One savors the feeling and overcomes it in the very recognition of inevitability. Ozu allows his characters to experience *aware*, at the same time allowing his audience to experience it along with them. *Aware*, at its essence, is revealed in a privileged moment from *Tokyo monogatari* (*Tokyo Story*, 1953). Noriko is being visited by her mother-in-law, Tomi. Noriko is a widow and thus no longer truly a member of Tomi's family. Nevertheless, Noriko treats Tomi with love and affection. Noriko prepares sleeping mats for herself and Tomi, bringing out her late husband's for the older woman. Tomi, seeing this, sighs contentedly, "What a treat—to sleep in my dead son's bed." The depth of such an emotion would be too much without the aestheticizing process of *aware*.

The narrative strategy of the classical mode is combined with associative allusions. These are typically drawn from nature and, as such, point to the idea of cyclical, mythic, and transcendental ideology. The titles of many films and novels in the classical mode are overtly drawn from nature. Ozu's *oeuvre* provides numerous examples: *Banshun* (*Late Spring*), *Bakushu* (*Early Summer*), *Soshun* (*Early Spring*), *Ukigusa* (*Floating Weeds*), and *Higanbana* (*Equinox Flower*). The same may be found in Kawabata's work: *Yama no oto* (*Sound of the Mountain*, adapted for the cinema by Naruse Mikio in 1954), *Yukiguni* (*Snow Country*, adapted twice), *Mizuumi* (*The Lake*), and *Senbazuru* (*Thousand Cranes*, also filmed twice). Another important associative technique may be found in the ending of Ozu's films. With rare exceptions (such as his last film, *An Autumn Afternoon*), Ozu's films tend to end on a still life, or coda. Such shots, of a field, clothes hanging on a line, a train passing, allude to human presence through absence. Such shots point to the transitory nature of individuals juxtaposed against the timelessness of nature, or the Zen-like absence of the human subject within a humanized context.

The linking of characters with nature, or the setting of a mood through a natural allusion, is often felt to be a part of Japanese "dailiness":

The seasonal sense is maintained in everyday life: in the care with which materials and colors of kimono are still selected and in the discrimination employed in choosing appropriate *kakemono* (hanging scroll) for the *tokonoma* (alcove) of the Japanese home. Many contemporary writers make use of these seasonal associations. A single reference to plum blossoms (the first winter flower), to the sound of the cloth-beaters' mallets (autumn), or to a certain variety of grass, is sufficient to evoke a mood, or to imply a character's feelings and actions.[15]

Such an aesthetic sense, even (especially) applied to daily life, not only aids the elicitation of *aware*, but also enables the attuned Japanese observer to participate in the greater harmony and awe of nature. Time is thus perceived not as linear but as cyclical in this "seasonal sense."

There is another consequence to this aesthetic strategy, however. There is also a specifically ideological dimension. For in seeing time as cyclical, one must also see history as myth—that is, history as an endless cycle of life-death-rebirth—rather than as the product of economic, social, and political forces. A reliance on decentered narrative, episodic plotting, and a cyclical view of life can encourage a disbelief in the validity of individual action, a devaluation in the idea of change. It was always in the best interests of the ruling class of succeeding generations to encourage a transcendental view of life. Much like the strategy of the medieval Catholic Church, the transcendental promise of a better life in the next world (heaven, nirvana) could defuse cultural tensions and political action in this one. The case of Mizoguchi Kenji is interesting in this regard. His prewar films, like *Gion no shimai* (*Sisters of the Gion*, 1936), are highly charged politically with an emphasis not on the classical model's mythic acceptance of one's situation but on personal, conscious rebellion against it. In the postwar era, the same basically proto-feminist view is suffused with the classical paradigm of narrative transcendentalism, thus deemphasizing the political aspects in favor of more spiritual ones. In this respect, Noel Burch's preference for Mizoguchi's prewar films can be supported not by suspect recourse to the formal aspects of the respective films, but on more concrete political grounds. Thus Ozu, typically called Japan's most Japanese director, emerges as one of its most conservative ones. An acceptance of life's problems through the elicitation of *aware* is also the acceptance of the political status quo.

In the shift from the classical to the modern paradigm, we find a shift in the attitude toward the status quo. From acceptance of life's problems, we find the emergence of the individual who fights against his circumstances; we find, in short, the emergence of bourgeois individualism. This individualism is expressed in a narrative mode which emphasizes chronological, causal, linear, and historical thinking. The paradigm here called modern is in all important respects modeled on the classical Hollywood style.

> The classical Hollywood film presents psychologically defined individuals who struggle to solve a clear-cut problem or attain specific goals. In the course of this struggle, the characters enter into conflict with others or with external circumstances. . . . The principal causal agent is . . . the character, a discriminated individual endowed with a consistent batch of evident traits, qualities, and behaviors.[16]

That the Hollywood mode should have been adopted in the immediate postwar era is hardly cause for surprise. Hollywood-style film narrative is clearly reflective of American ideology. And it was precisely American ideology which was imposed on Japan by the U.S. Occupation forces following World War II. Necessary to the "democratization" of Japan was a shift from feudal and transcendental values to a focus on the primacy and integrity of the individual. The films produced under the Occupation's aegis were "encouraged" to reflect this value system.

The paradigmatic director working in this mode is Kurosawa Akira; others include, as in Bock's chapter on the "postwar humanists," Kinoshita Keisuke, Ichikawa Kon, and Kobayashi Masaki. For Bock, these directors ushered in a second Golden Age of the Japanese cinema, and put forth "a new emphasis on the freedom of the individual and his encounter with the sometimes comic but often oppressive stodginess of the society at large."[17] Bock feels that a characteristic of this new generation was, stylistically, "faster pacing and more action," which was also (needless to say) modeled on the Hollywood style.[18]

An ideology cannot so easily be imposed on a culture, and it is the case that this postwar humanism and individualism already had roots in Japan planted by the theatrical mode of Shingeki. If perhaps too much emphasis has been placed by Western scholars on the Japanese cinema's relationship to traditional theatre, perhaps not enough attention has been paid to its relationship to Shingeki. Meaning "new theatre," Shingeki originated in the Meiji period (1868–1912), as part of an overall attempt to "modernize" Japan. The theatrical troupes instrumental in fostering a new theatre deliberately modeled themselves on European Naturalist theatre. Many Shingeki groups insisted on performing only European plays (in translation), especially the plays of Ibsen. The theatrical revolution inspired in Japan by Ibsen was thus of the same order as in the West—naturalism, psychological realism, representationalism. With the importation of plays by Ibsen came the importation of Western-style actor training. The Stanislavsky system was introduced in Japan in 1913 by Osanai Kaoru, who later joined Shochiku Films in 1919 and co-wrote the influential film *Rojo no reikon* (*Souls on the Road*, 1921).

The late 1920s saw the rise of a left-wing, overtly socially conscious theatre within Shingeki. This movement had a profound influence on the short-lived "tendency films"(*keiko eiga*) of the late '20s. Shingeki also helped spur along the introduction of actresses to the Japanese cinema, part of an overall move toward greater representationalism and psychologism. The influence of Shingeki on the prewar cinema, while it was profound, was never complete, of course.

Shingeki and the postwar modern cinema focused on the problems of the individual; instead of transcendental submission to life's cyclical essence, one found the conscious assertion of self. Tadao Sato neatly encapsulates the shift from transcendentalism to psychologism when he says of Kurosawa that he "sustained the people by his consistent assertion that the meaning of life is not dictated by the nation but something each individual should discover for himself through suffering."[19] The concept of suffering lends a more distinctly Japanese cast to Kurosawa, but the idea can also be related to the postwar existentialist movement in the West, as well.

The particular aesthetic and ideological boundaries of the modern/psychological narrative mode can be seen in Kurosawa's *Shichinin no samurai* (*Seven Samurai*, 1954). In this story of a group of swordsmen hired to protect a small farming village, Kurosawa tells a carefully plotted tale. The concept of plot is mirrored within the film itself by the use of plotting: Kambei, the samurai leader, constantly draws up plans and charts to plot the village's defense. The element of time, so inessential in Ozu, is crucial here, for the samurai are constrained by time: They must train the villagers and set their defenses before the fall harvest when the horde of brigands will return.

The samurai, each given individualizing characteristics and personalities, are subjected to historical time just as the narrative is subjected to plot. There is the fact that the samurai *act*; there is the fact that they lose—Kambei remarks at the film's end that only the farmers have won. Three of the seven samurai may have survived, but they did not win. And they did not win, furthermore, not because they have gained nothing, but also because it is just a matter of time (history) before the samurai class will be abolished. There is thus a certain pathos to be derived from the samurai, that is to say, a tragedy. They act as individuals and assert their will (they do, after all, have a choice about whether or not to help the farmers), but they are ultimately doomed to failure. This gives the film both a Japanese flavor of *aware*, but even more clearly, a Western existentialist cast.

The samurai, caught in linear time, the time of plot, are juxtaposed to the farmers who participate in mythic time. At the film's end, the farmers are seen in the communal ritual of rice planting, thus reestablishing the hierarchical values of community and the natural order. This serves to shift the focus of the Japanese audience from the samurai to the farmers; or at least to cause a hesitation between the two. Rather than reward the samurai for acting, Kurosawa, to an extent, aestheticizes their actions in favor of *aware* almost despite himself. The counterposition of the farmers and their transcendental quality exerts a mythic force on the audience and the film-maker—the force of "Japaneseness," of appealing to a cultural essence. The ultimate failure of the samurai is thus the failure of individualism. The failure of individualism in this film may be taken as emblematic of the failure of postwar humanism to take hold in the Japanese psyche; that is the attitude, at least, of the New Wave filmmakers, who sought to transcend the modern ideology which had failed modern Japan.

That humanism and postwar individualism never even came to dominate the Japanese cinema was the belief held by Masumura Yasuzo who, in 1958, "called for the destruction of the mainstream Japanese film because it advocated suppression of the individual personality. Mainstream films, he claimed, were totally congruent with the literary tradition of Japan. Characters in all of these narratives invariably submitted to the world around them and to a collective self."[20] Audie Bock points out that the New Wave directors desired to leave "behind the universal humanism of the earlier decade . . . (and) to overthrow the narrative and technical conventions established by the studio system."[21]

To Noel Burch, the New Wave directors made their break not by completely rejecting the Japanese tradition (for that would disgrace his thesis about the inherent radicalism of traditional Japanese art), but rather by extending certain practices already apparent.

> . . . we might say that these directors have combined the salient features of each of the previous generations, features which they have tended to *radicalize* [Burch's italics] in both senses of the term. Rejecting the academic transparency of Tadashi Imai, Kajiro Yamamoto et al., they none the less share these filmmakers' sense of political commitment . . . which they have radicalized in precisely the same degree that a whole generation of left-wing intellectuals, under pressure from the young, have moved to the left of the Communist Party. This political radicalization, moreover, has gone hand in hand with a rehabilitation, via the work of Kurosawa, of the aesthetic attitudes inherent in the work of the pre-war masters, a rehabilitation which is also a radicalization in that the ethos of transparency, rejected only partially by Ozu and Mizoguchi, has been radically disavowed by Oshima, Toshio Matsumoto, Yoshida, Shinsuke Ogawa and many of their contemporaries.[22]

This succinct but superb analysis by Burch represents a significant emendation to his earlier analysis in *To the Distant Observer*. For now Burch recognizes a change (radicalization) on the part of the New Wave filmmakers from the older film practice. But Burch nevertheless still subscribes to the notion that radical form equals, or yields, radical content. As Dana Polan expresses Burch's general attitude, "artists can make a revolution without realizing it (and often in works whose subject matter is reactionary) simply by creating non-narrative, non-illusionistic works."[23] Polan rejects the equation between radical form and politically radical content. He points out that

> Everyday life is often little more than a continual succession of disappointments, of subversions, all of which fissure our self unity and social unity as acting subjects. Art does not deny this malaise; it merely hides and denies its roots in historical forces. This is why contemporary culture can well accommodate formally subversive art; as long as such art does not connect its formal

subversion to an analysis of social situations, such art becomes little more than a further example of the disturbances that go on as we live through a day.[24]

Since traditional Japanese art is already formally subversive, a genuinely radical, political Japanese art must move beyond the merely formally subversive; but it must also move beyond the kind of radical content apparent in the prewar tendency films or the postwar humanistic, left-wing cinema of the 1950s.

The New Wave filmmakers were not alone in acclaiming the need to break away from the immediate and more distant past of artistic practices. In the theatre, too, a radicalization of traditional forms was attempted. This theatrical movement has been termed the "Post-Shingeki theatre" and it has much in common with the New Wave cinema (the subject of chapter 6). Suffice it to say for the present that the post-Shingeki theatre and the New Wave cinema take an acausal, dialectical, metapsychological view toward life and culture. Japanese critic Tsuno Kaitaro has called the artistic practice which reflects this view of life "multidimensional" and he says that "life . . . is not the coherent, one-dimensional process that modern theatre would have us believe it to be, but a complex, often chaotic, incoherent maze of many diverse, interacting dimensions. . . ."[25] Carol Sorgenfrei has described the work of playwright, screenwriter, and filmmaker Terayama Shuji as dealing with "the fragmentation of reality on the general level and the fragmentation of identity on the individual level. . . ."[26] The explicit rejection of the unified subject is a clear indication of the rejection of the humanistic ideal.

The rejection of humanism and Old-Left Communism and the artistic practices associated with them, are a function of a specific event in Japan in May-June 1960: the renewal of the Japan-U.S. Mutual Security Pact (Ampo). David Goodman maintains quite explicitly that the post-Shingeki theatre arose out of "the debilitating sense of impotence engendered by 1960 and the inability of the modern theatre movement, or for that matter modern political movements, to define modes of action and being that would not submerge humanity in some enormous, abstract, historical necessity."[27] Noel Burch also points out the significance of Ampo:

For a man of Oshima's generation and university background it was normal that the high-point of his own youthful commitment . . . should have been that second great defeat for the progressive forces of Japan: the renewal of the Japano-American Security Pact in 1959 [sic]. . . . Oshima made his debut as a director at the time of that struggle, the largest mass movement in the history of the country. It is not therefore surprising that the man and his films should have been marked by the great hopes it aroused—and by the great bitterness that followed on its failure. . . . The development of the Japanese cinema after 1959 is intimately related with these political developments. . . .[28]

Nihon no yoru to kiri (*Night and Fog in Japan*)
Oshima Nagisa, director. Shochiku Co., Ltd.

One of the paradigmatic films of the Japanese New Wave cinema is Oshima's *Nihon no yoru to kiri* (*Night and Fog in Japan*, 1960). The film is explicitly about the political protests surrounding the renewal of the Security Pact and about the politics that characterized the immediate postwar era. As if to insist on the difference between the generation of the 1960s and its immediate predecessor in the postwar era, Oshima's film juxtaposes two groups of student radicals—student Communists in 1952 and student protestors in 1960. In seeking to examine and transcend the previous generation, Oshima had to find a film style that would similarly highlight and disavow the past.

Night and Fog in Japan was Oshima's fourth film as a contract-director at Shochiku, and it was to be his last. For all the thematic and stylistic experimentation of his previous films, it is with this film about student radicals that Oshima made his most complete break with the past. That Oshima was allowed even to make this overtly political, stylistically radical film is something of an enigma. Bock, relying on Oshima and Sato Tadao, reports that Oshima convinced Shochiku that an "avant-garde" film such as he envisioned would appeal to a new audience. Shochiku also felt that since the film focused on a wedding, it could be exploited as a melodrama.[29] But it was clearly not a melodrama, and Shochiku just as clearly felt it could

not be exploited for any commercial potential; it was pulled from distribution on its fourth day in release. Shochiku claimed poor box office was
responsible; Oshima claimed it was a purely political maneuver, a response
to the assassination of JSP leader Asanuma Inejiro on October 12, 1960.
Certainly, Asanuma's assasination was a stunning blow to Japan. "In the
middle of a nationally televised pre-election debate and before an audience
of over 1,000, seventeen year old Yamaguchi Otoya leapt to the stage and
stabbed the Socialist leader to death. . . . Particular attention was drawn
to the fact that the killer's father was an officer in the Self-Defense Forces."
Young Yamaguchi committed suicide in jail shortly after.[30] Why Shochiku
should have withdrawn Oshima's film about the betrayal of the New Left
by the Old Left because of the killing of the Socialist party leader by a
young right-wing fanatic is unclear. The fact is that Shochiku did, indeed,
withdraw the film from circulation. (It was finally distributed nontheatri-
cally in 1963.) Oshima claims that he vowed to quit the company shortly
after; other sources say that Shochiku hesitated to entrust him with other
projects after this film, thus forcing him to resign.[31] Sato reports that, in
a neat replay of the wedding scenes from this film, at his own marriage to
Koyama Akiko, Oshima denounced the studio in a vindictive speech, thus
insuring his break from studio production.[32]

Dana Polan describes *Night and Fog in Japan* as a film dealing with the
problem of the past: "*Night and Fog in Japan* raises the question of *repetition*
[Polan's italics] as a problem for the political filmmaker: how does a filmmaker encounter tradition, and what is the relation between the weight of
tradition and the potential for cultural innovation?"[33] The repetition Oshima faces is the repetition of political action on the part of students in
response to a political crisis, and the repetition of a political filmmaker in
dealing with this response. Oshima's solution is a dialectical one, to compare past with present by juxtaposing two groups and focusing on their
respective responses. This dialectical process is noted by Burch when he
points out that "the film has two narrative levels: a *present* which takes
place shortly after the failure of the struggle against the Security Pact; a
past [Burch's italics] which takes place in the early 50s, at a time when the
Communist student movement was suffering from the combined effect of
the Cold War and the adventurist errors of the party's leadership."[34] Burch
goes on to define the present as the time in which we attend the wedding
of a member of the Communist past and a New Left young woman. The
present represents an attempt at synthesis as Old Left and New, via a
marriage, attempt to merge. But this union must first be preceded by conflict, by thesis and antithesis, a "duelling-ground for two generations of
the student Left."[35]

The dialectical struggle between past and present is complicated by another narrative level, one not mentioned by Burch, and that is the level of
the immediate past (the immediate past before the "present" of the wed-

ding)—the past, that is, of *Ampo toso*, of the struggle against the renewal of the Security Pact. Each narrative level, or time frame, is filmed in a distinct style. The '50s, the Communist Old Left, is evoked through what Burch amusingly calls the "miserabilist cinema of the period in which the action is situated"; the wedding scene is characterized by "extravagant lateral pans from one character to another," often with dramatic blackouts and eerie spotlighting.[36] In fact, these pans are quite extensive and lengthy (the whole film, in fact, relies on long takes, for there are only *forty-three* shots in the entire film). Unlike, for instance, the mechanical *plans sequences* of Godard's *One Plus One* (1969) in which the camera pans right to left, then left to right in ten distinct scenes, Oshima's camera is quite mobile. This mobility contrasts, per se, with the rigidly architectured setting in which the wedding occurs. The demonstrations, in turn, are handled in a highly stylized, suggestive manner. The flashbacks to the meeting of the Old Left journalist and the New Left bride-to-be take place in a hospital ward of stark, flat whiteness. The demonstrations themselves are suggested by banners, shouting, and martial music with a lone figure in Zengakuren combat dress (helmet, shield, and stave) illuminated by pastel blue and red lights against a black background.

Night and Fog in Japan begins in a highly dramatic fashion, with martial music over the credits to declare the film the center of a struggle. The action begins as the camera dollies through a fog-shrouded doorway into a wedding hall. The participants in the ceremony occupy rigidly formal positions. The bride and groom, best man and maid of honor occupy a dais in the center background. Along the left side of the CinemaScope screen are the groom's friends, those whom we later learn are the Communist student activists of the '50s; the bride's friends, the Zengakuren activists, are situated screen right. The foreground and middle ground of the center of the frame is unoccupied. This first becomes the territory of the camera which is an active participant, seeking out its subjects. In a single six-minute take, the camera virtually demands that the actors stand forth, drawing them to the center of the frame, while the use of CinemaScope enables the entire wedding party to remain in view.

The dialectical structure of the film, its recourse to flashbacks to the past of 1952 and the Ampo demonstrations, brings forward Tsuno's idea of a "multidimensional" existence. Initial flashbacks are disguised by formal devices. For instance, the first time change is hidden by the use of music as the first cut of the film takes us from the wedding back to 1952, the same song playing over the cut. The dialectical structure of the film is also highlighted by equivalent characters and by various forms of repetition. Two groups of student radicals face a crisis: In 1952, the Old Left Communists must deal with an alleged spy; in 1960, the New Leftists must deal with the Security Pact renewal. There are two weddings shown: the present wedding of Nozawa and Reiko, and the 1952 wedding of Kawayama and

Misako. There are two students in the respective groups who face serious consequences: Takao, who in 1952 killed himself over the spy incident, and Kitama, who was injured in the Ampo demonstrations. Two people confront Kawayama, the Stalinist Old Leftist: first, Ota, a New Leftist, than Toura, who poses as the ghost of Takao. Two times in which *Sensei* (the teacher of the Old Leftists) fails to exert his leadership, each time in his role as best man at the respective weddings; and two times in which Kawayama holds sway with his Stalinist rhetoric, in the past and in the present.

The wedding in the present is an attempt by Nozawa, the former Communist activist turned journalist, to expunge the past by merging with the present. Oshima disallows this effort by the constant interruptions by the various guests and the frequent intrusions of the past onto the present. Ota first interrupts the wedding on political grounds. He has been disillusioned by the violence and disillusioned by the betrayal of the cause by the Old Left. Ota acts as the conscience of the new generation as he confronts Nozawa and, especially, Kawayama for their part in the betrayal. Not only does Ota accuse Kawayama of betraying the new generation, but flashbacks gradually reveal that Kawayama betrayed his own generation, the '50s radicals. Toura, posing as the ghost of Takao, brings forward Kawayama's part in the spy case in which Takao was accused of allowing the spy to escape and so was hounded into suicide. Nozawa's wedding to Reiko is also interrupted by the vision of Kawayama's wedding to Misako, itself a function of Kawayama's betrayal of Nozawa, for we learn that Nozawa was in love with Misako until she was seduced away from him by Kawayama.

The wedding is also disrupted by Oshima's camera which acts in conflict with the formal arrangements. If the space of the wedding ceremony is formally harmonious, the constantly moving camera is disharmonious; it refuses to allow the symmetrical proceedings to remain unchallenged. Polan notes that "the camera movement neutralizes the wedding ceremony, revealing the extent to which a kind of political night and fog is actually present in the room. . . . not only do the radicals break into the wedding to remind the guests of a history of the struggle that they are denying by that very ceremony, but also the camera itself breaks in as well."[37] The perfect symmetry of the ceremony, its staging, is an attempt to deny access to the wedding of disruptive, disharmonious forces. Yet Nozawa discovers that he cannot deny admission, cannot, that is, deny the past. The intrusion of Ota from out of the fog, and the equally dramatic intrusion of Takao's "ghost," is the intrusion of offscreen space, implied at all times by the constantly moving camera which reframes the action.

This off-screen space is the intrusion of a historical consciousness onto the proceedings.

Nihon no yoru to kiri (*Night and Fog in Japan*)
Oshima Nagisa, director. Shochiku Co., Ltd.

Here when off-screen space becomes on-screen space through movement of
the camera, it is not an appropriation of the new by the old but, in direct
contrast, a challenge to the complacency of the old by the new. Against the
symmetry of the wedding which tries to deny history, the camera-movement
serves as a figure for the movement, the changeability of historical reality.[38]

The use of the long take foregrounds off screen space which then becomes
the place of radical possibility. The integrity of Oshima's camera, which
seeks out and isolates the characters, also functions to isolate the viewer
from the characters. In this respect, Oshima's use of the long take is similar
to Godard's as Brian Henderson explicates it: "Godard presents . . . an
admittedly synthetic, single-layered construct, which the viewer must examine critically, accept or reject. The viewer is not drawn *into* the image,
neither does he make choices within it; he stands outside the image and
judges it *as a whole*. [Henderson's italics]"[39] To refuse the viewer easy access
into the diegesis via identification with the characters and to demand a
critical stance toward the image as a whole is obviously a practice consistent
with Brecht. Polan, again, summarizes this aspect of Oshima's film:

What some critics have attacked as theatrical effects in the film . . . is in fact
evidence of the power of the film's cinematic codes to encourage a kind of
alienation effect. . . . If *Night and Fog in Japan* is "theatrical" it is so precisely
in the sense of Brecht's aesthetic: events are put into quotation marks, spoken
by an historical knowledge that is more committed and complete than the
knowledge possessed by the characters in the story.[40]

The possibility of radical thought or action thus belongs to Oshima and
not to the characters. At film's end, the characters are paralyzed into in-
activity, except for Kawayama. The wedding party enters the courtyard as
the police take Ota away. Kawayama begins to speak while the rest of the
guests stand isolated and apart, disrupted; the bride even begins to cry.
Kawayama exhorts the guests with his Stalinist rhetoric, but his words fade
out as the music fades up. Eventually, all is shrouded in night and fog as
the camera pans away from the wedding guests.

In *Night and Fog in Japan*, unlike some important later films of the New
Wave, there is a clear demarcation within the discourse between past and
present. The past intrudes on the present as offscreen space intrudes upon
onscreen space, thus creating a kind of offscreen time. And it may be that
this notion relates Oshima's film to Alain Resnais's documentary from
which Oshima took his title, as both Joan Mellen and Audie Bock assert.
Bock, in fact, goes on to claim a similarity of intention between the two
filmmakers: "Like the Alain Resnais short film . . . from which it takes its
name [*Night and Fog in Japan*] is a narration, a memory and an argument."[41]
In point of fact, the vagaries of memory and the intrusion of the past on
the present are operative here, for Resnais's film did not, in fact, have its
commercial premiere in Japan until October 1963. Oshima knew about the
film, read about it, and adapted its title *before* he actually saw it. Formally,
the films have much in common with their reliance on the traveling shot
in which the camera betrays the presence of the filmmaker, a questing,
questioning presence. James Monaco also provides a link between Resnais's
and Oshima's works which attempt to link past and present: " 'Nuit et
Brouillard' deals more with our memory of the camps, our mental image
of them, than with the camps as they actually existed, for the memories
are real and present, as are the physical remains through which his [Res-
nais's] restless camera ceaselessly tracks."[42]

If it strikes the Western observer as extreme to compare the horror of
the Nazi extermination camps with the feeling of having been betrayed by
the Old Left, it may be that at bottom it is the sense of betrayal that is
being highlighted in both films.[43] Implicit in Resnais's films is the utter
failure of European society which could give rise to such monstrous crimes;
explicit in Oshima's film is the utter failure of liberal-humanism and communism to bring any substantial changes to Japan, the failure to prevent

the return of feudalistic values and the failure to prevent the return of imperialistic aims.[44] If *Night and Fog in Japan* ends on a pessimistic note, it does so to encourage thought and reflection on the part of the audience; it encourages a political stance which demands an acknowledgment of the continuing spirit of Ampo. It brought to the Japanese cinema a sophisticated style capable of expressing a multidimensional, dialectical, metahistorical point of view; a style which completely disavowed *aware*, repudiated individualist tragedy and encouraged alienation—alienation from the characters in this specific film and alienation from the culture at large.

Night and Fog in Japan relies so strongly on the events immediately preceding its release, and upon events important to Oshima's own sense of betrayal (Old-Left Communism of the early '50s as well as the defeat of the Anti-Security demonstrations), that it is important to outline the origins of the Ampo struggle and situate it within the context of Japanese leftist movements. That the entire New Wave arose out of this movement (at least as an immediate response) further impels this summary.

To understand Ampo one must go back to September 8, 1951, when, with the signing of a security treaty in San Francisco, "the United States and Japan became allies for the first time in history."[45] The treaty was intended to go hand in hand with Japan's postwar constitution which, among other things, renounced war as a means for the Japanese of resolving international conflicts. The treaty placed Japan under the military umbrella of the U.S., which guaranteed to defend Japan's interests as well as its own. The treaty established various U.S. military bases and ports for the Army, Air Force, and Navy. Among the treaty's provisions was the periodic renewal every ten years, beginning with 1960, at which time the two signatories could discuss changes in the terms.

Along with the emergence of postwar democratic institutions in Japan came a strong labor union movement and the rise, after the Occupation, of a strong Communist party. Later in the 1950s, a strong Socialist party also arose. Another important political force to appear was a nationwide student organization.

> Each college (or, in large differentiated universities, each faculty) has an officially recognized student self-government association (*jichikai*) to which every enrolled student automatically belongs. The university acknowledges the *jichikai* by incorporating its dues into the tuition payment system. . . . All students are entitled to vote for delegates to the self-government association, who in turn elect a smaller committee to run it. . . .
>
> Simultaneously with the establishment of *jichikai* throughout Japan, an organization with close ties to the Japan Communist Party united all the *jichikai* into an All-Japan Federation of Student Self-Governing Associations (*Zen Nihon Gakusei Jichikai Sorengo*, abbreviated to *Zengakuren*).[46]

Zengakuren's leadership was drawn primarily from Japan's most prestigious universities. Patricia Steinhoff notes that "Elite universities have
been major centers of violent student protest, and the central ranks of the
more radical student organizations have been filled with highly intelligent,
competent, emotionally healthy students from stable homes."[47] The students' attraction to the Japan Communist party (JCP) at the time of Zengakuren's formation may be explained by the JCP's opposition to the
Second World War, the only recognizable (if small) group to oppose the
war vocally during the militarist era.

Zengakuren and the JCP were quite active together in the early and
middle 1950s. Some of the most spectacular (and notorious) incidents occurred at the prestigious Kyoto University. Among the participants in some
of these incidents was an officer in the *jichikai* named Oshima Nagisa. On
November 7, 1951, students from the university participated in a rally sponsored by a local labor union to celebrate the anniversary of the Bolshevik
Revolution. Following the rally, student protesters marched through the
streets and stoned the house of a moderate Socialist Party Diet (Parliament)
member who had supported the U.S.-Japan Security Treaty. The police
were called in and students clashed with them for the remainder of the
day, leading to many arrests.

A second incident became far more infamous throughout the country.
Known as the "Kyoto Emperor Incident," it had much impact on Oshima.
The Emperor was on tour throughout the Kansai region. At Kyoto University he was met by about one thousand students carrying placards and
shouting slogans, demands, and even insults. One source reports that the
conservatives throughout the country were angry over the students' use
of the word *kimi*, the familiar word for "you" to address the Emperor.
"Eight Kyoto students, allegedly leaders of the demonstration, were ex-
pelled."[48] According to Bock, the student association was also dissolved
as a result.[49]

There were a number of other protests and incidents leading up to May-
June 1960. Among them were the Popolo Theatre Incident of February 20,
1952, in which an undercover policeman was found taking notes on
attendance at a performance of the leftist-oriented theatrical troupe
while they performed at Tokyo University, and the "Bloody May Day" of
1952, in which approximately 20,000 unionists, the majority under JCP
leadership, tried to storm the plaza in front of the Imperial Palace.[50] The
confrontation between demonstrators and police left two dead, scores
wounded and led to 1,200 arrests.[51]

The peak of the protests in the 1950s was reached on November 5, 1955,
when leftist students and labor unionists clashed with police at Tachikawa
Air Base. The protests were spurred by the agreement between the U.S.
and the Japanese government to lengthen the runways at the base to accommodate the U.S.'s new, larger jets. To get the needed land, the Japanese

government began a survey of private land in Sunakawa, a small village that lies adjacent to the base. The students and labor unionists tried to block the land survey on the principle that the U.S. needed the runways for use in nuclear aggression against the USSR and Mainland China, and they claimed, further, that farmers were being "robbed of their hereditary land" for these objectives.[52] The Sunakawa Case, as it came to be called, interestingly anticipates the more massive protests at Sanrizuka (see chapter 5).

To the members of Oshima's generation, those who had been too young to fight in the war but who nevertheless experienced the militarist ideology, the actions of the government in these incidents "were seen as a consequence of the U.S. Occupation's reverse course and the return to power of the spiritual heirs of those who had led Japan through the tragedies of the 1930s and 1940s."[53] Along with the rise of student activism and the militancy of labor unionists, came a rise in activism, as a result of such governmental actions, among intellectuals, members of the academic, literary, and artistic culture whose record during the war years was not a proud one.

The period 1955–59 saw a lull in protest activity; the same period saw Oshima's tenure as an assistant-director at Shochiku. The spectacular rise in the standard of living in Japan led to a decrease in labor union protests, while student protests were similarly held in abeyance. But in 1959–60, a number of crucial incidents arose which plunged the country into near-turmoil, including the U-2 incident, a lengthy coal strike at Miike in Kyushu, and the renewal of the U.S.-Japan Mutual Security Treaty.

It is arguable that without the involvement of Zengakuren, the Ampo protests would never have reached such a peak. And it is possible that without the presence of Zengakuren, Ampo 1960 might not have had such an enormous impact on the arts. For it took not only the massive mobilization of organizations which represented a wide variety of constituencies to create the sense of frustration and betrayal engendered when the protests failed, it took the sense of youth's betrayal, the sense that the new generation of Japan would be dictated to and as oppressed as in the '30s, to foster an alienation and a rebellion from the mainstream of society. And this rebellion on the part of Japan's young would try to be an almost complete break from the past, a break not only from the resurgent Old Right which ruled Japan again, but from the Old Left, which had failed to prevent this return, which had, in fact, betrayed the young in favor of its own interests.

The vanguard of the political New Left (a term not used in Japan until later in the '60s) was created out of Zengakuren, whose leadership became disenchanted with the JCP. In fact, without the need to band together to protest the Treaty's renewal, the break between Zengakuren and the JCP might have been both less shocking and yet more complete. "Security

Treaty revision provided a unique opportunity for harmony, since the entire left wing agreed that the alliance with the United States must be ended."[54] The main coalition against the pact consisted of the Japan Socialist party (JSP; *Nihon Shakai To*), the JCP (*Nihon Kyosan To*), Sohyo (General Council of Trade Unions), and Zengakuren. Allied with this coalition was the smaller but influential group known as the *kakushi interi* (progressive intellectuals), an outgrowth of the increased social and political activity by academics, artists, and critics since the war. The progressive intellectuals were Marxist-oriented critics who "captured the attention of Japan's vast reading public with a new brand of sweeping social criticism and commentary."[55] This coalition of the major left-wing organizations formed a People's Council to provide the ideological and tactical agenda for coordinated protest activities.

Zengakuren had some immediate revolutionary aims at odds with the parent People's Council. Zengakuren hoped to lead the way toward a real revolution in Japan through "carefully planned violence" intended to deliver a "shock" to the people. "The leaders saw themselves engaged not in senseless violence (as it appeared to many) but in an intricate problem of revolutionary struggle in which the sparks flying from a well-placed incident might ignite the dry timber in Japanese society."[56] The Summer of 1959 saw one concrete example of differing strategies between Zengakuren and the People's Council.

> Zengakuren, increasingly impatient with its "weak-kneed" leaders, wanted to use the 5th World Conference Against Atomic and Hydrogen Bombs, a leftist-inspired gathering at Hiroshima on Aug. 5, 1959, to pass a resolution against treaty revision, but the JSP, JCP and Sohyo refused to go along . . . One writer . . . said later that the left wing forfeited here a great opportunity to merge the two elements ("peace and democracy") in the postwar leftist movement.[57]

As the year wore on, the split between Zengakuren and the People's Council widened, and the November 27 Incident served as virtually the final break between them. During a large demonstration organized by the People's Council outside the Diet building, approximately three to five thousand students rushed through the main gates and into the Diet compound, an illegal action opposed by the Council. There were many injuries to both demonstrators and police, although none serious. However, the "invasion" of the Diet compound swayed public opinion against the demonstrators.[58] Realizing this turn of opinion, the Communists sharply criticized Zengakuren activists, "calling them Trotskyites, adventurists and trolls of American imperialism among other things." The JCP tried to discredit the students in the Council and to put forth an image of itself as a responsible, civic-minded opposition party working against the security treaty and for the independence of Japan.[59]

With the split irreparable, Zengakuren felt free to organize its own demonstrations and upgrade the climate of confrontation. On January 16, 1960,
they staged the First Haneda Incident (as it later came to be called). Zengakuren went to Haneda airport (before Narita, Tokyo's main facility) and
tried to stop Prime Minister Kishi's plane from taking off for the U.S.,
where Kishi would sign the security treaty. The students erected barricades
in the main lobby of the airport, but the police broke through, making
many arrests. Among those arrested was a "small, quiet girl named Kamba
Michiko."[60]

Kishi's plane took off and landed in the U.S. on January 16. In the White
House on January 19, Kishi signed the treaty. It was announced then that
President Eisenhower and Crown Prince Akihito would exchange visits
later in the year, with Eisenhower traveling to Japan in mid- to late-June.
On the same date as the treaty's signing in Washington, D.C., Liberal
Democratic Party Vice-President Ono declared his intention "to eliminate
government-supported humanities programs which simply serve to support Zengakuren." In late January, Education Minister Matsuda put forth
a plan to eliminate humanities and social science departments from the
national universities and shift them to private colleges, while favoring science and engineering in the national schools. That particular idea was
opposed by virtually all of Japan's academic establishment, and was never
implemented.[61] It does serve, however, as a strong index of the government's displeasure over the protest activities on campus and a compelling
reminder of the place of the humanities in national affairs.

Both the Japanese government and the student activists had reason to
continue their respective efforts to work against and for change. Both sides
were keenly aware of events transpiring in South Korea where, beginning
on March 15, 1960, rioting by students commenced against Syngman Rhee.
On April 27, Rhee's government was overthrown. Certainly, no one could
attribute this event solely to the students' efforts, but it did provide much
inspiration for Zengakuren and the left in Japan. Interest in Korea, and in
Koreans in Japan, was increasingly occupying the attention of the Japanese
New Left in a general way, and following the disappointments of 1960,
would become quite central to their political concerns.

Although the Security Treaty was signed on January 19, the Diet continued to debate the issue until April of that year, when debate was closed.
On April 26, an organization lately formed to protest the treaty's provisions,
The Association for Criticizing the Security Treaty (*Ampo Hihan no Kai*),
staged coordinated protests across Japan "even posting a well-known figure like Hani Susumu at an important railway station in Tokyo to pass out
leaflets."[62] The debates thus went on in Japan despite the LDP's best efforts
to contain them.

The protests reached a tragic climax on the night of June 15. About fifteen
hundred students had broken through the South Gate of the Diet com-

pound about 7:00 P.M. At 8:30 P.M. there were some four thousand students inside the compound. The students fought with police, dragging police vans away from the gates and setting fire to them. At about 1:30 A.M., the police were instructed to use tear gas on the main body of the students, marking the first time such a tactic was applied in the Ampo struggles. There was sporadic police violence reported against demonstrators and reporters. By about 4:30 A.M., the *demo* (as the Japanese call it) was over, with eighteen police trucks destroyed, hundreds of injured on both sides, 196 arrests, and one dead.[63]

The dead demonstrator was Kamba Michiko, a twenty-two-year-old co-ed from Tokyo University. The left claimed she was strangled by police; the right claimed she had been trampled by rioting students. The circumstances of her death were never resolved, but few cared then exactly who was responsible. What was clear was that while the police reacted with admirable moderation throughout the bulk of the demonstrations, on June 15 things took an ugly turn. There was some resentment on the part of police against the well-to-do students, many of whom were the same age as they (in another premonition of a U.S. occurrence, Kent State). It is also the case that the police sustained numerous injuries from the rocks and clubs wielded by hard-core Zengakuren activists. Nevertheless, whatever lustre the protesters had lost due to the November 27 Incident of 1959, they more than regained on June 16. On June 18, some 300,000 demonstrators massed outside the Diet, along with 12,000 police, while inside, minus the presence of the JSP members of Parliament, the treaty passed without major incidents. On June 23, all the necessary signatures from LDP members and the Cabinet were collected. Prime Minister Kishi resigned his office.[64] Kamba Michiko's death became something of a martyrdom.

Although the Security Treaty was a fait accommpli, an Ampo spirit was just beginning to be felt. It made its way into the theatre: Abe Kobo, already a well-known playwright and an emerging novelist, wrote *Ishi no kataru hi* (*The Day Stones Speak*) for producer Senda Koreya, and the play was performed in Japan and Mainland China by a professional Shingeki troupe in the Fall of 1960. And in the cinema Oshima Nagisa, Hani Susumu, and Shinoda Masahiro similarly made films with the Ampo spirit. Oshima's *Cruel Story of Youth*, released just a few months before *Night and Fog in Japan*, dealt slightly, but significantly with the Ampo demonstrations, while Hani's 1962 *A Full Life* focused on a woman whose sense of self comes alive due to her participation in the demonstrations. These two films will be discussed at some length in succeeding chapters. But Shinoda's film, which followed hard on the heels of *Night and Fog in Japan*, deserves immediate attention.

Shinoda's *Kawaita mizuumi* (*Dry Lake*, 1960; U.S. title: *Youth in Fury*) was his second film for Shochiku Studios and it marked the first teaming of Shinoda with screenwriter Terayama Shuji. *Dry Lake* went into production about the same time as *Night and Fog in Japan*, obviously inspired by Oshima's *Cruel Story of Youth*. Like this latter film of Oshima's it had something of the flavor of a melodrama, Shochiku's bread-and-butter genre. Its roots in melodrama obviously inspired Shochiku to allow its continued theatrical release while it pulled the more radical *Night and Fog in Japan*. But *Dry Lake* transcends its generic roots, and it does so precisely via its Ampo spirit.

Audie Bock's brief plot description of *Dry Lake* is somewhat misleading. She says the film concerns a "student fanatic" who is a "little Hitler" frustrated revolutionary.[65] While the character of Shimojo, a Zengakuren activist with pictures of Hitler on his wall who goes around wearing an American-style leather jacket, is crucial to the film, the central character is unquestionably Yoko, a college student whose father killed himself because of a political scandal. A third character also figures prominently in the narrative, Michihiko, a disaffected young man with extremely wealthy parents. Shinoda and Terayama focus on these three characters, ultimately siding with Yoko.

Dry Lake belongs to the "youth film" movement in which most of the New Wave directors began their careers (and the subject of the next chapter). But Shinoda and Terayama focus quite specifically on the political issue of Ampo here. Shimojo, with his worship of Hitler and Fidel Castro, is an example of the Japanese would-be revolutionary inappropriately fascinated with the West. Shimojo, like Kawayama in Oshima's *Night and Fog in Japan*, is shown merely to be playing with political poses, the infatuation with the West a hollow façade. There is also, in Kawayama's adoption of Soviet culture and Shimojo's more indiscriminate infatuation with Western dictators, the notion that political change in Japan will not come about by adopting outside ideologies and ideologues, but must come from within the Japanese context. Michihiko, at the opposite pole of Shimojo, represents the decadence of the old ruling class, who are also represented in the film by the figure of Oseto, the Diet member. Instead of using his money (actually his parents' money) in a constructive, positive way, Michihiko wields his wealth like a weapon. At one point, a female classmate of his comes for a loan because her father needs ¥2000. To get the loan, she must strip and sing a song for Michihiko's amusement. Thus at another point in the film, Yoko, who has left home and needs money, goes to Michihiko's looking for a job. He demands that she have sex with him, and to help aid his "seduction," he plays a recording of "Ride of the Valkyries" on the stereo. Again, we see that the adoption of Western ways is hypocritical and hollow.

The only character in the film who goes through any significant change, who comes to an understanding of the society and her place in it, is Yoko. At the film's start, she learns that her father has committed suicide. She soon discovers that he was forced into the act by Oseto who actually instigated the wrongdoing but who feared a scandal if Yoko's father should tell the whole story. Yoko's sister, Shizue, has her marriage called off because of the scandal, and her family is soon besieged by creditors. Shimojo (in what might be considered a positive act) has a Korean friend beat up Shizue's former fiance, although not with Yoko's consent. Yoko's decision to leave home is spurred on when she learns that Shizue has become Oseto's mistress in exchange for monetary support of the family. It is then that Yoko turns to Michihiko only to be repelled by his sexual advances which are no better than Oseto's to her sister. She also rejects the violent actions of Shimojo who vows to plant dynamite during an Ampo demonstration. As Shimojo is arrested (not for terrorist activities but for hiring the Korean), Yoko joins the Ampo demonstrations. As she joins in the march, she seems invigorated, brought back to life and to hope.

The links drawn between Michihiko and Oseto clearly show the continuity of feudal values in newly economically triumphant Japan. But Shinoda and Terayama also link Shimojo with Oseto. Shimojo begins to frequent the same bar as the Diet member, attracted and repelled by the rich, powerful politician. He offers to pimp for the politician as he declares that members of the young generation are just as greedy as the old. Oseto's materialistic relationship with women is matched by Shimojo, who rejects his girlfriend, Setsuko (pregnant by him), in favor of his political activities. Shimojo is also linked to Michihiko not only by the fact that the two are friends, but by their equally heartless treatment of Mizushima, a poor student who idolizes Shimojo and who needs a job from Michihiko. Eventually rejected by both of them, Mizushima hangs himself. Michihiko's destructiveness (humiliating the girl who needed a loan and Mizushima) is linked to Shimojo's who wants to plant dynamite at the demonstration.

Thus it is only Yoko who breaks away from the corruption of Oseto and Shizue (a tragic victim, but a victim nevertheless), and from her equally corrupt friends. Yoko is the new generation of Japan, the hope that today's youth will refuse to be victimized and will break the cycle of repetition.

CHAPTER TWO

Cruel Stories of Youth

While it is absolutely essential to an understanding of the Japanese New Wave movement to see it within the context of its place in Japanese cultural and cinematic history, it is also apparent that its New Wave had much in common with other New Wave movements across the world. The Ampo demonstrations may have been the immediate catalyst for the sudden burst of the New Wave, but the seeds of rebellion had been planted in the middle 1950s by a variety of factors revolving around the question of youth. At virtually the same time in the United States, Great Britain, France, and Japan, the national consciousness turned toward a suddenly new social class, one not previously identified, let alone perceived as having, or being, a problem. This new focus on youth (children and teenagers) had many and varied origins, all inextricably linked. The peace and prosperity of the postwar world, especially in the U.S. and Japan, changing demographic habits of lifestyle, the postwar worldwide "baby boom," the availability of automobiles, and the invention of television all conspired and created an atmosphere in which ever-greater attention could be paid to the home, family, and offspring. Youth was identified, isolated, and coddled in the '50s; in the '60s youth was dominant. Perhaps nowhere was this clearer than in the cinema.

While youth had figured as the subjects of numerous films before the '50s, surely few would argue that the youth film came of age, so to speak, in the middle of the decade. In the U.S., this may be seen in the immediate cult status of *The Wild One* (1954) and *Rebel Without a Cause* (1955). For the moviegoing audience (ever dwindling because of television), Marlon Brando and James Dean represented not only new heroes, but a new kind of hero. Alienated, misunderstood, rebellious but ultimately powerless, this new kind of hero was *young*.

Great Britain and France saw the same phenomenon. The British New Wave was preceded by the "Free Cinema" movement, a series of important documentary shorts. Karel Reisz and Tony Richardson co-directed "Momma Don't Allow" in 1955, while Reisz went on to direct the longer "We Are the Lambeth Boys" (1959). Both films subscribed to the older British documentary tradition of leftist sociology, but were characterized as much by a focus on youth as on class. The focus on youth was later confirmed by the "Angry Young Men" movement, inaugurated in the theatre in 1956 and transferred to film in 1958. The more famous French *nouvelle vague* directors similarly focused on youth in their early short films and initial features. Truffaut's "Les Mistons" (1957), *Les Quatre Cents Coups* (1959) and "Antoine et Colette" (1962), and Godard's "Tous les Garcons s'appellent Patrick" (1957) and *Le Petit Soldat* (1960; not released until 1963) demonstrate a fundamental concern with the emerging generation of young people.

Contemporary with the Hollywood youth films of Brando and Dean, with the documentaries of the Free Cinema movement in Britain and the early short films of the French *nouvelle vague*, Japan's Hani Susumu was beginning his own documentary explorations of the world of children. *"Kyoshitsu no kodomotachi"* ("Children in the Classroom," 1954) and *"E o kaku kodomotachi"* ("Children Who Draw," 1956) brought a new style and attitude to the world of Japanese filmmaking which culminated in Hani's *Furyo shonen* (*Bad Boys*, 1960), one of the fundamental films of the Japanese New Wave. "Children Who Draw" could easily have had a direct influence on then assistant-directors working at Shochiku Studios, and others, as the film was somewhat uncharacteristically released theatrically to play before feature films.[1] A much more direct influence on the New Wave, and the immediate inspiration for the Japanese cycle of youth films, came from the novels of Ishihara Shintaro.

Donald Richie notes the coincidental appearance of the world youth cycle and the importance of Ishihara's influence in Japan: "As in most other countries, the middle years of the 1950s saw a revolt on the part of youth. This was particularly pronounced in Japan, and a young novelist, Shintaro Ishihara [sic], became the spokesman for the discontented generation. He also saw most of his novels made into films."[2] Ishihara's works were classified by the appellation *taiyozoku* ("sun tribe"). The derivation of this term stems, in part, from Ishihara's novella *Taiyo no kisetsu* (*Season of the Sun*) and from the powerful, mythic image that the Sun has in Japanese culture. Thus the term describes Japanese youth who feel themselves cut off from their past yet part of a new, mythic culture, the culture of youth.

Season of the Sun was made into a film in 1956 by Furukawa Takumi at Nikkatsu studios, then a relatively minor company seeking to establish itself in the commercial sphere. This is worth noting in that Nikkatsu would, just a few years later, completely commercialize the newly emergent youth film. In 1956 two more Ishihara novels were transferred to film. *Shokei no heya* (*Punishment Room*) was brought to the screen by Ichikawa Kon at Daiei. Anderson and Richie claim that Daiei's interest in the *taiyozoku* genre was strictly commercial, an extension of their sex films made possible by the easing of censorship codes under the U.S. Occupation.[3] Yet the film also fits into Ichikawa's emerging interest in youth as he begins to develop his own distinctive authorial personality.

The most important of the sun tribe films was undoubtedly *Kurutta kajitsu* (*Crazed Fruit*, aka *Juvenile Passion*), the debut film of Nakahira Ko, also produced at Nikkatsu. Like many of the *taiyozoku*, the film is situated at a summer resort (another index of sun tribe) and focuses on teenage sex and sensuality. While *Punishment Room* had aroused much controversy, *Crazed Fruit* seems to have inspired a genuine mass reaction; both films brought out a fear of uninhibited teenage sex combined with social alien- ation. *Crazed Fruit* proved inspirational to Oshima Nagisa, who said that it was this film that helped point the way toward a new Japanese cinema: "I felt that in the sound of the girl's skirt being ripped and the hum of the motorboat slashing through the older brother, sensitive people could hear the wails of a seagull heralding a new age in Japanese cinema."[4]

Outside of the *taiyozoku* genre, Imai Tadashi's *Mahiru no ankoku* (*Darkness at Noon*—not derived from the Arthur Koestler novel), also in 1956, fit into the "juvenile delinquent" cycle of films being produced worldwide. In this fact-based film which tells of five teenaged boys accused of a brutal murder, Imai accuses the police and courts of corruption. Considering that the case on which the film is based was still pending, it was interesting (if possibly prejudicial) for Imai unequivocally to show the youths innocent of murder. Anderson and Richie castigate the film for its "tear-jerking" qualities and its unabashed willingness to wring sympathy from the audience.[5] This comment fails to take into account the surrealistic aspects of the film which look forward slightly to Oshima's *Death by Hanging* (1968) and, oddly enough, to Robert Bresson's *L'Argent* (1984). In addition, the film overtly challenges the authoritarian attitudes of the police, prosecution, and ju- dicial officials, a quite radical stance compared to the usually submissive Japanese attitudes to authority. In 1958, Imai directed another film within the juvenile delinquent cycle, *Jun-ai monogatari* (*The Story of Pure Love*). This film focuses on young pickpockets sent to reformatories and on one par- ticular boy who is helped by a kindly policeman to get a good job. The boy falls in love with a girl from a similarly deprived background. While the boy struggles to keep on the straight-and-narrow path, the girl, who suffers from radiation sickness, gets sicker and dies. This kind of film is typical of the old-style social problem film in Japan (what little tradition there is of it) in that it links together, usually melodramatically, a number of current issues, here the problem of youth and the atomic bomb. Imai, a Com- munist, was particularly prone to this habit, but while the New Wave filmmakers singled him out as a target of their rebellion, he nevertheless had a profound influence on the emerging youth cycle and the social cri- tiques it inspired.

Also of major significance as a prelude to the New Wave was Ichikawa

Kon, whose version of Ishihara's *Punishment Room* was in the center of the *taiyozoku* genre. Ichikawa occupies a place firmly within the generation of postwar humanist directors, like Kurosawa and Kinoshita Keisuke, but has much in common with the New Wave. He emerged preeminent among the immediate postwar directors as a social critic. This side of his varied directorial personality emerged precisely with his attachment to the sun tribe films. He followed *Punishment Room* with *Manin densha* (*A Crowded Streetcar*, 1957), a darkly hilarious look at contemporary Japan as seen through the eyes of a recent university graduate. Ichikawa tackled the problem of troubled youth in a more serious vein in *Enjo* (*Conflagration*, 1958), an adaptation of Mishima Yukio's *Kinkakuji* (*The Temple of the Golden Pavilion*). The story of an acolyte priest who is driven mad by the hypocrisy of the family and religious system until he finally burns down the magnificent temple structure neatly captures the ambivalence felt by the young toward Japan's cultural heritage.

Kobayashi Masaki, another of the liberal-humanist directors against whom the New Wave would rebel, can also be seen as an important precursor of the movement. For instance, his *Kuroi kawa* (*Black River*, 1957) focuses on petty thievery and prostitution which surround the U.S. military installations in Japan. The film starred Watanabe Fumio, who would become a central player in Oshima's cinema. More importantly, the film is a clear, if more melodramatic precursor to Imamura's New Wave masterpiece, *Buta to gunkan* (*Pigs and Battleships*, 1961).

Shochiku Studios, home to Kobayashi, was also home to Kinoshita Keisuke, who, aside from Ozu, was the studio's most important director. In 1956, hoping to both cash in on and critique the *taiyozoku* craze, Kinoshita made *Taiyo to bara* (*Sun and Rose*). Kinoshita's ambivalence about siding with youth clearly came through; in any case, Kinoshita's strength was then (as now) in dealing with the image of women and the family. Kinoshita was to have a profound, if equally ambivalent, relationship to the emerging New Wave.

The most immediate influence upon the New Wave directors-to-be was Masumura Yasuzo. Masumura made his directorial debut in 1957, after spending a few years studying at the Centro Sperimentale in Rome. The influence of neo-realism was made clear in his preference for location shooting and his focus on the lower classes. On the other hand, like many of the neo-realist directors, he shifted his focus slightly, concentrating on how human desires can change one's environment seen through a juxtaposition of the freedom of the individual against the contraints of the social system.[6] His shift away from the humanist directors who were his contemporaries is seen in his debut film, *Kuchizuke* (*Kisses*). The youthful hero is from the masses; he is poor, alienated, angry, little given to much self-expression or introspection, seeking instead for immediate thrills, among which are riding his motorcycle and romancing a young woman of similar back-

Kuchizuke (*Kisses*)
Masumura Yasuzo, director. Kawakita/Japan Film Library Council

ground. A freshness of style is achieved by the location shooting and the reliance on hand-held camerawork. The film is clearly a forerunner not only of the youth films of the New Wave directors in Japan, but looks forward to the first features of the French New Wave, as well. Oshima Nagisa has this to say about *Kisses*: "In July, 1957, Yasuzo Masumura's *Kisses* used a freely revolving camera to film the young lovers riding around on a motorcycle. I felt now that the tide of a new age could no longer be ignored by anyone, and that a powerful irresistible force had arrived in Japanese cinema."[7]

Masumura followed *Kisses*, which was not a big hit in Japan, with *Danryu* (*Warm Current*, 1957) and *Kyojin to gangu* (*Giants and Toys*, 1958), the latter bringing Masumura to public acclaim. This film is, according to Anderson and Richie, "a fast moving and at times trenchant attack on the advertising racket in Japan. . . . [It] bravely attacked a prevailing materialistic social philosophy and . . . showed the cynicism and corruption of the world of mass communication."[8] As well as providing one of the immediate cinematic models for the New Wave, Masumura would remain on a parallel with them; his films of the '60s tackled the subject of women, as did many of the New Wave filmmakers.

In seeking to understand the intimate link between the New Wave and the focus on youth, the particular characteristics of the Japanese film industry of the time must also be taken into account. And in so doing, one can better understand the sentiments expressed by earlier critics, like Audie Bock, who see the New Wave as a reaction against the preceding generation of film directors. For beyond political differences, beyond a sense of Japan's failures to deal with the modern world in a democratic manner, comes the recognition that in concrete ways these young filmmakers actively rejected their forebears. Many of the most important directors of the New Wave, primarily, Oshima Nagisa, Shinoda Masahiro, Imamura Shohei, and Yoshida Yoshishige, began their film careers as assistant directors at Shochiku and consciously rebelled against their mentors.

To understand the dynamic involved in attempting to reject the immediate past one can turn, if only for the sake of illustration, to Harold Bloom's thesis of "the anxiety of influence." Just as the powerful poets of the Romantic era sought to remain uninfluenced by their equally powerful predecessors, so too the New Wave assistant directors, working for Ozu, Kinoshita, Kobayashi and other established filmmakers, actively sought their own voice in their own anxiety of influence. A quote from Imamura illustrates this: "I wouldn't just say I wasn't influenced by Ozu. I would say I didn't want to be influenced by him."[9] This anxiety of influence has clearly Oedipal overtones as the younger poets seek to rebel-kill the older poets. This psychological dynamic may help explain the sympathy for youth expressed in the New Wave films. But we need not involve Freud in our attempts to place the Japanese New Wave filmmakers as sons to the liberal-humanist fathers. Another, even clearer factor contributed to establishing the New Wave filmmakers as something like sons to the established fathers, and that is the essentially feudalistic nature of the assistant-director system.

Whereas in the American film industry there have traditionally been a number of ways to rise to the status of film director (among which is *not* to start out as an assistant director), in the Japanese system one began as an assistant, having first passed a competitive exam. After a period of apprenticeship, the young assistant was eventually promoted. This assistant-director pattern seemed so important to Anderson and Richie that in their pioneering history of Japanese film they felt compelled to print what is virtually a genealogy of film directors and their assistants.[10] While this makes for fascinating study in itself, the important point in the system is the essentially feudalistic attitudes held by the directors toward their assistants. Kinoshita Keisuke, for instance, talks about the attitude toward his assistants manifested by Shimazu Yasujiro, Kinoshita's mentor, an attitude duplicated, in turn, by Kinoshita toward his assistants.[11] Assistant directors soon learn that their abilities and opinions, which got them their positions in the first place, are of no value, are, in fact, unwanted in their jobs. Instead, they are there to learn the company system in a general way (the practice of changing studios was relatively rare, a manifestation of the Japanese corporate ideal of lifetime employment) and the particular directorial habits of an individual director in specific. By the 1950s, the system of linking up assistants to one senior member was breaking down. The intention at that time, as Yoshida has said, was to become involved first in a variety of projects for different directors with different groups of assistant directors.[12] However, eventually one settled with a single director and only rarely worked with another. So it was that Yoshida worked with Kinoshita on eight films as an assistant director. This kind of practice encouraged the young assistant to fit his style into the company practice via the approved working methods of the senior staff member. And since virtually all the films fit into one genre or another, and since most directors are either typecast or are themselves only interested in particular genres, the assistants were similarly encouraged to find, and stick to, a particular niche.

In retrospect, many of the New Wave directors denigrate the assistant-director system. Imamura, for instance, has said, "For the first three years assistant directors talk a lot of theory and aesthetics and feel resentful toward the older established directors. . . ."[13] Such feelings of resentment are no doubt natural when others occupy a position one wants, but it also takes on the flavor of youthful resentment and jealousy. Here is Oshima complaining about the job: "I never became a 'great assistant director' who runs hard at the director's bidding. . . . If I thought the work was boring, I'd quit and go home."[14] And Shinoda, who was less overtly rebellious, and who seems to have earned a strong reputation as a "great assistant," nevertheless discovered that "unlike in the university, intelligence meant nothing and he was best off keeping his ideas to himself while doing everything he was told."[15]

The realization that the assistant director's job at a film studio was at odds with one's experiences as a college student, brings us to another factor explaining the interest in youth taken by the New Wave directors, who were approximately thirty when they made their first films—which is not so old, of course, but which should not automatically imply an interest in the problems of college students and college-age youth. All the New Wave directors thus far mentioned, Oshima, Shinoda, Imamura and Yoshida, were graduates of prestigious universities. Yoshida mentions that of the assistant directors hired by Shochiku in his year, five were graduates of Tokyo University (Japan's most prestigious school), two were from Waseda and one was a graduate of Keio University.[16] (Oshima, a graduate of Kyoto University, began his assistantship the year before Yoshida; Shinoda, a graduate of Waseda University, began one year before Oshima.) Almost without exception, these men had majored in literature, mostly foreign (French, German, and Russian were the most popular) or in theatre, giving them a wider experience of world culture than their seniors.

There is some controversy, or at least some doubt, about how unified the New Wave movement was at Shochiku Studios itself, where it basically originated. It is quite common for the participants of the movement to deny any intention to start a "new wave." Shinoda stated:

> I never felt part of a New Wave—there was never really a "school" of New Wave art. But we [the so-called New Wave directors] did all have one thing in common: the older generation of directors were confident of what they were depicting. The younger generation were not so optimistic, were suspicious even of themselves. . . . Kurosawa's generation of humanists demonstrated conclusions to contemporary problems; the New Wave does not possess this certainty.[17]

Shinoda also feels himself apart from the New Wave directors in that he was never as "radical" as Oshima. He says that in some sense, "the 1960s made me." Elsewhere on this subject, Shinoda has said, "filmmakers . . . should bear witness to the politics of their age."[18] Seen in the context of the 1960s, Shinoda was not part of a school, but a movement—the New Wave.

Oshima maintains "that there were too few 'new directors' to constitute a 'wave,' and moreover that they were all working within the restrictions of the company system." Oshima also claims that it was merely coincidental that both he and Yoshida used alienated students as the protagonists of their first films.[19] But was it strictly coincidental; was there no "movement" building before the directors had a chance to make their first films? In fact, even before the Ampo demonstrations provided immediate inspiration to Oshima, Shinoda, and Yoshida, there was a conscious movement at Shochiku, a banding together by many of its then-assistant directors, those whose university backgrounds in literature and theatre gave them a critical disposition.

Yoshida credits Oshima as the political inspiration for the New Wave movement. Oshima helped initiate some of the labor changes of Shochiku's assistant director system, for instance, and, as the first of the group of young assistants to direct a film, he set a tone and standard for the rest to live up to. It is also true that Yoshida himself was quite active in initiating the movement. Since his college days, Yoshida had been active in artistic-political groups. Yoshida and three classmates at Tokyo University established a literary magazine dedicated to publishing original fiction, translations (Yoshida majored in French literature), and essays. Another member of this coterie was Ishido Toshiro, a Chinese literature major, who would become an assistant director at Shochiku along with Yoshida, and who would, more importantly, emerge as Oshima's co-scenarist on four of the latter's most important early films. (Yoshida claims that the character of Takao, the student who commits suicide in *Night and Fog in Japan*, was based on a fellow classmate of Ishido's who killed himself in 1952.)[20] At Shochiku, Yoshida again formed a journal with his fellow "classmates" in the fall of 1956. While assistant directors were at the directors' bidding during the making of a film, they were also expected to write scenarios and one advanced to full directorship partly on the quality of one's scripts. Yoshida, along with Oshima, decided to "stir up an original scenario movement" to provide a forum for scripts which veered away from Shochiku's pat formulas. Yoshida asked Ishido and Tamura Tsutomu to join the venture. Tamura accepted, but Ishido refused on the basis that he would soon leave the studio. Oshima enlisted Tanaka Jungo, an assistant director in Oshima's class and a graduate of Keio University. (Yoshida mentions that Tanaka committed suicide shortly thereafter.) Yoshida also involved Takahashi Osamu, Saito Masao, and an assistant director named Uemura who was at that time Kinoshita's chief assistant.

The journal they formed was called *Shichinin* (Seven Men), and it was funded by a combination of monies removed from the assistants' salaries and sales to the company and senior directors. Yoshida reports that Kinoshita donated ¥20,000 of his own money to the group. The journal lasted a few years, until the time most of the group graduated into directing.[21] The theoretical discussions they had and the scripts they wrote were clearly harbingers of things to come. For out of this group, in addition to the films of Oshima and Yoshida, came Takahashi Osamu's *Kanojo dake ga shitte iru* (*Only She Knows*, 1960) and *Shisha to no kekkon* (*Marriage with the Dead*, 1960), along with Tamura Tsutomu's *Akunin Shigan* (*Volunteering for Villainy*, 1960). Tamura later left directing and became Oshima's primary screenwriter, beginning in 1966.

Thus we might conclude that if there was no conscious movement, no formal announcement as such, on the part of the handful of younger Japanese directors to create a "New Wave," the combination of the culture's interest in youth, the backgrounds of the young directors, the particular characteristics of the Japanese film industry, and the massive protests surrounding the Japan-U.S. Security Treaty renewal conspired, in a sense, to bring about a new look, form, and feel to the Japanese cinema. This new look, form, and feel, presaged though it may have been by Masumura's *Kisses* and the *taiyozoku* cycle of films, came clearly into view with the first directorial effort of Oshima Nagisa.

Shochiku production head Kido Shiro selected Oshima's script *The Boy Who Sold His Pigeon*, a script which might be described as a Japanese version of Britain's "Angry Young Man," as the first film to be directed by a member of the "Seven Men" group. Kido changed the title of the script to *A Town of Love and Hope* (*Ai to kibo no machi*). Despite the title change, and Oshima's heartsick reaction to it, the film was a critical success.[22] Shochiku, however, apparently simply dumped the film into small theatres and denied Oshima his next directing assignment for half a year. In those same six months,

while awaiting his next directorial opportunity, Oshima joined forces with
Ishido Toshiro and wrote two scripts, in addition to a script of his own.
In 1960, Oshima was again allowed to direct, while fellow assistants Yoshida, Shinoda, Takahashi Osamu, and Tamura were also promoted (at least
temporarily). Once again, events seemed to have conspired to bring about
a New Wave at the beginning of a new decade.

Once again Oshima was in the vanguard as *Seishun zankoku monogatari*
(Cruel Story of Youth) was the first New Wave film to reach the screen in
1960. Its treatment of the theme of alienated youth, its acknowledgment
of the Anti-Security Treaty demonstrations and the intergenerational conflict, and the exemplary use of color and CinemaScope make this film a
virtual paradigm of the New Wave cinema. *Cruel Story of Youth* received
strong critical praise, although Oshima was already hard at work on his
next film, working with "journalistic speed"[23] to capture the spirit of the
times.[24]

If *A Town of Love and Hope* thematically resembled the Angry Young Man
movement in Britain, then *Cruel Story of Youth* seems to be a Japanese *Rebel
Without a Cause*. Sato Tadao feels that the young couple upon whom the
film focuses "are portrayed neither as sad victims of society nor as daring
rebels. In a society as evil as this one their rebellion merely takes the form
of meaningless delinquency, which is what is 'cruel' about their story."[25]
Of course, it is precisely what makes Japanese society "evil" that gives
these two young rebels their cause. And what makes society evil are those
factors—political, social, and economic—over which they have no control.

Cruel Story of Youth is clearly an extension of the *taiyozoku* cycle with its
focus on youthful sex and violence. Oshima, however, counted on the
context of the film to communicate to Japanese audiences that behind the
protagonists' action rests the "disappointment and depression at the failure
of the post-war democratic revolution."[26] To create this political tone, Oshima sets his story against the backdrop of the Ampo demonstrations and
other worldwide events. News headlines can be seen behind the red titles
which open the film. A newsreel featuring a student clash with police in
South Korea forms the film's second sequence, a newsreel which is non-
diegetic in that none of the protagonists are viewing the footage and it
does not relate to the film's plot. Color footage of the Ampo demonstrations
then reveals the two young heroes. Thus, although the basic plot of the
film is not politically motivated (unlike, obviously, *Night and Fog in Japan*),
Oshima creates a political tone, a strong context, in which the film must
be viewed.

Oshima is careful to demonstrate his characters' disillusionment. Kiyoshi
and Mako are not especially politically motivated. Oshima compares them,
on the one hand, to another couple their age, and to an older couple of
the 1950s student-generation. Mako's friend Yoko, and a Zengakuren ac-
tivist-friend of Kiyoshi's, are heavily involved in the Ampo demonstrations.

Seishun zankoku monogatari
(*Cruel Story of Youth*)
Oshima Nagisa, director
Shochiku Co., Ltd.

Alone together in Kiyoshi's apartment, this couple discusses the relationship between politics and love; in another sequence, we see the four young people together and come to see Kiyoshi's and Mako's pessimism compared to the optimism of their friends. On the other hand, there are Mako's sister, Yuki, and her ex-lover, Dr. Akimoto, the former student-radicals who lost their ideals in the '50s. Akimoto, in fact, has become an abortionist (a powerful symbol of pessimism) and he performs one such operation on Mako. At one point, Akimoto tells Kiyoshi, "We were young, we made mistakes. We tried, but the wall stayed firm." Later he speaks again of the futility of the student demonstrations of the 1950s as if to say that similar actions in the '60s are also doomed. But Kiyoshi answers back, "We have no dreams, so we'll never be like you." This is a chilling statement, indeed, from a college student, an index not only of his own particular situation, but the possible situation of the entire '60s generation. To ensure that we understand Kiyoshi and Mako are not simply rebelling against the '50s generation, Oshima also includes Mako's father, who represents the war generation that has never truly subscribed to postwar democracy.

In place of political action and in place of dreams, Kiyoshi and Mako substitute desire. At the film's start, Mako expresses a curiosity about sex, men, and thrills. Kiyoshi satisfies her curiosity about all three in a famous rape/seduction sequence by a riverside. Oshima films Kiyoshi and Mako in a single, high-angle take as he pushes her into the river among floating logs and refuses to let her out of the water until she agrees to make love with him. During their lovemaking, Oshima cuts away to a shot of the sky, with the sound of airplanes offscreen. One wonders if the scream of the jets is to be understood as the presence of the U.S. Air Force—a subtle contextualizing of the political realities.

The relationship between sex and thrills is seen when Kiyoshi and Mako begin an intimidation scam whereby Mako allows herself to be picked up by men while hitchhiking until Kiyoshi comes along on his motorcycle and tries to extort money from them. The first time they perpetrate this scam is a big success, and the two ride off together on Kiyoshi's bike while rock music blares on the soundtrack—Masumura's *Kisses* is clearly invoked. This scheme of theirs is clearly an index of their nihilism, as is Kiyoshi's unfeeling attitude toward an older woman from whom he gets money in exchange for sexual services. This older woman is herself a symbol in Oshima's hands of the emptiness of Japan's moral and economic structures, although her kindness and sensitivity evoke much pathos. She, too, had an abortion when she was young; her marriage to a wealthy man does not satisfy her, as if to say that such an intelligent and sensitive woman is bound to experience pain and disillusionment in a social system such as Japan's.

Kiyoshi's ultimate undoing is brought about by a group of young gangsters under the leadership of a slightly older man. These gangsters make their headquarters in a bar frequented by Kiyoshi and Mako. Early in the film, Mako is accosted by a gang member who forces her to dance with him. Kiyoshi comes and challenges him to a fight, defeating the gang members. This action inspires Kiyoshi and Mako sexually and they make love in a junkyard. This same junkyard is the locale at film's end for another fight between Kiyoshi and the gangsters, only this time they beat him to death. The junkyard is clearly an overdetermined symbol of society's attitude toward alienated youth: The youth may express themselves physically, in sex or violence, but must do so away from society's center, amidst the detritus of modern civilization.

Cruel Story of Youth shows Oshima's fascination with the links between sexuality and violence, a motif common to the New Wave. Kiyoshi's initiation of Mako into his world is close to a rape; the first fight with the gang inspires them to make love; the dangers involved in the hitchhiking scam provide them with thrills akin to sex. The other young couple in the film begins the exploration in Oshima's work, and in the New Wave, of the links between sex and politics. Thus we have youth, sex, violence, and politics—the essence of the New Wave and the essence of the '60s.

While the use of color and CinemaScope was typical of the Japanese commercial cinema at the time, Oshima's handling of them was not. In one sequence, Kiyoshi comforts Mako following her abortion. Oshima frames them in a close-up, while Dr. Akimoto converses with them from offscreen. In the following sequence at the seashore, Oshima composes

Kiyoshi and Mako lying horizontally stretched across the frame. Oshima not only favors the long-take, but also hand-held shots, the most interesting of these in the sequence when Kiyoshi is released from jail and he walks with Mako through the streets. The camera leads them as they talk in a straight-on shot, walking in front of them, looking back. Sato attributes this general style of Oshima's to a desire to "apprehend their irritation through jittery camera moves that echo their own moves, thus becoming one with them."[27] This reading seems a bit mechanistic. Rather, the refusal to mount the camera on a tripod despite the widescreen ratio (where hand-held camera shots are extremely noticeable) is a rejection of the Japanese tradition of quality, the long, graceful takes of Mizoguchi, for instance. But it equally rejects the "subjective" camera of Kurosawa, who also employs a long-take, hand-held camera sequence in CinemaScope in *Yojimbo* (1960), where the device has a precise relationship to character and theme. The stylistic plane is not reducible to the thematic plane; it radicalizes earlier film form as the plot radicalizes earlier film content.

If *Cruel Story of Youth* was a pessimistic vision of the possibilities for youthful energy and dreams surviving in contemporary Japan, Oshima's next film was no more optimistic. *Taiyo no hakaba* (*The Sun's Burial*) was released just a few weeks after *Cruel Story of Youth*, a remarkable achievement considering the film's elaborate recreation of Osaka's notorious Kamagasaki slum.

The title, *The Sun's Burial*, is a highly allusive one. It refers to the image of the sun as a symbol of Japan, Land of the Rising Sun; the Japanese flag is alluded to by the frequent shots of the rising or setting sun blazing red in the sky. The recurrent use of the Japanese flag is an important visual motif for Oshima in this film and in many later works. The burial of the sun might also refer to the burial of the sun tribe, the genre of the youth film; youth destroyed by the commercial-materialistic society that Japan has become.[28] For in this film, people are reduced to mere flesh and blood, valuable only for how much these are worth on the black marketplace.

The Kamagasaki slum that is the film's main setting clearly stands in for Japan as a whole; the slum itself was created, Oshima pointed out, "when the Meiji emperor, who was going to Hiroshima on his way to Russia, did not wish to see any slums on his way. The slums were gathered together in one community."[29] In the film, there is nothing other than the slum; the protagonists never leave its confines, nor do they dream of any other life. They dream of survival, success, or the resurrection of a (mythical) past, all within the confines of the slum. All of the protagonists are criminals who justify their actions according to their needs. The petty thieves under the control of the militarist fanatic justify their actions as necessary to resurrect the Imperial army. The small-time gangsters define themselves by the gangster (*yakuza*) code; the vibrant heroine need not explain herself, for she is a survivor.

The Sun's Burial is even more nihilistic and absurdist than *Cruel Story of Youth*. The films ends in a conflagration as much of the slum is set ablaze. The hopelessly inept young hero—an incompetent gangster, an incompetent procurer, and an incompetent blood securer—has been killed. Even the heroine, who has discovered the joy of sex and the thrill of survival finds, as Oshima says, "that vitality is not enough."[30] But at least vitality enables her to survive while all around her perish in the face of the degrading materialism of the new Japan.

Oshima here brings to the fore another important motif of the Japanese New Wave: the gang. A gang appeared in *Cruel Story of Youth* and led to the hero's death. In *The Sun's Burial* the gang is ubiquitous, a clear metaphor for the Japanese social structure which virtually precludes individualism (the most frequently noted, even clichéd, image of Japan held by the West). And it is precisely the gang, with its codes of loyalty and obeisance, which leads to the destruction of its members. In Oshima's film, the youth gang is compared to the militarist band (gang), thus making it clear that the gang is a microcosm of the nation-state. What Oshima shows is that while the gang demands absolute loyalty from its members, the gang can, and does, betray an individual gangster. The single citizen owes loyalty to the State, but the State need not, does not, reciprocate. Gangs are formed for economic purposes and in so linking the gang with the nation, Oshima is demonstrating the fundamentally economic-materialist basis of the modern State. And, of course, the fact that the various gangs in the film find the trading in human blood to be their most lucrative activity, merely makes the allegory stronger and more overt: The State trades on the life's blood of the people.

The motif of the gang, apparent in these early films by Oshima, and recurrent in films by Shinoda and Imamura Shohei, finds a more commercial reappearance in a popular formula which appeared shortly after the New Wave: the *yakuza* film. The image of the gang in Oshima's films could not be more diametrically opposed to the romanticization of the gangster found in the *yakuza* film except in one crucial area, the disparity between the loyalty of the gang member to the gang, and the gang's loyalty to him. The *yakuza* film, which appeared in 1962–63, and "whose success is unparalleled in the history of Japanese film," throws into relief the problem of *giri*, or obligation.[31] The problem is insurmountable; loyalty is not reciprocated. The *yakuza* film thus has a nihilistic quality to it, much as Oshima's films. What separates Oshima from the *yakuza* genre is that while Oshima politicizes the context of his films, the *yakuza* film ritualizes it. The *yakuza* films, with their highly repetitive, highly coded actions and plots, sets itself in a closed world and through ritualized action serves as a catharsis for its audience of primarily urban, working-class males.[32] Oshima's films are intended not to be cathartic, not to close themselves off, but to open themselves up.

Koi no katamichi kippu
(One-Way Ticket for Love)
Shinoda Masahiro, director
Shochiku, Co., Ltd.

Oshima's third film of 1960, the ill-fated *Night and Fog in Japan*, continued his exploration of youth's search for meaning this time within the specific context of the Anti-Security Treaty demonstrations and the critique of the JCP. In a sense, *Night and Fog in Japan* answers the questions posed in the earlier films of that year: why does today's youth find no solution in school or in politics? The defeat of the protests, or, to put it another way, the triumph of the ruling class, taught Oshima that the nation-State was more powerful than he had conceived. Oshima notes, "I had known the existence of the large system called 'the nation' all along, but until 1960 there was still room for social change within that system. However, it seemed from that time onward this large system became increasingly conspicuous in Japanese society."[33] In *Night and Fog in Japan* we see retrospectively that the youth in the earlier films have only "thrills" to depend on. Sex and violence provide the only meaning available for young people to come to terms with an increasingly meaningless existence.

The failure of Shochiku to release *Night and Fog in Japan* properly inspired Oshima's move toward independent production. In the meantime, however, other directors at Shochiku and elsewhere were also turning their attention to youth, to the question of meaning within a politicized context.

In the wake of the critical success of Oshima's *A Town of Love and Hope*, Shinoda Masahiro was given a chance to direct his first feature, *Koi no katamichi kippu* (*One-Way Ticket for Love*, 1960). According to Bock, the film was based on a song by American pop singer Neil Sedaka.[34] Shinoda however, when asked specifically about that, instead claims that this rock 'n' roll saga arose out of his anger at the false promotionalism of the music world.[35] Regardless of the inspiration, Shinoda's first directorial effort focused on youth, and the specifically youthful world of rock 'n' roll. In the middle '50s, the U.S. saw a cycle of rock movies (*Rock Around the Clock*; *Don't Knock the Rock*; *Rock, Rock, Rock*, etc.) and Japan experienced a similar, short-lived cycle in the early '60s. While the New Wave actually had little interest in rock 'n' roll as a site of countercultural activity (compared, for instance, to American films of the late '60s), the use of rock music occasionally had a symbolic significance. In terms of music, the New Wave directors, Shinoda and Yoshida in particular, leaned toward deliberately avant-garde, contemporary compositions. Shinoda commissioned Takemitsu Toru, Japan's premier contemporary composer, to do the score for *Dry Lake*. As an essentially foreign import, rock 'n' roll may simply lack a radical position within Japanese culture.

It was *Dry Lake* (discussed in the previous chapter) which enabled Shinoda to establish himself permanently in the directors' ranks; a film which Shochiku allowed him to make following the success of Oshima's *Cruel Story of Youth*.[36] Shinoda's vision in this film is far more optimistic than that in any of Oshima's. *Dry Lake* addresses the range of options open to Japan's youth with its three central characters. The rich young man maintains the feudalistic values of the past couched in materialistic concerns; the radical terrorist seeks solace in violence, his political actions are merely an excuse to turn to extreme behavior. Only the young woman who rejects both the past and violence, can find solace, even contentment, when she joins the Ampo demonstrations. The issue of the Security Treaty itself is less important than her willingness to join in an effort aimed at achieving a positive end, in demonstrating that she believes in a future.

Shinoda and screenwriter Terayama also reveal, in *Dry Lake*, an understanding of the connection between the radical Right and the radical Left in Japan. Shinoda claims that he and Terayama confronted the fact that whereas the rightists in Japan typically resorted to terror and violence (as in the assassination of JSP leader Asanuma), the emerging left was similarly becoming so inclined.[37] This insight of theirs in the early '60s points the way toward an understanding of the attraction certain figures of the Right have held for the Japanese Left: Kita Ikki and Mishima Yukio are two examples.

Working within the strictly commercial confines of Shochiku, Shinoda directed three films a year for two years focusing on youth, or youth-gangs. His first film following *Dry Lake* was *Yuhi ni akai ore no kao* (*My Face Red in the Sunset*, 1961). With another script by Terayama, this offbeat action film about a *yakuza* hired by a corrupt contractor to kill a woman journalist, lumped together social protest and the emerging *yakuza* form. The world of *yakuza* was used again in 1962 for *Namida o shishi no tategami ni* (*Tears on*

Namida o shishi no tategami ni (*Tears on the Lion's Mane*)
Shinoda Masahiro, director. Kawakita/Japan Film Library Council

the Lion's Mane), which featured a rock 'n' roll score by Takemitsu Toru. The film is based partly on *On the Waterfront* (1954), but here Shinoda sees management as corrupt, not the union, as in the Hollywood film (whose anti-union message Shinoda attributes to the Red Scare of the postwar era). Shinoda also claims that he was inspired to model the character of the hero, a youth who tragically succumbs to the feudal tradition of *giri*, on Mishima Yukio. He initially wanted to make his hero homosexual; the studio refused that idea and Shinoda settled for a "second-rate *yakuza*."[38] Shinoda's tribute apparently pleased Mishima, who, in a number of films he wrote later on, adopted the image of a second-rate *yakuza*. Shinoda's interest in the world of *yakuza* culminated in 1963 with *Kawaita hana* (*Pale Flower*), considered by many in the West to be among his major works.

Between these *yakuza* forays, Shinoda dealt with both working-class and middle-class youth, trying to accommodate himself to Shochiku's essentially melodramatic plot structures. The most interesting of the films made before 1963 is probably *Shamisen to otobai* (*Shamisen and Motorcycle*, 1961). Through this story, which is pure soap opera in structure (romantic betrayals, coincidences, dark family secrets), Shinoda begins what we might consider to be his most significant authorial characteristic: the comparison between traditionalism and modernism (in terms of both social norms and

Rokudenashi (Good-for-Nothing)
Yoshida Yoshishige, director
Shochiku Co., Ltd.

aesthetic practice). In this film, Shinoda juxtaposes the moral values of the prewar and postwar eras in this tale of a young woman who discovers the truth about her parentage and who is finally allowed to marry the man she chooses. Too many assignments like this one, however, inspired him to leave Shochiku in 1965.

Yoshida Yoshishige also benefited from the early critical success of Oshima. In 1960 Yoshida directed his first film, *Rokudenashi (Good-for-Nothing)*; the film that Oshima said was merely "coincidentally" about alienated students. But just as Shinoda's *Dry Lake* seems remarkably Oshima-like, so, too, *Good-for-Nothing* is a variation on *Cruel Story of Youth*. In Yoshida's film, four university friends rob the secretary of a company president, who is the father of one of them. They do it basically for kicks ("recreation" is their term); and it is for kicks that one of them, Kitajima, starts up a sadomasochistic sexual relationship with this secretary. When his three friends decide to rob her again, this time threatening her with a pistol, Kitajima stops the robbery only to be severely wounded. Kitajima runs over his friend with his car, and gives the money back to his lover. She reveals that her purse was stuffed with newsprint to lure them out. Kitajima dies, claiming everything was mere "recreation."

Yoshida followed this lively film with two Shochiku-imposed social melodramas for which he wrote original scenarios. While both contain elements of protest, they are more reminiscent of films by such solid liberal filmmakers as Yamamoto Satsuo or Masumura Yasuzo (the latter having retreated from his stance of the late '50s). In 1962, Yoshida directed his most

Akitsu Onsen (*Akitsu Hot Springs*)
Yoshida Yoshishige, director. Shochiku Co., Ltd.

important film of this early period, *Akitsu Onsen* (*Akitsu Springs*). While the film is most significant for the portrayal of the female character (discussed in Chapter 4), Yoshida demonstrates an interest in youth and youth's increasing disillusionment with the postwar world. Yoshida follows a love affair beginning on the home front in World War II and continuing on and off until the present day. The hero, Kawamoto Shusaku, is nursed back to health by Shinko at the end of the war. The film then spans seventeen years as Shusaku and Shinko continue their relationship. Shusaku's dream of writing great philosophical novels gradually dissipates as does any sense of optimism about the world. Yoshida's film is relatively depoliticized in context compared to Oshima's works, but it is clear nevertheless that Shusaku is emblematic of the 1950s generation which saw its dreams shattered by the war years and then Japan's failure to repudiate those years. The increasing materialism of Japanese society is also condemned as the hero becomes something of a wastrel.

In *Arashi o yobu juhachinin* (*18 Roughs*, 1963; the title translates as "18 Who Stir Up a Storm"), Yoshida, as Oshima and Shinoda before him, combined the youth film with the gang film to tell the story of one young man's efforts to try and keep a group of eighteen *yakuza* from wreaking havoc on the job and on the town. The hero's love for a young waitress is threatened when she is raped by one of the eighteen. Although he is unable to find the rapist, the hero succeeds in convincing the girl to marry him. The eighteen roughs leave town to work and wreak havoc elsewhere. Unlike the heroes of *Cruel Story of Youth* and *The Sun's Burial*, Yoshida's youthful protagonist does not succumb to the nihilism and violence of his fellow-alienated youth. Instead, he allows himself to feel love which not only redeems him from a life of crime or anti-social behavior, but which rescues his girlfriend from despair as well.

Yoshida followed *18 Roughs* with a film closer in spirit to the nihilism of Oshima; closer in spirit, as well, to French New Wave mentor Jean-Pierre Melville. *Nihon dasshutsu (Escape from Japan, 1964)* is a violent and grim gangster story of a young man, Tatsuo, who works as a "roadie" (assistant) for a famous pop singer. He gets involved with a drug addict named Takashi, who introduces him to Gota, a former bicycle racer, and Yasue, who works as a maid in a bathhouse. The four plan a robbery of the baths at which Yasue works, but in pulling the job, Gota kills a policeman (shades of Godard's *Breathless*, itself inspired by Melville's films). The gang begins to disintegrate and Tatsuo kills Gota for abusing Yasue. Tatsuo and Yasue dream of escaping to America on board a U.S. ship bound for Korea and then to the states, but Tatsuo is betrayed by a *yakuza* and Yasue is arrested while trying to board the vessel. Yoshida says that the basic story idea was given to him by Shochiku President Kido. Yoshida deliberately avoided making a standard *yakuza* film (by this time dominating Japanese screens) and avoided, too, the style of a samurai action film. Yoshida's final scenes of the hero's madness in prison were removed from the release prints of the film and Yoshida left Shochiku shortly thereafter as a result. He had long realized that such a move was inevitable, especially after Oshima's earlier departure.[39]

Also working within a commercial context which attempted to capitalize on the youth cycle was Imamura Shohei at Nikkatsu Studios, arguably the most resolutely commercial company of them all. After working as an assistant at Shochiku, Imamura arrived at Nikkatsu with a bit more freedom than might otherwise have been the case despite some assisting work initially assigned to him. Critics see his first four films as preludes to the more important work to follow, detecting in them emerging authorial characteristics. While this is sound, these films also have a place within the youth film. Three films (!) in 1958 rely on various aspects of the youth cycle then in full swing, and look forward to the early films of Oshima, Shinoda, and Yoshida. The first of these films, *Nusumareta yokujo (Stolen Desire)* concerns a traveling theatrical troupe (Imamura's original title was "Tent Theatre" but the company changed it).[40] The hero is an intellectual producer-director who has quit college for love of the theatre. Imamura claims that this character was modeled on himself.[41] The hero develops a strong attraction to the wife of the troupe's leading player, but is in turn romantically pursued by her younger sister. Bock describes the film as a "ribald comedy,"[42] but we can also see the focus on the young hero and his increasing disillusionment with the theatre and its rules (its rules of performance and its rules of offstage romance) as a metaphor for the emerging alienation of the young filmmakers and the young generation.

Imamura's next film, *Nishi ginza eki-mae* (*Nishi Ginza Station*) was a strictly commercial star-vehicle for popular singer Frank Nagai.[43] The rather slight plot focuses on Nagai as a henpecked drugstore owner who daydreams about a native woman he met on an island during the war. The image of the native woman merges with that of his clerk. A friend advises him to have an affair. Comic complications ensue, including an idyll on a tropic island which turns out not to be a tropic island. Something like a reunion of husband and wife occurs at the end—this is, after all, a comedy. Dave Kehr notices that the island paradise image will recur in *Kamigami no fukaki yokubo* (*The Profound Desire of the Gods*, 1968).[44]

The third film of 1958, *Hateshi naki yokubo* (*Endless Desire*), has some resemblances to Oshima's later *The Sun's Burial* with its grim humor and deathly betrayals. The relationships between the gang members anticipates *Buta to gunkan* (*Pigs and Battleships*, 1961), while Bock sees in the character of the widow "the first of Imamura's ruthlessly determined women."[45] The image of the gang and the legacy of World War II clearly anticipate the developing thematics of the New Wave.

Nianchan (*My Second Brother*, 1959, aka *The Diary of Sueko*) was Imamura's first critically respected film, the kind of liberal indictment that Japanese critics laud (witness their love of Imai, for instance). Based on a diary written by a ten-year-old girl, the film is set in a coal-mining village and focuses on a family of Korean descent. The discrimination they encounter is a function of prejudice against Koreans (see Chapter 5) and part and parcel of a life of poverty. The film emphasizes individual determination and the essential bonds of the family—the father dies and care of the family is left to the older children, especially the older brother who returns to care for his siblings.

With *Pigs and Battleships*, Imamura produced his first genuine masterpiece and abandoned forever the touches of simplistic humanism that appeared in *Nianchan*, and extended the blackly comic vision that distinguished *Endless Desire*. Contemporary with the gang-style films of Oshima, Imamura's film focuses on a youth gang living and working in the shadows of the U.S. military at the Yokosuka Naval Base. *Pigs and Battleships* is something of a rarity in the Japanese cinema as it is an out-and-out political satire, as funny as it is pointed. The film clearly pokes fun at Japan's economic reliance on the U.S. and condemns not the Americans, but the Japanese themselves for pimping and prostituting themselves before the mighty U.S. dollar.

The film's hero is Kinta, an energetic, likable, somewhat slow-witted

Buta to gunkan (Pigs and Battleships)
Imamura Shohei, director
Kawakita/Japan Film Library Council

youngster whose true ambition is to be a band leader, but who has done some pimping and who is now involved in a bizarre pig-raising scheme. The petty gangsters with whom he is involved decide to raise pigs, feeding them garbage from the U.S. naval ships, and sell them on the black market. Kinta's girlfriend, Haruko, tries to convince him to leave the gang and move with her to Kawasaki City to work in a factory. When he discovers that Haruko is pregnant, Kinta refuses, opting for the gang. The inevitable falling out of the gang members occurs, leading to a surrealistic climactic confrontation on the streets of the red-light district, replete with a stampede of the hogs and a shoot-out. Kinta's dramatic death scene occurs in a Japanese-style toilet, an obvious but comically effective metaphor.

Pigs and Battleships is clearly intended as an indictment of Japan's postwar prosperity, but it is not simply a condemnation of materialism, or even a commentary on Japan's reliance on the U.S. Rather, the film points out the bitter irony of the fact that Japan's riches stem from U.S. militarism—the continued presence of U.S. servicemen on Japanese soil, the U.S. involvement in the Korean war and its further forays in Asia.

The issue of economic prosperity through militarism is refracted through Japan's partial, even twisted, adoption of U.S.-style democracy. The American presence in Japan is shown to be ubiquitous; certainly it is in this film set near a U.S. naval base. The Japanese literally prostitute themselves to the U.S. soldiers. Haruko, at one point angry at Kinta, pretends to be a prostitute and goes with a sailor to a hotel. When the serviceman discovers that she has no intention of sleeping with him, he and two of his fellow shipmates rape her. The three men then take a shower together, singing "I've Been Working on the Railroad" as they do so. Haruko tries to rob them; the three sailors discover this, beat her up and have her arrested. The American presence is alluded to in more subtle ways. The film opens with the "Star-Spangled Banner" playing on the soundtrack as the camera pans across the harbor. At another point, U.S. war planes prompt the comment that "Americans are great." American ideology is invoked when the gang members convince themselves that by stealing pigs from their own boss they are "democratizing" the gang.

Imamura also relies on black comedy to get his points across. Cannibalism is evoked in a grotesquely funny scene when the gang members discover, at one point, that the pig they are eating has been fed the corpse of a murdered man. The comedy of death-and-dying is utilized in a sub-plot involving the gang leader who believes that a mild case of indigestion is really an incurable cancer. Unable to face the pain, he decides to kill himself. However, he is equally unable to commit suicide, so he hires a Chinese assassin to kill him. Then, when he discovers that his X-rays have been inadvertently switched and that he is not incurably ill, he also finds himself unable to cancel the contract. These are not the *giri*-driven gangsters of the *yakuza* film!

The only survivor of this world of corruption, deceit, prostitution, and comic incompetence is the young heroine, Haruko. She looks forward to Imamura's innocent heroines who survive their ghastly worlds. But we should not find an image of hope in her eventual exodus to the promised land of Kawasaki City, for the image of the youthful hero, Kinta, his head in the porcelain of the toilet, remains more firmly etched in our minds. Kinta's youthful optimism and energy have been sapped by the competition for material gain, the false democratization of Japan, the hypocrisy of postwar Japan's disavowal of militarism, and the continued group-orientation of the Japanese people. Kinta's essential innocence has been inevitably corrupted by deceit, and he strikes back in anger and violence which can lead only and inevitably to death. The blackly comic tone prevents the Japanese audience from finding Kinta's death pathetic and heroic. We may not wallow in our pity, giving vent to our feelings. The cold eye of satire and irony that Imamura brings to this film makes its message clear and powerful; and it makes the rest of his cinema uniquely suited to an examination of Japan in the postwar world.

Imamura abandoned his focus on youth after this in favor of explorations about the nature of Japanese identity and the exploration of the essence of the spirit of Japanese women, the latter a theme he would come to share with a number of other New Wave directors, as we shall see later. Contemporary with Imamura, Oshima, Shinoda, and Yoshida in the youth realm, however, was another important force in initiating the Japanese New Wave, a force which came slightly from outside of the commercial mainstream in the form of Hani Susumu and his first feature film, *Furyo shonen* (*Bad Boys*, 1960).

As we briefly discussed above, Hani's career was launched through the route of documentary shorts, a preparation for directing features unique among this group of New Wave directors. (In fact, Matsumoto Toshio, who has directed only three features, is the only other New Wave director who made short films as a prelude to features—and he has since returned to making experimental shorts.) *Bad Boys* shows its roots in documentary. Based on a slightly fictionalized study of juvenile delinquents, *Wings that Couldn't Fly*, the film uses nonprofessional actors, black and white, hand-held cinematography, and location shooting.[46] Joan Mellen reports that among the locations used was a real reformatory and that the actors were all ex-reform school boys who created much of their own dialogue. Hani, in fact, maintains that the boys basically acted out their real lives, including a sequence in which he staged a robbery as part of the film, during which the young actor playing the thief went into a jewelry shop and stole three rings as the camera photographed him from outside.[47]

The film is something of a "case study" as it focuses on Asai Hiroshi, an eighteen-year-old boy whose father died in the war and whose poverty-stricken mother abandoned him. What we see clearly is that Hiroshi is not a "bad boy," that society is incapable of admitting its failures and so chooses to incarcerate him to remove him from sight. First we see that Hiroshi is implicated in a jewel theft; the flashing lights of the amusement district in Asakusa (one of Tokyo's poorest sections) boast of thrills that Hiroshi cannot afford. A movie poster prominently displays the latest exploits of youth-star Ishihara Yujiro (a nice, ironic touch). Hiroshi and his friends rob the store, partly from the desire to experience some of the fun they see around them. Hiroshi's accomplices to the crime are all released into the custodies of their families; having no family, Hiroshi is sent to a special reformatory after he pleads that he wants to live a decent life.

The reformatory is introduced by a shot of the Japanese flag, a link between this institution and the State. The institution is run like an army training camp replete with strict discipline, rigorous physical exercise, para-military rules (like saluting), and a hierarchy which is detrimental to the younger, newer inmates. Hani himself believes that such treatment as Hiroshi receives is indicative of "the spirit of totalitarianism, which is still deep rooted in modern Japanese behavior."[48] Hiroshi's rehabilitation is ironic in that he *resisted* prison life, a resistance which enabled him to grow up.[49]

However, the film is somewhat more ambivalent about Hiroshi's maturation due to "his own inner strength."[50] In the reformatory, Hiroshi is well fed, which contrasts to his own memories as a young boy when he was always hungry. He also experiences kindness in the boys' school. After he is transferred from the prison laundry, he goes to work in the woodshop, where Mr. Ohkuma, the teacher, treats him kindly. He also makes friends with another inmate, Debari. The kindness and friendship he experiences in the woodshop recall to him how he was befriended as a child by a bar girl with a G.I. boyfriend. Debari's description of his life before the reformatory, when he lived with a girl and three other boys as part of a gang who made money by extortion and petty thievery (shades of *Cruel Story of Youth*), is also filled with ambivalence. The feeling of community he experienced as part of a gang is something he misses, but he recognizes that a life of crime is no life for a youngster. Hani's point is that life inside and outside the reformatory is filled with ambivalences; kindness and exploitation exist inside the walls of the prison and without.

The perception of ambivalence is a very Japanese characteristic. In *Bad Boys*, as in some of Hani's later films (espeically *She and He*), it is not allowed to dominate as it does, for instance, in the works of Ozu in which the *feeling* of ambivalence is allowed to overwhelm the perception of it, the political, social, and economic realities which give rise to it. Things are not so clear and simple: A system which gives rise to hypocrisy and encourages a cycle of exploitation (the young inmates are exploited by the older ones; when they replace the older ones who leave, they, in turn, exploit the newer arrivals) also contains within it the seeds of kindness, a pure essence which can flourish in trying circumstances. The focus on youth by Hani is a focus on the moment when ambivalence is held in balance: Hiroshi can turn in either direction, to a life of crime, a life where he is both exploited and exploiter, or he may look to a better future, of integrity and self-confidence.

The militaristic ideology of the reformatory in *Bad Boys* indicates the potential negative effects such training can have on the young and stands as an implicit indictment of fascistic leanings in postwar Japan. This is a common expression of dismay on the part of New Wave directors who gave even clearer vent to their feelings in films specifically set in the war years. While the protests surrounding the renewal of the U.S.-Japan Mutual Security Treaty provided, as we have seen earlier, much of the immediate context, and some of the content, of the New Wave cinema, the spirit of 1960 did not remain an intense force—how could it? The intense fervor aroused inevitably dissipated, resurging from time to time throughout the '60s in a variety of organized protests, especially of U.S. involvement in Vietnam. Of much greater lasting significance in molding the ideology of the New Wave filmmakers were the war and postwar years, when virtually all of them were coming into adulthood.

The influence of World War II on the young is the subject of two films by important New Wave directors: *Shiiku* (*The Catch*, 1961), by Oshima, and *Shokei no shima* (*Punishment Island*, 1966; aka *Captive's Island*) by Shinoda.

Shiiku (The Catch)
Oshima Nagisa, director. Kawakita/Japan Film Library Council

Oshima's film, adapted from a short story by Oe Kenzaburo (who shares many crucial thematic concerns with the New Wave), marked his first effort as an independent producer; *Punishment Island* similarly marked Shinoda's first independent production after leaving Shochiku. While Oshima's film is not especially well thought of within the context of his canon (Japanese critics liked it well enough), many feel that Shinoda's film is among his best.[51] It is interesting that both Oshima and Shinoda should turn to a war story for their first independent effort, and that both would structure their films around the war's effect on the young.

Ian Cameron notices the centrality of the young in *The Catch*: "At various moments of violence, Oshima dwells on the presence of children, stressing the effects which both the specific events and the general situation must have on them and hence on the future—or, from our view-point, the present." Cameron goes on to point out that the central role of the young boy is meant clearly to correspond to Oshima, who, in 1945 when the film takes place, was the same age as his protagonist.[52] The film tells the story of a downed black U.S. airman captured by the citizens of a small village. Told by the village headman to wait for the Military Police to come for the airman, the villagers hold him prisoner. The MPs never arrive and the villagers deal with the situation themselves, their dealings culminating in killing the airman. To justify their actions, the villagers supply various pretenses, thus revealing their essential hypocrisy and cowardice.

The presence of the airman brings forth hidden tensions and conflicts within the community and the black man becomes something of a scapegoat for dissatisfied villagers. To the children, the soldier is both fascinating and frightful, although they eventually begin to treat him as a person, something the adults never do. For them he remains an abstraction, a promise of hope for reward from the authorities, an image of fear onto whom they can project their own inadequacies. As the children observe the actions of their elders, their disillusionment grows, culminating at film's end in one of the youngster's complete disassociation from the group.

It is clear that this lone village with its single POW is meant to stand as a microcosm for Japan during the war. Oshima has said about this film, "In this case the responsibility for the war was not the responsibility of the generals or the military men but of the people in general."[53] The hypocrisy, the self-delusion, the pettiness of the villagers and the excuses they find to justify almost every despicable action becomes increasingly clearer to the young people. Thus, Oshima is saying, it was no surprise that in the early '50s, such youth (his generation) would rebel against their traditions. And as the postwar world came increasingly to resemble the war years, save only that Japan was not engaged in armed conflict (though it was allied with the U.S. who was), more and more young people would come to feel increasingly alienated.

The war in microcosm appears even more strongly in Shinoda's *Punishment Island*. Here the story concerns a young man of about thirty who returns to the site of his youthful torment as a ten-year-old prisoner in a reformatory on Kojima Island, the punishment island of the title. Saburo (called Sabo as a child) returns to search for Otake, the vicious head of the school who "worked boys even the reformatory couldn't handle." The film alternates between Saburo's search for and confrontation with people still on the island who did not help him then, and flashbacks which reveal the incredible cruelty he endured at the hands of fellow prisoners and, most especially, Otake. The scars on Saburo's back attest to the vicious beatings he received; his anger at the current primary school principal remains palpable. At one point, in the present tense of the film, he tells the man to "just be an onlooker like you always were." Flashbacks reveal the then schoolteacher's unwillingness to stand up to Otake when young Sabo ran away and sought refuge with him. Only his wife, now sickly, tried to intervene. This indictment of the principal reflects the New Wave's condemnation of the previous generation of intellectuals who did not stand up to the militarists. Similarly, the figure of Matsui, a man who takes pleasure in hunting for escapees from the island's new reformatory, reflects the cycle of exploitation common in Japan (revealed so compellingly in *Bad Boys*, as well). In flashback, we see that Matsui was a primary tormentor of Sabo; in the present he is just as vicious and cowardly.

The major confrontation, however, is reserved for Otake. Saburo reveals to Otake's daughter that before coming to the island, Otake was a Military Policeman (*kempeitai*). Among his actions was the murder of Saburo's family because the father was an anarchist. The military, embarrassed by Otake's actions, dispatched him to Kojima to hush up the affair. Otake's cruelty to Sabo culminates when Otake hurls the young boy into the sea from a high, rocky cliff. Of course, Sabo did not die as everyone thought. Saburo finds himself now unable to kill Otake, a mere shell of his former self, but he does demand that Otake make some kind of restitution. Saburo accepts Otake's right thumb as payment (a variation on *yakuza* penance of removing the first joint of the little finger). He then hurls the finger into the sea from the very same cliff.

That the island of Kojima is to be taken as a microcosm of Japan is made especially clear by the fact that the island, seen from a distance in the opening scene, resembles Mt. Fuji, that most beloved symbol of Japan. Otake stands in for the patriarchal system. He represents official authority (in the flashbacks he is always wearing his uniform) and he is a father (where his wife is, is never mentioned). He also should be a father-figure to the boys (as the Emperor was said to be during the war), but he is cruel almost beyond belief to Sabo. The primary school principal and his wife represent the basic citizenry, some weak, some stronger, but ultimately ineffectual in the face of rampant militarism. Matsui is the brutalized youth who become brutalizers in the present; perhaps he stands, too, for the unregenerate war criminals reintegrated into mainstream society. Saburo represents the new generation, a man who has finally, by film's end, exorcised the past; he has exacted revenge and can now put the past aside. Of course, if we extend the allegory of Kojima as Japan, what are we to make of the fact that Saburo leaves (leaves again) the island? Need today's generation abandon Japan? Yes, Shinoda is saying, the past that is Japan; bury this Japan, throw it into the sea, and live one's life free from its memory.

The inability to escape the brutal, militarist past is however, a severe problem according to Oshima in his extraordinary international success of 1969, *Shonen* (*Boy*). This film, Oshima's most famous as it was the one which introduced him to the Western world, deals with another cruel patriarch, a World War II veteran whose wife, and then his ten-year-old son, participate in a scheme to feign being hit by moving cars to extort hush-money from the drivers. The father claims that war injuries prevent him from working. He beats his wife, denies his son any pleasure, lies to the boy and makes him feel guilty and unwanted. The boy retreats into a fantasy life, imagining himself an alien from the galaxy of Andromeda. He tries to run away, but is returned to his family. He eventually determines that if he gets hit by the cars his wounds will look more realistic and so the family will be able to extort more and more money. In each town, the authorities soon become suspicious, so the family must continually move, the film following them on a northward course until they reach the northern tip of Hokkaido. As Joan Mellen points out, the boy's comment, "Is this the end of Japan?" is an ironic double entendre, the wish to be rid of Japan perfectly understandable and desirable.[54] Their scheme comes to an end amid death and capture.

The boy's youth is robbed by the legacy of the war and by the continuing patriarchy and militarism of the postwar world. The boy's imagination and artistry are constantly shown as he weaves his fantasy life for his younger brother. But this inner world is increasingly constricted by the outer world which comes ever closer to destroying him. Oshima contrasts this lively inner world with the drab outer world not only through the contrast between the boy's fantasy and his reality, but through the constant reminders of Japan's material growth. Oshima posits an inverse ratio between material growth and spiritual growth. The more Japan succeeds economically, the poorer its inner life. The more patriarchy is allowed to continue, the more youth will be destroyed. The film is a bleak indictment, but a cogent one, made even stronger by the knowledge that the film is based on an actual incident. Oshima's films based upon historical circumstances or actual cases, like *Death by Hanging, Boy,* and *In the Realm of the Senses,* are his most powerful works; even the early, extraordinary *Night and Fog in Japan* has a firm grounding in fact.

A condemnation of the way war, or at least the Second World War and its militarist ideology, robbed young people of their youth is brought home by a wonderfully eccentric work of film art by Suzuki Seijun in 1966, *Kenka ereji* (*Elegy to Violence*; aka *The Born Fighter*). This stylish, comic, black-and-white CinemaScope film stands at an angle slightly askew from the central works of the New Wave by virtue of its origination in the ranks of the youth exploitation films of Nikkatsu. Director Suzuki himself stands just to the side of the New Wave, trying to deal with many of its primary issues while being subjugated to genre films. Noel Burch reflects that Suzuki's *Tokyo nagaremono* (*Tokyo Drifter,* 1966) may be compared, in terms of its cult status, to Robert Aldrich's *Kiss Me Deadly* (1955).[55] Suzuki's status as an auteur may be likened to that of Don Siegel, another director confined to genre who has transcended formula by virtue of certain eccentricities and insights. In fact, however, the best comparison to a director in the West (and Suzuki's virtually unknown status here probably requires some comparison) would to to Sam Fuller.[56] Both directors start from a generic base—war, gangster, thriller, and so on—and both impose their own personality on the material. More significantly, both have what can only be called an offbeat sense of humor, of *theatrics.* Burch (naturally) ascribes these characteristics of Suzuki to "distancing effects" and likens them somewhat to Oshima's *Night and Fog in Japan*.[57] Within the context of the routinely generic, what can be made of Fuller's *Verboten!* (1958) or his post- Godardian *Dead Pigeon on Beethoven Street* (1972)? No more nor less than of Suzuki's *Irezumi ichidai* (*The Life of Tattoo*, 1965). A full understanding of *Elegy to Violence*, with its seemingly weird swings of tone and its patently unrealistic fight scenes leading up to a brilliant denouement of great insight and seriousness, can only come about via a brief tangent through the world of Nikkatsu's genre films about youth.

The interest in youth which arose in the late '50s not only had an influence on the management at Shochiku, which allowed Oshima, Shinoda, and Yoshida a chance to direct, but it also affected the more commercially oriented Nikkatsu. It was Nikkatsu, after all, which launched the first wave of *taiyozoku* films. In the late '50s, Nikkatsu produced a group of films called the "Nikkatsu Action series," which featured a new generation of young male stars, the most important of whom were Ishihara Yujiro (younger brother of *taiyozoku* novelist Ishihara Shintaro) and Kobayashi Akira. (Ishihara and Kobayashi created Nikkatsu's "Diamond Line" of "Mighty Guys,"[58] along with a third young star, Akagi Keiichiro, who died in a traffic accident in 1961 at the age of twenty-one.)

Ishihara Yujiro rose to fame in the 1950s on the strength of his starring roles in the films adapted from his brother's sensationalist novels, *Season of the Sun* and *Crazed Fruit*. Following these successes, Ishihara starred in five or six films a year throughout the remainder of the 1950s and well into the '60s, and during those years he was unquestionably the most popular movie star in Japan. His image was that of a moderately rebellious youth who breaks away from the rules imposed by society and his family, but only up to a point. He was both heroic and sensitive; Sato Tadao feels he combined the best traits of both *tateyaku* and *nimaime* roles.[59] A typical film of his, contemporary with the New Wave, might be *Shimizu no abarenbo* (*The Wild Reporter*, 1960), which features Yujiro as a radio newsman who exposes a narcotics ring.

Slightly below Yujiro in popularity came Kobayashi Akira. He made a group of films known collectively as the "*wataridori*" (migrating bird) series. Among the most important of these are *Wataridori itsumata kaeru* (*When Does the Migrating Bird Return?*, 1959) and *Guitar o motta wataridori* (*The Wandering Guitarist*, 1960). The bulk of Kobayahsi's films were directed by Saito Buichi, and featured Akira as a guitar-playing wanderer, dressed in an American-style cowboy outfit. In between songs, on the soundtrack or performed within the plot (Kobayashi had a music-and-film career similar to Elvis Presley), he would become involved in adventures, many of them stemming from the days when he was a police detective who was forced to resign. In *The Wandering Guitarist*, for instance, he exposes a narcotics ring in Hakodate, Hokkaido, headed by the woman he loves. He exposes the gang and leaves at the end. The wandering aspect of his character gives his screen image a built-in pathos, and also provides the filmmakers with a chance to show off the location photography. Both aspects look forward in some ways to the (in)famous *Otoko was tsuraiyo* series (known in the U.S. as the "Tora-san" series) of Yamada Yoji at Shochiku. Kobayashi, unlike Tora-san, however, is a two-fisted action hero, but his homelessness and wandering imbue him with emotionalism, at least to the Japanese. This idea of wandering was also seen in his films like *Umikarakita nagaremono* (*A Drifter from the Sea*, 1962) and *Kanto mushuku* (*Kanto Wanderer*, 1963; Kanto is the name of the large plain on Japan's main island which contains Tokyo and its massive urban sprawl). The latter film was directed by Suzuki Seijun, and might first have seemed appropriate to Nikkatsu's interesting but nevertheless routine youth-action pictures. Suzuki, however, had other things in mind.

Akira plays a bouncer in a gaming house, which provides an opportunity for many fight scenes, at which Suzuki excels. Sato describes one fight in the gambling club:

> When the bare-chested hero suddenly swishes his sword and the two *yakuza* fall with a thud, everyone flees and all the *shoji* (paper-covered sliding doors) of the large room fall away in a wafting motion. The surrounding corridor is then revealed bathed in brilliant red light. The scene changes in the next shot, and the screen is filled with snow. In the midst, shaded by a Japanese paper umbrella, the hero is striding forth to fight his enemies single-handedly.[60]

This description of a scene from *Kanto Wanderer* reveals Suzuki's particular contribution to the youth cycle. The climactic scene of *The Life of Tattoo* finds the hero challenged to a fight on a city street. The lighting changes suddenly and the protagonist and his enemies are standing on a stage bathed in colored spotlights. One thinks, too, of the final sequence of *Tokyo Drifter*. This time it is a gunfight in a deserted nightclub; the lighting of the scene switches to a bright yellow for the climactic shoot-out. Obviously, such scenes are overtly theatricalized, which prompts Sato to launch into a short disquisition on Brecht, and it is this sort of thing which prompts Burch to place Suzuki within the same context as Oshima (and other New Wave directors who employ the "theatrical sign"—the subject of my Chapter 6). What should be noted is that the Nikkatsu audience would find such *outré* moments quite acceptable (and supports Burch's theses in his chapters on traditional Japanese aesthetics). It was also these moments of overt stylization which made Suzuki a "cult" favorite in the '60s, a status reserved for very few other Japanese directors. When Suzuki was fired by Nikkatsu in 1968, there were organized protests by thousands of young film fans in a Japanese equivalent of the French "l'affaire Langlois" (Henri Langlois, director of the *Cinéma thèque Française* was fired by the government in 1968). On the other hand, not all Japanese filmgoers were comfortable with Suzuki's "Brechtianism." Max Tessier notes that Suzuki was fired by Nikkatsu President Hori Kyusaku because his films were "incomprehensible for the public."[61]

Until he was fired from Nikkatsu, Suzuki was an incredibly prolific director working primarily in two variations on the youth film: the *yakuza* and "pink" films which came to dominate Japanese screens in the '60s. There seems little doubt that *Elegy to Violence* is Suzuki's most important film; the Japanese critics of *Kinema Jumpo* certainly think so.[62] To Nikkatsu in 1966, save for its unique use of black-and-white cinematography, *Elegy to Violence* might have been no different than any of their other films, or at least no different from Suzuki's oeuvre. The film stars Takahashi Hideki, who was seen at this time as the next Yujiro or Akira (he is ten years younger than Yujiro, seven years younger than Akira). Takahashi's greatest fame came in a series of ten films known at *"Otoko no monsho"* (Male's Crest) in which he played a youthful *yakuza oyabun* (boss). While Nikkatsu may have understood the black-and-white cinematography as appropriate for the setting in the past (1935–37), one doubts they perceived its perceptive understanding of the links between the Japanese educational system and Japanese militarism.

With a script by Shindo Kaneto (most famous in the West as the director of *The Island* and *Onibaba*), *Elegy to Violence* has an overt political level concerning the clash between traditional Japanese and Western religions. The hero, Kiroku, nicknamed "Fighting Kiroku" because of his love of violence, lives with a Catholic family in Okayama in 1935. He is torn between the purity of his love for Michiko, the daughter of the family, and his increasing sexual desires for her. He sublimates his sexual desires and uses the energy in outbursts of violence, delivered in typically high style and humor by Suzuki. In fact, until the end, the fight scenes are staged more like cartoons, replete with bouncy music, rather than the theatricalized fights described earlier. The film is structurally similar to the Chinese Martial Arts movies which became popular in the U.S. in the early 1970s with the films of Bruce Lee and (closer to Suzuki's style) the Shaw Bros. productions. Like Chinese Kung Fu movies, *Elegy to Violence* focuses on a youthful hero who is concerned with perfecting his skills as a fighter and who seems to spend more time, in school and out, studying martial arts than anything else. Youthful insubordination to his school's military instructor gets him transferred to Aizu, a northern prefecture. In Aizu, he meets a man named Misa, who claims to be a haiku instructor and who is having an affair with a beautiful bar waitress. Kiroku comes to admire Misa, who turns out to be Kita Ikki, the ideologue behind the *ni-ni-roku* (2–26, or February 26) Incident of 1936. While Michiko decides to enter a convent, Kiroku decides to head for Tokyo with Kita, to get into a really big fight. Sato claims that no doubt this big fight will be the Sino-Japanese war, but

Kenka ereji (*Elegy to Violence*)
Suzuki Seijun, director
Kawakita/Japan Film Library Council

one thinks that Suzuki means all of World War II, for nothing short of global war will serve as an elegy to violence.[63]

Japanese critic Oshikawa Yoshiyuki, felt that the introduction of the *ni-ni-roku* Incident ruins the film.[64] On the contrary, it is Suzuki's most brilliant stroke, which he himself added to the film.[65] Suzuki thereby demonstrates that an educational system which encourages violence and conformity to the group leads to the possibility of global adventurism and that, moreover, youthful idealism is easily swayed. It is the case that the writings of Kita Ikki had their most profound influence on younger Japanese army officers who were becoming increasingly alienated and dismayed by what they perceived as perversions of the Japanese way of life. For Suzuki, regardless of the content of Kita's works, the betrayal of the young officers who staged an attempted coup d'etat in February 1936, by the Japanese government represents another instance of official hypocrisy and the betrayal of youthful ideals. This particular elegy to violence is an elegy for all the Kirokus whose youthful energy and idealism were channeled by an educational system which encouraged their natural impulses for boyish violence into a massive fighting force cynically manipulated by old men for political ends.

That Suzuki, whose basic sympathies are anti-militaristic and essentially Leftist, could allude to the betrayal of the Right-wing army officers to condemn the Japanese establishment is indicative of Japanese radical politics. Commitment is more admirable than hypocrisy; idealism is preferable to cynicism. This same ideal, seen in the attraction many of the New Wave felt toward Mishima Yukio, is expressed by the Socialist Student League in 1960 who, in seeking to understand the failure of the Communist Party leaders of the 1930s, turned to the writings of Kita Ikki in search of an ideology indigenous to Japan that might foment social change.[66] Kita Ikki himself became the central subject of *Kaigenrei* (*Martial Law*, 1973; aka *Coup d'etat*) by Yoshida Yoshishige. The *ni-ni-roku* Incident is also invoked, it should be noted, by Oshima's *In the Realm of the Senses*. It therefore seems important to discuss Kita's writings, which led to an attempted coup d'etat in 1936.

Writing in 1919, while in Shanghai, Kita put forth a plan which came eventually to be called the *Nihon kaizo hoan taiko* (Outline Plan for the Reorganization of Japan). The plan called for the limitation of private property and corporate holdings; the government should nationalize those properties deemed to be "excessive." Moreover, the government should plan the national economy while providing for social welfare and free education for both sexes (although only men over the age of twenty-five should have the right to vote). Company profits should be shared by employers and employees.[67] If this sounds like communism, one should realize that Kita appealed to Japanese conservatives with this plan. The plan was not communistic in essence, for it rested on a firm foundation of *kokutai*—the national polity, with the Emperor enshrined as the deific figurehead of the nation-family. Japanese conservatives despised communism, but recognized

> that as long as there was suffering in Japan, there would always be social unrest. The best way to check the spread of revolutionary ideas and restore social harmony . . . was to eliminate the roots of exploitation and injustice. . . . Right-wing radicals objected to *both* the capitalist system and its left-wing opponents. Their aim was to restore *kokutai* on a popular basis, through national reform . . ." [emphasis added].[68]

It was sentiments such as these, and the belief that Japan had deserted her true self in favor of blind imitation of the West, that motivated the young military officers to stage a coup d'etat.[69] They intended to bring about a new Meiji Restoration and to accomplish this, to restore Japan's soul and spirit:

> On the snowy morning of Feb. 26, 1936, about 1,400 Japanese troops, led by junior officers, seized the center of Tokyo and murdered a number of prominent officials. The rebels announced that they would not retreat until a new cabinet bent on carrying out sweeping reforms was set up. After three days of hectic negotiations, an Imperial order was issued for the suppression of the rebellion. . . .[70]

A few days later, Kita Ikki was executed for his part in the failed coup d'etat.

Yoshida's *Martial Law* is no straightforward biography. The film is situated clearly within the avant-garde tradition that Yoshida had been working toward since the late '60s which culminated in his "trilogy" examining major figures and events in the twentieth century: *Eros purasu gyakusatsu* (*Eros plus Massacre*, 1969), *Rengoku eroica* (*Heroic Purgatory*, 1970) and *Martial Law*. The first film of this trilogy focuses on the Taisho-era anarchist, Osugi Sakae; the second film, a rather baffling, dense work, looked at the 1950s activism of Yoshida's college days. *Martial Law* focuses on the militarist era of the '30s.[71] In contrast to the color and CinemaScope mandatory when Yoshida was a contract director at Shochiku, this film, co-produced by Yoshida's *Gendai eiga-sha* and the Art Theatre Guild (ATG), relies on black-and-white cinematography and the standard (1.66) aspect ratio. The film boasts an avant-garde music score by frequent collaborator Ichiyanagi Yasushi, a major contemporary composer in Japan's lively music scene. Yoshida extends the decentered compositions that seem to have been as much influenced by Michelangelo Antonioni as by a certain stream of traditional Japanese art.

The story is told through large narrative ellipses and allusion, but nevertheless basically examines events in Kita's life between 1921 and 1936 as he comes to provide ideological inspiration and leadership to an emerging group of military men who want to restore Japan to its true spiritual greatness. We see at the start, one of Kita's followers murdering the millionaire head of the Yasuda financial group; he commits suicide following the assassination. His sister brings his clothes to Kita to honor her brother's last request. Kita himself sends a present to the Crown Prince who acknowledges the gift with a blank receipt. Kita solicits a bribe from the son of a *zaibatsu* (major corporation) head to finance the cause. Early in 1932, Kita, his devoted acolyte Nishida Zei, and a cadre of military officers, plan a series of terrorist acts and murders to culminate on May 15 when twenty-four members of the group will assassinate Prime Minister Inukai Tsuyoshi.

Kita is torn between genuine idealism and personal gain. To punish himself for dreaming that he is the Emperor, he cuts his arm with a razor. And when he becomes frightened by the talk of revolution he asks to be punished for his cowardice. His group is constantly watched by the secret police, but the *kempei* never act to prevent the conspirators from meeting or carrying out their plans. Finally, on February 26, 1936, the young officers proclaim their desire to bring forth a "Showa Restoration" (Showa is the reign name for Emperor Hirohito), and they assassinate a number of high government officials. Their troops, 1,400 strong, occupy major government offices. During this period, Kita is extremely nervous, even psychotic, yet he has enough presence of mind to advise his followers to hold their positions. At first, the men are elated as the Emperor acknowledges their

Kaigenrei (*Martial Law*)
Yoshida Yoshishige, director. Kawakita/Japan Film Library Council

motives. But the government then declares martial law and Kita's troops
are isolated and surrounded. Over the course of three days, the men's
resolve weakens, many commit suicide, others simply abandon their posts.
On February 29, the insurrection is suppressed and Kita is arrested by the
kempei, who claim to be acting on the Emperor's orders. Kita and Nishida
are then executed. Kita's execution shows him tied and kneeling with a
white handkerchief covering his eyes; then blood pours over the handkerchief.

As if to encapsulate the entire issue of youth in the New Wave, *Martial
Law*, while sticking closely to the historical record, adds to the story a
nameless young soldier who wishes to join the cause. The youth is willing
to do anything, including self-sacrifice, to bring about Japan's moral rebirth.
The young soldier clearly looks to Kita as a spiritual father, desperately
seeking his approval and acknowledgment. Given an assignment to blow
up a power station on the May 15 Incident, he fails and seeks a strong
condemnation from Kita. Later, the soldier goes to Nishida claiming to
have become a *kempei* spy and wants Nishida to execute him. After the
collapse of the coup, the soldier confronts Kita saying that now he has
indeed become a spy because earlier he was never even suspected of being

a spy. In this young soldier's relationship to his wife, one sees elements of Mishima Yukio's story and film version of *Yukoku* (*Patriotism,* 1967), a highly romantic, graphically violent tale of a young army officer who commits *seppuku* (ritual suicide; hara-kiri) with his wife when the February 26 coup dissolves. The link between erotic love and love of country made explicit in Mishima's story is similarly highlighted by Yoshida. The intensity of this love leads to the intensity of the feeling of betrayal. Kita Ikki feels betrayed by the Emperor who did not support the young officers who tried to seize power in his name; the young soldier feels betrayed by Kita Ikki who could not live up to the idealism the youth so fervently held. The soldier's very namelessness and his very youthful optimism and idealism are paradigmatic of the New Wave filmmakers' understanding of the way youth seems inevitably to have been betrayed by adult hypocrisy and political expediency.

CHAPTER THREE

Ruined Maps

Identity, Sexuality, and Revolution

A concern about youth, a fundamental characteristic and defining feature of the New Wave, leads inevitably to a concern about the problems of youth. One such problem is a concern with identity, with coming to terms with an emerging self. Part and parcel of this self-concern is a growing awareness of one's sexuality. As identity is so strongly intertwined with gender, one cannot separate the problem of identity from the problem of sex.

The conflation of identity and sexuality, normal in the best of times, was complicated by a number of factors in the Japanese 1960s. The question of identity *for the Japanese* was becoming an increasing cultural concern. American anthropologists and sociologists have long noted the Japanese propensity for self-examination, for raising, and trying to answer, the question of "Japaneseness." Such internal questioning perhaps seems an obvious result of Japan's loss of the Pacific war and its subsequent occupation by a foreign power. The enormous changes wrought by the aftermath of World War II, including postwar democratization, the ideology of individualism and humanism (and existentialism among the intelligentsia), and the increase in materialism had scholars of Left, Center, and Right persuasions raising the issue of national identity. The issue was further exacerbated by the events surrounding May-June 1960 and the formation of the Japanese New Left, a movement with certain aims and goals similar to youth movements in the U.S. and Europe (simply known today as "the 60s"). To the problem of identity and sexuality was added the issue of revolution, the question of bringing about social change. To change society, one first had to define society; to change one's self meant first defining this self. And whatever else the self was, it was (at least partly) a product of society.

Among youth in the 1960s, the links between self and society were often expressed in the form of open rebellion on the part of the individual from society. Rebelliousness, as a characteristic of youth, is a function of ego-formation, an emerging self trying to assert uniqueness and self-integrity. From the Japanese viewpoint at the time, there was a kind of double rebellion. In a culture in which individualism is not a standard of value, assertions of the individual ego take on a dialectical force. To be sure, the promulgation of individualism was an Occupation-derived ideology, but the generation of the 1950s in Japan managed to subsume this ideology under the guise of economic rebuilding and materialistic pursuits. It took postwar prosperity to bring forward the latent ideological underpinnings of individualism, quite similar in this respect to the youth rebellion in the U.S. at the time. The assertion of self was a major feature of the era, a rebellion against the "plastic" culture, the culture of conformity that characterized the 1950s. For the Japanese, moreover, *open* rebellion was a blow against the facade of peacefulness, against the picture of placidity and homogeneity the Japanese like to project to the outside world. The radical individualism of the New Wave filmmakers was not a bourgeois individualism which posited a transcendental subject outside culture; rather it was the assertion of a will already formed by culture struggling with that culture. The form of rebellion this assertion of will took was often "spectacular," a rebellion in the realm of spectacle, most typically in the realm of sexuality.

In the world of film, the question of identity has been handled somewhat obsessively and unilaterally by Teshigahara Hiroshi. Although Teshigahara's work is precisely contemporaneous with the New Wave (he directed his first feature in 1962), he stands outside of it by virtue not only of his independent status (a characteristic of the New Wave directors only *after* they had established their careers), but by his relationship with Abe Kobo. Teshigahara directed four feature films in the 1960s and all four are adaptations of Abe's works. *Otoshiana* (*Pitfall*, 1962) is based on a television drama, while *Suna no onna* (*Woman in the Dunes*, 1963), *Tanin no kao* (*The Face of Another*, 1966), and *Moetsukita chizu* (*The Ruined Map*, 1968) are all, in Keiko McDonald's words, "faithful renditions of Abe's novels."[1] As the novels were published first (typically a year before the films were released) and each film has a screen adaptation by Abe himself, the literary aspects have a priority over the filmic aspects, despite the evident stylishness of Teshigahara's camera work. This does not disgrace the films by any means, nor is it meant as a critique of Teshigahara as an *auteur* (an issue, in general, with which this study is not concerned). In fact, it strengthens the notion that questions of identity, along with other of the New Wave's major motifs, were important cultural concerns at the time. On the other hand, it is worth noting that Abe Kobo, despite some au courant thematic elements, as a novelist has perhaps more affinities with the West than with his Japanese contemporaries. (This might explain why virtually all of Abe's works have appeared in English, translated by E. Dale Saunders, whereas more important Japanese novelists, like Oe Kenzaburo, have seen only a portion of their work appear.) Abe's links with the West and Teshigahara's overtly stylish films help explain the "cult" popularity of *Woman in the Dunes*.

Noel Burch wants to disgrace *Woman in the Dunes* by damning it with faint praise and by castigating it for its popularity in the West. Abe's novel is characterized as a "symbolic fantasy," and Teshigahara's film adaptation features an "aggressive aestheticism and sensuality." But this is no real praise, for the film's style is "achieved by what was in fact no more than a technically masterful revitalization of the decorative style of the 1930s." Its reception in the West was due to its origins in Japan *instead* of in the West, from whence it could just as easily have originated. As for the rest of Teshigahara's work, it is "even more extravagantly chic. . . ."[2] Other critics, contrary to Burch, favor *Woman in the Dunes* precisely for its decorative style and its Western-style themes.

For many, *Woman in the Dunes* is seen as an allegory (Burch's "symbolic fantasy"). The question becomes, an allegory of what? To the Western youth audience of the 1960s, when the film achieved its cult status, the film encapsulated their own feelings of meaninglessness and entrapment. The hero of the film is literally entrapped in a sand pit, forced to remain there by hostile villagers. Thus he experiences the feelings of powerlessness felt by youth. The many certificates and identity cards the hero initially carries symbolizes the increasingly bureaucratized, depersonalized quality of modern life—the "plastic culture" (of credit cards, primarily) that was a '60s watchword. The sexuality on view, relatively explicit compared to mainstream American films of the era, was a valorization of the increasingly free expression of sexuality that also characterized the decade. Of course, in the film the display of sex, the acts of making love, were aestheticized through the visual motif of the sand, transforming the act of sex into a graphic pattern. But this, too, had a '60s counterpart: the transformation of life (including sex) into "art." The ending, in which the hero decides to stay in the sand dune with the woman, was clearly an existentialist parable, a Sartrean variation on "No Exit."

Keiko McDonald finds the film a celebration of "contemporary man's courage to fight the encroachments of society, however absurd his personal battle may be."[3] The film for her is thus an allegory of the struggle between "the threat of society to . . . existence" and the preservation of "intrinsic human nature." Alongside, and perhaps a necessary component of, this struggle is "contemporary man's constant effort to maintain [that] love is more important than the achievement of [goals]."[4]

Discussing the novel, Arthur Kimball also sees an existential allegory in the text. He maintains that "Among Japanese writers, no one except Kobo Abe has been so preoccupied, one might even say obsessed, with the identity theme."[5] For Kimball, the main character of *Woman in the Dunes*, identified only at the end as Niki, his name significantly removed from him until after he accepts his entrapped status, must strive to make meaning out of his existence: "Niki must find what else there is to life, for in the sand society he meets the tedium of everyday life in concentrated form." Kimball sees a particularity to Niki's sand existence relating to Japanese culture as he recognizes that "relatively uncomplicated as life in the dunes is, it nonetheless soon confronts Niki with the problem of obligation."[6] Niki develops an obligation (*giri*) to the woman, for though she tricked him into staying with her that first night (in conspiracy with the villagers), she has treated him well, fed, and cared for him, despite his initial unwillingness to work in clearing the sand each evening. In addition, Niki and the woman have obligations to the rest of the dune-dwellers (unseen but referred to) and to the villagers in that if they do not clear the sand away from their hut, somehow all the dunes will be imperiled. There is, of course, something of the myth of Sisyphus operative here, hence the connections to existentialism. But their Sisyphean task impacts upon others so that the concept of *giri* is very much present. Kimball retreats from this implicit Japanese interpretation of the symbolism (an allegory about co-operation and the need for *giri*) and returns to a more existential one: "Out of the apparent absurdity of life [Niki] has learned to extract meaning. He has been 'set free' in the metaphysical sense, and 'escape' is no longer necessary."[7] The meaning he "extracts" (a nice expression on Kimball's part) is a function of the water he has learned to extract from the sand. This valorizes the idea of individualism, a reading consistent with the '60s attraction to the film and with McDonald's.

In terms of seeing this film in relation to its Japanese context, one could compare the notion of how one finds meaning in existence despite the "tedium of everyday life" with the same question in Ozu's films. In so doing, one sees that the transcendental vision of Ozu, in which a participation in the natural cycle enables one to find ultimate meaning, is replaced by the ideology of liberal-humanism more consistent with Kurosawa, especially *Ikiru* (1952). Kurosawa's film is often thought of as an existentialist parable. Watanabe, the hero, finds he is dying of cancer and embarks on a search for the best way to spend his remaining months of life. In the actions taken by Watanabe, who decides to build a playground on the site of a swamp, one can see the existentialist idea combine with the liberal one of social relevance. This, too, may be comparable to Niki, whose ability to extract water from the sand is a valuable discovery in an arid climate and not simply the existentialist idea of action for its own sake.

Despite its essentially liberal-humanist ideology and its roots in the tradition of *giri*, the stylization of the film makes it at least interestingly tangential to the New Wave. One wants to resist the too easy allegorizing of the sand itself. McDonald has not resisted this temptation. For her "the sand itself is society."[8] The sand, which is everywhere, even in the pores of the skin, represents the fact that "society sifts even into the very core of human existence—the love between man and woman—thus dooming every individual to alienation."[9] But if the sand exists as a thing apart, as a graphic patterning for the camera's eye, and not the novelist's theme, then *Woman in the Dunes* compares, at this level, to the works of Oshima, Yoshida, and Suzuki.

Woman in the Dunes highlighted the problem of identity by transposing it into the meaning of action. *The Face of Another* and *The Ruined Map* deal more directly with the question. In the former film, Abe and Teshigahara focus on a man whose face has been horribly disfigured in an industrial accident. He finds that his relationship to those around him has changed; he responds differently to them partly as a function of his belief that they respond differently to him. The idea that his lack of a face causes his social alienation stems from the reliance of the film on first-person point of view. The question of identity has been psychologized. The loss of the man's face results in his feeling of the loss of his identity. The getting of a new face, a lifelike mask, results in his feeling of a new identity. This new identity, however, does not enable him to reintegrate into society. In fact, he feels further apart by virtue of the recognition that he wears a mask, a public face, a face apart, the face of another.

The idea of a "mask" is another '60s motif, the commonly expressed view that we all put up a front, a facade, to prevent others from getting to know the "real" us. If we would all stop wearing this "mask," if, that is, we would let our real selves be seen, somehow this would all bring people closer together. *The Face of Another* demonstrates that the social formation of the self makes such sentiments appear naive. The film turns around the question of who defines the self, the main character discovering that he has no inner-self apart from a social self. When society rejects him (or when he thinks society rejects him, which amounts to the same thing), his self disappears.

The disappearance of the self is the theme of *The Ruined Map*, a modernist detective story. The use of the familiar genre of the private investigator (the private "I" in this case) enables this film to work well as a compelling story alongside the allegorical intentions (as opposed to the earlier films which are only allegories). The plot begins straightforwardly and generically: A detective is hired to find a missing husband. There is not much amiss at the start and the husband's disappearance is not necessarily attributed to foul play. In fact, the film and novel relate themselves to a Japanese social phenomenon in which an average man, a businessman, husband, and father, suddenly takes off, runs away. The phenomenon is known as the "vanishing man" and it is taken up by Imamura Shohei, as well. The detective is drawn ever more into a complex web of interlocking events, few of which actually relate to the case. Unable to find the missing man, the detective finds himself slowly occupying the husband's place. An attraction to the man's wife, his own divorce (that is, his own version of having "vanished") and other similarities to the disappeared man serve to transform him into that man. The detective's own hold on his identity was always tenuous, his job a transposition of his own search for himself into the search for others, for other selves. In *The Face of Another*, the man's identity is irrevocably lost when his wife leaves him; in *The Ruined Map*, a new identity is found when a new wife is found. Identity is, then, always a function of relationships, a tension between an inner-self and a self which interacts with others.

The Ruined Map clearly has connections with other modernist variations of formula stories, such as the novels of Alain Robbe-Grillet or Thomas Pynchon (another index of Abe's affinities with the West). In 1972, Teshigahara tried to address the question of identity and the relationship between self and society in a non-allegorical, non-modernist form, in his first film apart from Abe, *Summer Soldiers*, written by John Nathan. The film focuses on American deserters from the Vietnam-era army who are expatriates in Japan. The film demonstrates, among other things, the social and cultural gaps between the Americans and their Japanese friends who are trying to help them adjust to life in a foreign country. One of the motifs that emerges is the Americans' increasing sense of alienation; they have deserted their own country, their own culture, their own selves, and can find no sense of belonging in Japan. In an interview, Teshigahara speaks of one particular soldier about whom this is especially true. At one point, the soldier is trying to make love to a prostitute and is unable to perform. It is here that "his isolation and suffering reach a peak. I contrasted this misery, the reality of human alienation, with the quiet, serene, and beautiful Kyoto as it is viewed from the outside."[10] *Summer Soldiers* eschews the stylization of the earlier films, and Teshigahara uses non-actors for the leads (as compared to the film stars he used in the earlier films, Okada Eiji, Nakadai Tatsuya, and Katsu Shintaro). The film suffers, in a curious way, by its overt focus on identity and cross-cultural relationships, for it ignores the greater political ideology. Whereas the earlier films are even more guilty of ignoring the political realm (in favor of the allegorical), it was their very stylization that won them favor. *Summer Soldiers*, lacking Teshigahara's pictorialism and lacking the political dimension screenwriter John Nathan tried to inject, became a film whose flaws were only too clear. Nevertheless, the film demonstrates the continuity of the question of identity, highlighting the intercultural confrontation which gave rise to it in the postwar era.

We might briefly mention Shinoda Masahiro's *Chinmoku* (*Silence*, 1971), an adaptation of Endo Shusaku's novel about Portugese missionaries in medieval Japan, and *Setouchi shonen yakyudan* (*MacArthur's Children*, 1984), which details the clash of cultures on a small island when the American Occupation forces arrive in 1945. While neither film is particularly successful (both rank among the director's most minor efforts), they, too, show the ongoing concern with identity.

The question of identity also interests Imamura Shohei who wants to seek out and explore the essence not of individual identity, but of "Japaneseness," the question of what it means, what it is, to be Japanese. Allan Casebier intriguingly puts forth the notion that irrationality is a key to the Japanese essence for Imamura. Irrationality is defined as the mystery, and incomprehensibility in all things (derived from the metaphysical and aesthetic concept of *yugen*). Irrationality is rooted in the instinctual, emotional, and intuitive processes of human behavior.[11] The appeal to the irrational might imply a connection between Imamura and Ozu, whose Zen-like codas call forth not only *mono no aware* but also *yugen*, an essential component of Zen. But the sense of mystery, of irrationality, in Imamura often stems from the structures. Casebier has isolated a series of oppositions which characterize Imamura's work: irrational vs. rational; primitive vs. civilized; spontaneous vs. conventional; the lower classes vs. the upper classes; authentic vs. contrived. To these we might add documentary vs. fiction (related to the last opposition of Casebier's, although he refers to the actions of the characters, not the techniques of the films). Casebier maintains that in the oppositions he has isolated, "Imamura believes the first of these conflicting elements to be the locus of value."[12] Only in the opposition documentary vs. fiction, which I have isolated, is there no clearcut demarcation, no clearly defined value. The lines between the two are vague, and this explains Imamura's attraction, like Oshima Nagisa's, to real-life incidents and characters.

Nowhere is the merging of documentary and fiction more complex than in *Ningen johatsu* (*A Man Vanishes*, 1967), a film remarkably similar in theme and treatment to *The Ruined Map*. *A Man Vanishes* involves the search for the disappearance of a "vanished man," except that here the "detective" is a professional actor. In a sense, like the detective in Teshigahara's film, the actor, too, loses his identity when, to the actor's consternation and confusion, the woman whose fiancé is missing falls in love with him. A confusion of roles ensues in Imamura's mix of fact and fiction: "an actor can become a real-life subject, and a real-life subject can become an actress."[13] The confusion of roles and the partial abandonment of the search, which is an abandonment of the film's narrative, its ostensible subject, highlight the essentially irrational nature of human behavior, discourse, and interaction. And while the film implies that the older sister of the woman may have been involved with the man's disappearance, the disappearance is ultimately left unsolved, as it might be, and typically is, in similar real-life cases—cases themselves which are tinged with the irrational.

The merging of documentary and fiction forms an interesting undercurrent to Imamura's earlier *Jinruigaku nyumon* (*The Pornographers*, 1966). This motif is visualized through the use of a film-within-a-film structure, first, as Imamura himself presides over a screening of *The Pornographers*, in the opening and closing sequences, and, second, through the use of films within the main narrative—a narrative concerned with the making

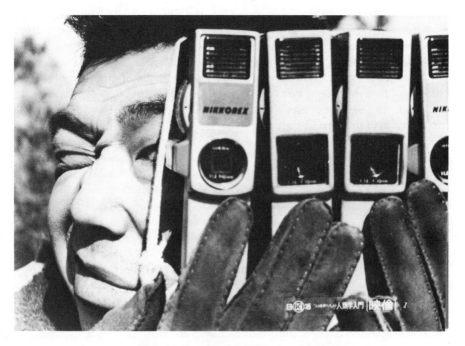

Jinruigaku nyumon (The Pornographers)
Imamura Shohei, director. Kawakita/Japan Film Library Council

of pornographic films. There is a strong self-consciousness manifested by Imamura about the nature of pornography whose appeal to its audience clearly rests on a foundation of voyeurism. Imamura uses a series of long-takes which not only heighten the "realism" of the scenes, but which refuse to allow us to look elsewhere (there is nothing else to see save that which he shows us). Furthermore, many of these scenes are shot through windows, the camera looking voyeuristically in from the outside. There are also important variations of this strategy: the camera looking through a gate onto an alley; a restaurant sequence in which screens are set up around the protagonists, the camera on the other side of the screens. Another interesting variation on shooting through windows is a particularly creative handling of CinemaScope. At one particular moment, a group of businessmen in their office, screen left, watch a group of office girls, screen right. We look at them looking, and we look at the objects of their look. Signficantly, many voyeuristic moments are *not* confined to scenes which feature sexual activity. We are also voyeurs to more prosaic goings-on, especially the interaction of family members. And this is Imamura's most subtle and brilliant insight—the link between familial and sexual relationships.

This link between familial and sexual relationships (and the issue of voyeurism) finds its core expression in the motif of incest. This is something of a recurrent motif in Imamura's work, but it has also found expression in films by Oshima, Yoshida, and Shinoda. One hesitates to make too many generalizations from this, but it is the case that Japan's primary creation myth (from the Shinto tradition) attributes the birth of the Japanese archipelago to a marriage between a brother and sister god (Izanagi and Izanami). The homogeneity of the Japanese people and their traditional insularity also encourages an image of incest as marriage within a tribe. There is, too, the metaphor of the nation-as-family, and its reversal, the family-as-nation, with the Emperor and the Father ensconced as the head of the household/nation. In addition to this, as in the West, one's initial experiences in the sexual realm are directed at family members—Freud's Oedipus complex and the Primal Scene. This issue is complicated in Japan, in a strange way, by traditional Japanese architecture and the nature of the home itself, where concepts of privacy do not hold sway as they do in the West. Shoji (paper) screens may have the function of walls, but they certainly do not act as walls. The problem of incest is further complicated by the relationship of the Japanese mother to her children, especially sons. (This latter aspect has created a highly ambiguous, sexually charged image of women in Japanese cinema, which will be dealt with in Chapter 4). The motif of incest and the realm of familial sexuality impacts on the question of identity and its relationship to the political/ideological realm.

In *The Pornographers*, sex and the family are examined through the eyes of middle-class, modern Japanese, subject to various manifestations of *giri* and other social codes. The main character, Ogata, is a salesman who deals not only with the supply of medical instruments, but in the production and distribution of pornographic films and the procurement of young girls for businessmen. He lives with a widow, Haru, but desires to sleep with her daughter, Keiko. Haru refuses to marry Ogata ostensibly because she believes (and we have no real reason to doubt her) that her husband's spirit has been reincarnated in a carp which Haru keeps in a large fishtank. Haru's son, Koichi, is also an obstacle between Ogata and Haru. Joan Mellen notes how "Koichi . . . fondles and caresses his mother . . .,"[14] but fails to note that in one sequence, he gets into bed between his mother and Ogata and snuggles up to Ogata's bosom! Similarly, while Ogata desires Keiko, when he finally does make love to her, she cries out with pleasure, "Otoochan" ("Father Dear"). While such incestuous desires strike the Western viewer as perverse, Imamura does not think that this problem, the problem of incest, is at the root of this family's troubles.

Mellen attributes the root of their troubles to "the puritanical censorship of a society which places so many obstacles in the way of fulfilling basic needs."[15] This is seen most especially through Imamura's frequent shots taken from the point of view of the ever-present carp. The carp who is inhabited by the dead husband's spirit is Imamura's way, according to

Mellen, of satirizing the idea of ancestor worship "as well as the unnecessary waste and pain resulting from the injunction that widows not remarry."[16] The carp is also felt to be responsible for Haru's illness which is clearly psychosomatic in origin. In the first instance of her becoming ill, Imamura shoots a night-time sequence through the fishtank and also uses sound reverberations to endow the carp with evil intentions. Mellen attributes Haru's illness as a function of the deeply repressive forces which are "rooted in her being."[17] Shortly before her death, Haru goes insane in an extraordinarily powerful sequence which shows her having hysterics on a balcony, an act which draws a crowd below. Disjunctive rock music plays on the soundtrack and we are given a completely interiorized, fantasized scene of Haru transported to a desert. A freeze-frame at the end of the scene implies her death.

Fantasy sequences are also delivered via Ogata's interior point of view. Toward the end of the film, he makes love to Keiko fantasizing that, far from making love to his stepdaughter, he is making love to his mother. In this manner, fantasy is partially conflated with memory in which Ogata has a flashback wherein he is caressed by his mother. Flashbacks have been used earlier—Ogata remembers an accident in which Keiko injured her leg. However, the style of the flashback (odd angles, freeze-frames) resembles the fantasy sequences showing a conflation between memory and fantasy. Keiko does have a scar on her leg from the accident, but the force of memory becomes confused with the desires of fantasy.

The intermingling of fantasy and memory is a variation on the opposition between fiction and documentary which is further reflected in the film by the use of pornography. Imamura in a sense documents the fantasy of pornography as he details the production and consumption of pornographic films. In one instance, a rather long take details the editing of a blue movie, except that the camera is outside of the editing room. In another sequence we watch Ogata's all-male clientele as they watch a pornographic film. In another long-take scene, we sadly view a young retarded girl, dressed in a school uniform, being coached into "acting" for a sex film.

The intermingling of fantasy and reality reaches a comic conflation at the film's end. Following Haru's death and Keiko's marriage to a *yakuza*, Ogata begins the elaborate and painstaking construction of a life-size rubber doll. Working diligently aboard a small houseboat tied to a dock, Ogata acquires human hair from a nearby beauty shop and sews the hair on the doll's head and pubis. So entranced and enamored of the doll is he that he does not notice, one day, when the boat's mooring is slipped and he goes drifting out to sea.

Most critics writing about *The Pornographers* see Ogata as basically an ordinary, even decent, man. Raymond Durgnat describes him as "a middle-aged middle-class quiet amiable and average man . . . ," who attempts to be "a friendly, unauthoritarian father-figure to his mistress's children."[18]

Joan Mellen finds the pornographic movies he makes "pathetic, essentially innocent."[19] Ogata's intermingling of sexual desire for his stepdaughter with the memory of her accident is not "perverse" but "funny" because "[l]ove is intermingled with lust in all of us, good motives with selfish ones."[20] While it is undeniably true that Ogata is a pathetic man, as much victim as victimizer, Imamura's attitude must be seen as ambivalent. The scene with the young retarded girl must strike the sensitive viewer as sad, a reminder of the essentially exploitative nature of pornography. In *Behind the Mask*, Ian Buruma's tour through the often outré world of Japanese popular culture, there is a description of a contemporary *toruko* (short for Turkish bath) in which, for a hefty fee, the Japanese businessman is passively serviced by a *torukojo* (bath girl). Buruma notes that many of these establishments are geared to male fantasies. The facades of the buildings resemble, for instance, a jet plane, the girls inside dress as stewardesses; another bath house resembles a bank, the girls inside wear company uniforms. He also mentions the "Young Rady" schools (high-class girls schools) which feature girls in tennis outfits, or other up-scale fantasy images.[21] The schoolgirl uniform worn by the retarded girl in *The Pornographers* is clearly one such fantasy image. But in satisfying such fantasies, a child has been abused.

Imamura cannot resolve the contradiction of the "good man" in a "bad job." While Ogata is punished in a way, Ogata himself never comes to terms with his trouble. The retreat out to sea recalls the man who vanished in Imamura's 1967 film. And one wonders if Oshima (the name of the man who vanished) and Ogata are destined to meet in Kuragejima, the island setting for Imamura's most important film, a film set in a place Imamura himself seems to want to retreat to—a mythical place where much of the essence of the Japanese spirit still resides.

Kamigami no fukaki yokubo (*The Profound Desire of the Gods*, 1968; aka *Kuragejima: Tales from a Southern Island*) is Imamura's most overtly anthropological film, as well as his most overtly auteurist. This anthropological interest is shown in the use of a singer at the film's start, and again in the final scene, who chants the legend of Kuragejima (Kurage Island), a legend which finds this island, like Japan itself, the product of incest between a brother and sister god. The concern with origins also appears as a concern with customs, the customs of the island people whose culture contains aspects of the past which intersect with the modernization process. Through the figure of an outsider, Mr. Kariya, the engineer, Imamura is able to view the island life from the outside, while clearly sympathizing with it. Such sympathies appear not only in plot, but also in the fact that (as no previous commentators seem to have noticed) Kariya bears a strong resemblance to Imamura himself. When Kariya is seduced by the island's ways, especially by the young girl, Toriko, Imamura seems to be indulging not only in a sympathetic treatment of traditional values, but also (perhaps) some wish-fulfillment.

The film is basically structured around the principle of tradition vs. progress. For Mellen, this issue is one-sided; every instance in which something is amiss on the island, Mellen claims Imamura attributes to "modernization." For instance, when Nekichi kills fish with dynamite, he is punished by the islanders for his refusal to stick with the old methods. Most of the community, Mellen feels, try "to live in symbiosis with nature, taking only what they need."[22] And indeed there are other instances in which the islanders try to resist modernization and stick to tradition. The village headman, Ryugen, orders Nekichi and his family to sabotage the engineer's work in the sacred forest. During a time of drought the water in the island's shrine is left untouched and the islanders refuse to allow the engineer to construct a pipeline to draw water from the shrine for use by the projected sugarcane processing plant. Thus it might at first seem that Imamura straightforwardly sides with the traditional against the modern. This is not the case, however; ambivalence is again the operative term.

The islanders are embarrassed by Nekichi's family for their practice of incest. They believe the gods punished Nekichi for practicing incest with his sister, Uma, by thrusting a giant phallic rock into the middle of his rice paddy. Ryugen (who has made Uma his mistress) commands Nekichi to dig a hole around the rock until it falls. Uma, on the other hand, is respected as a *noro* (priestess) and she participates in the communal rituals. The Nekichis are thereby set off as both inferior and superior, appropriate sacrificial victims for the islanders. Just as Imamura makes it clear that in the traditional culture various cruel methods were used to control the population and to appease the gods (a bell would be rung and late arrivals to a certain spot would be killed; pregnant women were tossed off a cliff into the sea), so too, today's islanders kill Nekichi and Uma when the two set off for God's Island to start a new race (an obvious reference to Kurage's and Japan's creation myth). Nekichi and Uma are overtaken by the islanders who wear fearsome masks, beat Nekichi to death with their oars and set Uma adrift at sea, tied to the mast of her boat. While Imamura clearly sees much to admire in the islanders' attempts to maintain traditional ways, he also sees that these traditions have a degree of cruelty about them that cannot be ignored. The only way around the insoluble contradiction of tradition vs. progress is through recourse to the irrational.

The irrational is alluded to most clearly in the film's final sequence. Kariya, having left the weeping Toriko (Nekichi's and Uma's daughter), returns to the island after an absence of five years. Toriko has since died and the islanders maintain that her spirit inhabits a rock which seems to be waiting for the engineer's return.[23] Kametaro, the only remaining member of Nekichi's family, has himself returned from Tokyo to become the engineer of the island's new steam train, which takes tourists through the cane fields. Among the tourists in the final scene are Kariya and his wife. The train, as Mellen points out, seems to be chasing the ghost of Toriko.[24] Only Kametaro can see her; when he pulls the emergency brake to keep from hitting her, no one else, not even the engineer who was her lover, can see her.

While Imamura clearly explored the roots of Japanese tradition and the question of identity, seen in the struggle of Kariya to retain his identity as a modern man or lose it in carefree lovemaking to a slightly retarded, yet magically possessed, young woman (the struggle to hold on to his identity recalls *Woman in the Dunes*, while the retarded Toriko brings forth an uncomfortable reminder of the filmmaking sequence in *The Pornographers*), some Japanese critics found significant drawbacks to the film. Nagabe Hideo stated, "Imamura Shohei understands the world, but I wonder if he tries to change it."[25] Another critic, Okamoto Hiroshi, complained that the island to which Uma and Nekichi try to retreat could not exist in a vacuum, that the island, wherever it was, had a political reality Imamura ignored. "It does not matter if it is American territory or Russian territory to them." Imamura is as guilty as Nekichi and Uma in trying to retreat from political realities: "A revolution comes from one's will to obtain freedom within human relationships. A revolution cannot be obtained through the behavior of escaping from human relationships."[26] Such criticism as this must be seen in light of the then-current controversy surrounding the return of Okinawa (arguably the "Southern Island" on which the film takes place) to Japan, and the increased militarization of Okinawa (then under U.S. control) during the Vietnam War. Student protests at major Japanese universities and the May '68 Revolution in France were very much on the minds of such critics, although the Okinawa allusion was fundamental to their critiques. While Imamura is unquestionably, as Mellen asserts, "a man of the left,"[27] he is also, as Bock notes, concerned with "the need for a feeling of cultural-emotional unity. . . ."[28] Perhaps applying Western political labels is again self-defeating, for like many of the Japanese New Wave directors, Imamura seeks the potential for revolutionary change from within the deepest roots of Japanese tradition.

Teshigahara's concern with identity is clearly less politically motivated than Imamura's. While the indictment of the conformity of contemporary culture lent *Woman in the Dunes* its appeal to the counterculture of the 1960s, such issues have since also been taken up by the Right. And, in Teshigahara's films in general, the problem of identity is posed in existential terms which, if nothing else, has the strategy of removing the issue from political discourse. Imamura's films are more tied to particularities, better able to pose the question of identity within the specifically Japanese context. But Imamura abandons issues of the moment for more broad-based anthropological concerns. The question of identity was posed more politically, more immediately, by Oshima Nagisa.

Five films by Oshima in particular, pose this question in dynamic ways: *Etsuraku* (*Pleasures of the Flesh*, 1965), *Hakuchu no torima* (*Violence at Noon*, 1966), *Muri shinju nihon no natsu* (*Japanese Summer: Double Suicide*, 1967), *Shinjuku dorobo nikki* (*Diary of a Shinjuku Thief*, 1969), and *Ai no koriida* (*The Realm of the Senses*, 1976). These films posit an implicit link between identity and sexuality, and equate a liberating sexuality with political liberation (an important motif in America in the 1960s, as well). Conversely, then, for Oshima repressed sexuality has a repressive political dimension (an insight with which Imamura would agree). Oshima also demonstrates, however, that a balance between the sexual and the political is crucial. For while repressed sexuality must have a repressive political force, an overemphasis on sexuality has an equally damaging effect on the political realm.

Pleasures of the Flesh may be said to inaugurate a new phase in Oshima's career by virtue of the fact that it was the first feature film he directed after a three-year absence (having released *Amakusa Shiro Tokisada* in 1962). During the interim between features, Oshima worked in television, making half-hour documentaries and an information series. While *Pleasures of the Flesh* was a complete financial failure and something of a disappointment to Oshima himself, it does introduce a number of emerging motifs in his work. The film is a clear, if obvious, condemnation of the great economic miracle of Japan since the 1950s. Oshima shows that economic achievement does not necessarily mean moral affluence—quite the reverse, in fact. It also posits a connection between the ills of society and the formation of criminals. And it introduces an equation between society's outcasts—criminals, Koreans, the poor—and disaffected, alienated, educated youth.

Pleasures of the Flesh centers on Wakizaka, a recent college graduate who has a low-level, white-collar job. He is jilted by Shoko, whom he has loved for many years. Unknown to her, Wakizaka had murdered a man who was blackmailing her. (The man had raped Shoko when she was younger and was blackmailing her to keep *his* silence.) Hayami, a government official, witnessed the murder and now he blackmails Wakizaka, except in this instance, Wakizaka is sentenced by Hayami to hold ¥30,000,000 that Hayami has embezzled, while Hayami is sentenced to prison.

Wakizaka lives in misery for four years, pining over Shoko and nervously hiding the money. Finally, he can stand it no longer and begins a series of affairs with bar hostesses. Increasingly paranoid about having spent most of Hayami's money, Wakizaka learns that the man has died in prison. At this point, he meets Shoko, who offers to have sex with him in exchange for a loan. Forced to turn her down (since he has spent all the money), Wakizaka tells her of the murder he committed for her and the life he has since led. Angry at being rejected, Shoko turns him in to the police.

Etsuraku (Pleasures of the Flesh)
Oshima Nagisa, director. Shochiku Co., Ltd.

Oshima's intention is not to blame Shoko for her betrayal of Wakizaka. Rather, he wants to show how this victim (raped, blackmailed, caught in a marriage with a bankrupt husband) becomes, in turn, a victimizer. That Hayami is a government official must be taken to be overtly symbolic, so that Wakizaka's betrayal is the betrayal of postwar youth cynically manipulated by the government and victimized by members of their own class, equally victims of the social system. While the symbolism is clear and the message in keeping with the emerging politics of the New Wave, the film is certainly one of Oshima's minor efforts, an interesting attempt to develop the interlocking themes of sexuality, criminality, violence, politics, and the question of identity.

If *Pleasures of the Flesh* is an interesting failure, Oshima's next film, *Violence at Noon* is a fascinating success. That the film has never had a U.S. release may account for the lack of critical writing on this film (save for Noel Burch's typically intriguing yet eccentric approbation), but that should not keep us from acclaiming this as one of Oshima's most important works. For Burch, the film is significant for a number of reasons, among them that the film contains over two thousand separate shots, though it is of moderate length (ninety-five minutes); its decoupage extending "certain aspects of the radical editing of Eisenstein's silent films."[29] (By my rough calculation, both *Violence at Noon* and *Potemkin* average 2.8 seconds per shot.) The film manifests the "Shoin complex," a term derived, as Burch tells us, from Yoshida Shoin, "a celebrated reformist, fiery pamphleteer and agitator," who put forward an image of madness and foolishness: "In the last years of the Tokugawa shogunate, men of high purpose . . . found no alternative than to represent themselves and their exploits as mad and foolish." Accounting for the prevalence of mad/foolish heroes in the New Wave cinema, Burch maintains that "It is characteristic of the new cinema to portray madness and/or innocence as a form of revolt."[30] The revolt on the part of mad heroes is accompanied by an overtly "arty" or "gratuitous stylization" (in Burch's words, "manipulation of the signifier"). Finally, Burch valorizes the fact that "almost no account is taken of orientational matching; eyeline position and direction are disregarded more often than not."[31]

It is characteristic of Burch to ignore the content to which such "excessive decoupage" (his term) is put, save to say only that the film "relates the failure of an experiment in rural communal living by a group of urban intellectuals, and its tragic aftermath," and that "Sato Kei, one of the principal members of Oshima's troupe, plays a psychopathic rapist/ killer."[32] Presumably, by these two hints a full page apart at the content of the film, we are to understand that due to the failure of the group, Sato's character becomes a rapist/killer (the "floating ghost" of the Japanese title, which translates as "Floating Ghost in Broad Daylight"—floating ghost being a metaphoric characterization of a rapist). Oshima is, in fact, drawing a connection between failed political attempts and failed romantic attempts; the mad-fool floating ghost is the tragic aftereffect of lost ideals and failed political commitments. Recognizing this, we can see a relationship between *Violence at Noon* and *Night and Fog in Japan*. Whereas the 1960 film relied on "excessive mise-en-scène" (forty-three shots constitute the entire film), *Violence at Noon*, similarly structured around flashbacks, relies on "excessive decoupage." And the secret of the failure of postwar democracy, which could only be revealed at night in the earlier film, is here exposed to the light of day.

A plot synopsis of the film cannot communicate the disjointedness of its presentation. Frequent flashbacks combine with "fantasy" scenes, such as when the dead Genji talks to Matsuko at his gravesite. Nevertheless, there is a discernible plot line here: a phantom rapist is pursued by a police detective, the two women who know he is the killer choose not to turn him in. The complexity of the film's presentation is a function of Oshima's insights into the complex network of factors which may be said to "cause" or lead to criminal acts. In *Violence at Noon*, the criminal is formed because socialist ideals fail to take root in postwar society. The failure of socialism is not simply attributed to the hegemonic power of capitalism nor is it a

Hakuchu no torima (*Violence at Noon*)
Oshima Nagisa, director. Shochiku Co., Ltd.

function of fate—the flood which destroys the communal farm is an index
not of nature's dissatisfaction, but of the failure of individuals to band
together in an idealistic manner, their failure to maintain their spirit of
idealism. There is also the fact that their idealism may be said to be naïve.
Matsuko maintains to Eisuke (who will become the floating ghost) that
"love is voluntary," a sentiment that looks forward to Yoshida Yoshishige's
examination of the "free love" ideals of another failed idealist, Osugi Sakae
in *Eros plus Massacre* (discussed in Chapter 7). The acknowledgment of the
link between political liberation and sexual liberation is an important characteristic of the communal farm. But a failure to account for basic human
emotions (love is not really voluntary) has the effect of impacting on the
political success of their venture.

The attempt by Genji and Shino to commit *shinju* (lovers' suicide) when
the farm fails, and Eisuke's turn to violent crime, are both "excessive" or
"spectacular" responses in personal ways to political failures and they have
a particularly unique Japanese cast to them. However, it would be a mistake
to claim any simple direct cause for the hero's actions. This would reduce
the film to a single symbolic reading which would be clearly insufficient
to account for its complexities. Equally excessive and equally not reducible
to any single symbolic function is the complex series of lateral pans in-

scribed by the camera at the film's end as Matsuko and Shino sit facing each other on a train. The semicircular and circular motions, not motivated by characterization or dialogue (the camera's motions made more spectacular by the CinemaScope ratio), "stop" our attention but without any special reason for doing so; or at least not any reason that is clear, much like the presentation of the events in this film, much like the actions taken by the characters in the film, much like the action taken by human beings in their search for meaning and identity.

Japanese Summer: Double Suicide brings back into play the conflated elements of sex and death within a political context. The "double suicide" of the title is an allusion to classic Japanese tradition, but the two central characters here are nothing like the star-crossed lovers who populate the world of playwright Chikamatsu. In fact, the two modern-day would-be lovers are extremely neurotic, alienated loners, the man looking to die at the hands of a woman, any woman, the woman looking for someone to make love to her. The two become involved, as victims, in a terrorist hijacking. Sex, death, and revolution are thus roped together, implicitly compared, and when the two commit double suicide just before they are killed by the police, we realize that the mad energy involved in defying cultural convention (revolution) underlies defying sexual convention. We may understand that the police confusion which mistakes these victims for terrorists, is, in fact, the desire on the part of official culture to repress such sexual energy. Sex and revolution are understood by officialdom as two sides of the same liberating force.

The links between sex and revolution form the structuring basis of Oshima's *Diary of a Shinjuku Thief*, one of his most important films. It is also among Oshima's best-known works, and has been dealt with quite well by others. It is important to realize that Shinjuku was (and partly still is) the center of youth culture in Japan. Burch calls it "the entertainment quarter," but that is something of a misnomer as many sections of Tokyo can boast of this.[33] At the time the film was made, Shinjuku was the center of the various *ungura* (underground) movements in theatre, art, and cinema. In fact, Japanese commentators who wonder where the spirit of the '60s has gone, have formed the question, "Has the culture of Shinjuku been replaced by the culture of Harajuku?"[34] Harajuku, a fashionable Tokyo neighborhood, boasts chic boutiques and eateries, and a variety of outdoor dancing in the parks on weekends. *Ungura*, the implication of the question is, is clearly no longer in fashion.

Oshima's main point in *Shinjuku Thief* seems to be that "sexual frustration is just one of the many sorts of frustration that go with the various forms of rebellion."[35] The film parallels the search for sexual identity and liberation by the two youthful protagonists with "more general feelings of frustration among the student population" at the time. The film also parallels a theatrical performance staged within the film with actual footage of a massive student protest/riot in Shinjuku, the parallel suggesting that "both are revolutionary activities." It may be said that a student riot is a direct and practical action of a revolutionary nature while the theatrical performance concerns a revolution of the imagination.[36] Connecting the theatrical performance with the student riots is the search for sexual identity which is itself sifted through the idea of theft. Oshima "stole" the title of his film from a work by Jean Genet; the main character, Birdey Hilltop, steals books from the famed Kinokuniya bookstore; and the play within the film concerns Yui Shosetsu, who tried to "steal" Japan through a coup d'etat. Theft provides Birdey with sexual gratification, a motif extended from *Pleasures of the Flesh* and *Violence at Noon* (and apparent as early as *Cruel Story of Youth*), except now Oshima makes clear at what level "revolution" is to take place: imagination, "the idea that something that starts with imagination can change reality."[37] Crime and sexual problems, theatre and the student rebellion, are linked in a reciprocal relationship revolving around a dialectic between reality and fiction (imagination). And it is this "revolving around" that causes the film's complexity, that makes this "revolving around" a "revolution."

The sexual dysfunction that characterizes Birdey Hilltop and Umeko, the young protagonists, stems from a confusion of sex roles. A sexologist they consult diagnoses Umeko as possessing "lesbian tendencies" (i.e., aggressive or masculine characteristics) while he feels that Birdey has a feminine streak in him. The sexologist advises them not to rid themselves of these tendencies, but, on the contrary, to allow these tendencies into the relationship. For Oshima, "a male being a female figure was the most significant aspect or spirit of that time, the era of the demonstrations from 1968–69." Oshima disavows homosexuality, instead merely claiming that "the male figure . . . is getting weaker and gentler and soft."[38] For Joan Mellen, this is clearly a positive step toward social change:

> The liberation of the male from traditional Japanese ideas about masculinity thus becomes analogous to the political protest. The movement recognizes, at least implicitly, that once Japanese society begins to be immersed in political upheaval with its end a more democratic society, the Japanese could also begin to free themselves psychologically from rigid, traditional, and repressive attitudes toward sexuality.[39]

Oshima's actual presentation of Birdey's dysfunction is, however, more ambivalent than Mellen allows. As Raymond Durgnat notes, there is a strong degree of masochism in Birdey's sexual problem. Birdey tries to "sell" Umeko to Mr. Tanabe, the president of Kinokuniya, after she is raped by Watababe Fumio and Sato Kei who have apparently slipped from playing themselves to portraying characters who rape Umeko. Birdey seems to revel in his powerlessness, an index of his masochism. When he demands that

Shinjuku dorobo nikki (Diary of a Shinjuku Thief)
Oshima Nagisa, director. Kawakita/Japan Film Library Council

Mr. Tanabe buy Umeko, he confronts the older man with his (Birdey's) inadequacy.[40] This sequence has Birdey wearing Umeko's skirt over his pants, and he comes to the realization that, "I want to become a girl and that Umeko wants to become a boy."[41] Role confusion, per se, therefore, does not necessarily have a revolutionary aspect. Birdey and Umeko do not consummate their relationship until *after* they have become involved in the theatrical performance,"stealing" the role of Yui Shosetsu from Kara Juro. The imaginary revolution they participate in invigorates their sexuality, just as the imaginary revolution in the theatre invigorates (by virtue of Oshima's crosscutting) the student riots.

Oshima may have exaggerated when he claimed that a male being a female figure was the most significant aspect of the late '60s, but it was certainly an interesting aspect of the time. Of course, one must note that role confusion, or role-*playing*, is a dominant characteristic of Japanese theatre, the famous *onnagata* of the Kabuki theatre (in which there are no women), and its reverse, the Takarazuka theatre (in which there are no men). In the 1960s, the tradition of the *onnagata* and the Takarazuka theatre (started in 1914) were alive and well, part of Japan's "official" culture.[42] Slightly apart from the official culture, but still part of an apparently large segment of the popular audience, is the tradition of transvestite performing.[43] An intermingling of the theatrical and the performance modes can be seen in a fascinating film directed by Fukasaku Kinji, *Kurotokage* (*Black Lizard*, 1968).[44]

Black Lizard stars famed female impersonator Maruyama Akihiro in the title role, portraying a female jewel thief who is pursued by a relentless detective. The Black Lizard is a collector of "living statues," people she kills, embalms, and mounts. (Shades of Roger Corman's *A Bucket of Blood!*) The detective has fallen in love with her and she with him. The film takes on more interest for the Westerner than merely the appearance of a transvestite actor (common, for instance, in films by Andy Warhol and John Waters, though neither filmmaker can be considered mainstream, like Fukasaku). The film is based on a stage version of a story by Edogawa Rampo (a Japanization of Edgar Allan Poe) adapted especially for Maruyama by Mishima Yukio. Mishima makes a cameo appearance in the film as one of the "living statues." Mishima's presence subtly invokes all the concerns for which he was notorious: the conflation of identity, with returning to the "Japanese spirit," sexuality (his body-building and homo-eroticism), and the cult of death.

Elliott Stein, reviewing *Black Lizard* as part of the Gay Film Festival in New York in 1984, claimed the film is "camp and a half."[45] While camp may be a positive value to some, there is something a bit condescending in such a judgment. Maruyama Akihiro's image, as Ian Buruma notes, is not camp. Akihiro's appeal rests on the idea of artificiality rendering "her" more beautiful. Akihiro's sexual attraction "is enhanced by a certain amount of ambivalence," an idea which seems to be "a universal truism."[46] Her transvestite art is an extension of the official art of the *onnagata* of the Kabuki theatre, and of the less official, but possibly more popular, Takarazuka tradition. Sex roles are deliberately theatricalized, highlighted in their social essence, and so provide a starting point for a radical critique of the dominant culture's attitudes toward sexuality. Transvestism may thus be seen as one form of "spectacular" rebellion.

It is this spectacular rebellion which characterizes the transvestism of *Bara no soretsu* (*Funeral of Roses*, 1969), Matsumoto Toshio's first feature. The film stars another well-known transvestite star who calls himself Peter, here portraying a male prostitute. Burch praises the film for its avowed Brecthianism.[47] An index, however, to the *popular* appeal of Peter (if not necessarily Matsumoto's challenging style) is the fact the he appeared as "The Fool" in Kurosawa's *Ran* (1985), the famed director's adaptation of *King Lear*. For Donald Richie, the links between this world of spectacular sexuality and contemporary Japan is clearly stated by Matsumoto: "*Funeral Parade of Roses* [an alternate title] made the world of male prostitution a paradigm for contemporary Japan."[48] Ambivalence, so important in the sexual attraction of crossdressing, also functions in this film as a political category.

The links between eroticism and violence, sex and politics, and the ambivalence about sex roles, all come together in Oshima's most explicit film—explicit sexually and explicit about its political implications: *Ai no koriida* (*The Realm of the Senses*, 1976). Of course, the film was made after the New Wave was over and it attests as much to Oshima's personal explorations of the connections between sex, death, and culture as it does to a common point of cultural contention in the 1960s. It is also worth noting that Oshima's version of the fairly famous story of Abe Sada was not the only film version produced at the time. Tanaka Noboru's *Jitsuroku Abe Sada* (*The True Story of Abe Sada*) was released in 1975. Tanaka's film uses a flashback structure and, like Oshima's, makes oblique reference to the *ni-ni-roku* (February 26) Incident. Such a reference seems unavoidable (although Oshima handles it more subtly and hence with greater force) since the Abe Sada case came to light on May 16, 1936. In fact, some Japanese critics insist that the interest the case aroused at the time was a function of the political issues of the day as people sought relief from the violent military events in this sad, comical, outrageous incident. The case is also deemed to be significant in that it seems to have caused something of a re-thinking on the part of many Japanese about traditional sex roles.[49] The fact that Abe Sada came to dominate her sexual relationship with Ishida Yoshizo (or Kichizo), strangled him to death, and castrated him broke down the stereotype of the Japanese woman as submissive.

Most critics writing on *The Realm of the Senses* (Oshima prefers the French title *L'Empire des sens* which he claims is a pun on Roland Barthes' *L'Empire des signes*[50]) see the film as primarily concerned with sexual politics. Peter B. High may be taken as representative of this critical view. High links Oshima with directors like Mizoguchi, Shindo Kaneto, and Imamura who are all concerned with examining the image of women in Japanese film and culture. For High, Oshima ultimately subscribes to the "Queen Bee Complex" in which women kill their mates. Abe Sada initially represents a vision of "the end of male domination" which is necessary to bring about "complete libidinal liberation." High maintains that Sada's "power over men is the lure of her absolutely uninhibited sensuality, a promise of Heaven in an earthbound, erotically subjugated world. It is liberation through the extinction of the outside world—a secret craving of the male. . . . " Unfortunately, coupled with this vision/desire for "unimaginable pleasures of the flesh" is the horror of liberated female sexuality: "claustrophobia, suffocation and castration." These fears, realized when Sada strangles and castrates Kichi "throw doubt on the desirability of Kichizo's action." Thus, to High, Oshima ultimately rejects Kichizo as an example of true liberation: "true liberation from the sexual repression of male-dominated society is not to be found in its opposite exteme."[51]

If High's interpretation is correct, then we are left, once again, with ambivalence over sex roles. Yet, just as in *Diary of a Shinjuku Thief*, there is a specifically political dimension to this work. In this instance, politics is present by its absence. As High correctly notes, the process Oshima puts us through, via Sada and Kichi, is one of ever-increasing claustrophobia. Except we must note the sequence in which Kichi leaves their room to journey through the streets. Marching soldiers, on their way, perhaps, to stage the February 26 Incident, cause Kichi to cower against a wall. As Dana Polan notes about this scene, Oshima often "gives the spectator information that the characters do not possess."[52] The retreat by Sada and Kichi into sexuality, into the realm of the senses, is a retreat from the outside world, the realm of the political. Polan: "I think we can find in *Realm of the Senses* a practice of film that calls into question the obsession with the personal and with the 'liberatory' possibility of sexuality per se."[53] We must conclude that any relationship which tries to deny the outside world by creating a private world (at one point Kichi says to Sada, "We are not in town, we are still at home") is doomed.[54] Once again, then, there is a strong link between sexuality and politics, except in this instance a *liberated* sexuality is being practiced against a background of *repressive* politics; hence the importance of 1936 for Oshima. It is precisely by ignoring politics that such repression in the social sphere may exist; and this in turn dooms the private sphere. The private is political in more ways than one; if you wish to foment a revolution, you must not retreat into the realm of the senses.

The Realm of the Senses needs to be understood as an outgrowth not only of Oshima's concern with sexuality, politics, and identity, but also in its relationship to other films similarly concerned, in particular, the Japanese genre of the "pink" film and its more radical extension, the "roman porno" (romance pornography). The beginning of the pink film (*pinku eiga*) is typically placed in 1964, which caused something of a scandal in Japan as this was to be the time of Japan's greatest postwar international triumph, the Tokyo Olympics. Neo-pornographic films hardly seemed to put forth the kind of image the Japanese government wanted to show off. Nevertheless, Shochiku, Nikkatsu and, soon after, Toei, began the production of pink films, which quickly came to dominate the home market. By the mid-1960s, pink films accounted for fully one-half of domestic production.[55]

The first important director of pink films was Takechi Tetsuji. In 1964, he directed *Hakujitsumu (Daydream)* and *Kokeimu (Dream of the Red Room)*, both adapted from stories by Tanizaki Junichiro. In 1966, he produced an erotic version of *Genji monogatari (The Tale of Genji*—which is, like Tanizaki's works, already erotic, if not sexually explicit). His most important and controversial contribution to the pink film was *Kuroi yuki (Black Snow, 1965)* which brought a political element into the genre.

Black Snow focuses on a young Japanese man, the son of a prostitute who serves the soldiers at the U.S. military base in Yokota. The boy is impotent, able only to make love while holding a loaded gun. He shoots a black GI and then is, in turn, gunned down by American soldiers. In June 1965, Takechi was prosecuted on a charge of public indecency. In court he claimed:

> The censors are getting tough about *Black Snow*. I admit there are many nude scenes in the film, but they are psychological nude scenes symbolizing the defencelessness of the Japanese people in the face of the American invasion. Prompted by the CIA and the U.S. Army they say my film is immoral. This is of course an old story that has been going on for centuries. . . . In fact it [is] a matter of rank political suppression.[56]

Intellectuals and filmmakers alike, including Mishima Yukio and Oshima Nagisa (who would face similar charges in 1976 surrounding a book version of *The Realm of the Senses*), rose to Takechi's defense. Takechi won his court case and the pink film continued to dominate Japanese screens.[57]

Suzuki Seijun, while he continued to produce his offbeat variations of Nikkatsu's youth exploitation films, also turned to the production of pink films. His *Nikutai no mon* (*Gate of Flesh*, 1964) was the second film version of a powerful postwar play about an organized gang of black marketeers and prostitutes. Suzuki used the pink film to make an anti-war statement in *Shunpu-den* (*Joy Girls*, 1965). This film focuses on a platoon of Japanese soldiers in Manchuria and the prostitutes attached to the unit (a repressed part of Japan's war history, alluded to briefly in Chapter 5, the subject of Imamura's 1973 documentary, *Karayuki-san*, and the popular fiction film *Sandakan #8*, 1974, by Kumai Kei). The sex scenes are clearly merely generic, the anti-militaristic tone dominating. Suzuki directed at least half a dozen more pink films at Nikkatsu before he was fired in 1968, with such titles as *Suppadaka no toshigoro* (*Age of Nakedness*) and *Subete ga kurutte iru* (*Everything is in Chaos*).

The most important director to emerge in the pink film genre was Wakamatsu Koji. A contract director for Nikkatsu, he directed twenty films in a two-year period, 1963–65. What turned out to be his last film for the company found Wakamatsu entering the area pioneered by Imamura Shohei and becoming a growing concern for Oshima, the connections between sexuality, identity, and politics. *Kabe no naka no himegoto* (*Secret Act Inside Walls*, 1965) was submitted to the Berlin Film Festival without the endorsement of the Japan Film Federation (Eiren—the organization also refused to submit Kurosawa's *Ran* for Best Foreign Film Oscar consideration). The submission of Wakamatsu's film to Berlin created a scandal in the official film culture of Japan, since pink films were held in low esteem (despite their complete dominance in the marketplace). Predictably enough, the film proved a *succès de scandale* and thereby lent a certain respectability to the pink film. The release of Takechi's *Black Snow* that same year also aided the cause of upgrading the pink film, or at least showing the potential the pink film held for politically minded filmmakers. The release of *Secret Act Inside Walls* coincided with the release of Wakamatsu from Nikkatsu to go into low-budget (*very* low-budget) independent film-making.

Secret Act Inside Walls is the story of a student studying for his college entrance exams, a time of severe anxiety for Japanese youth. This particular youth finds release in masturbation and voyeurism. One day he enters an apartment and, in spite of the woman's consent to have sex with him, kills her. Voyeurism and rape are two common motifs in the pink film, and two recurring characters (for somewhat obvious reasons) are college-age youths and housewives. In this film, Wakamatsu begins to bring in a specifically political dimension to these formulaic figures. The student is especially anxiety-ridden over the entrance exams due to his working-class origins. Denied access to a first-rate secondary education, he is at a severe disadvantage on these tests. While the "bored" housewife (a generic characterization of housewives) may not exactly be a symbol of modern Japan against whom the student feels resentment, she nevertheless brings forth a host of political, economic, and psychological associations.

Taiji ga mitsuryo suru toki (*The Embryo Hunts in Secret*, 1966) brings a psychological inflection to the pink film in a spectacular (if possibly unpleasant) manner. It was this film which prompted Noel Burch to characterize Wakamatsu as a "primitive," a characterization that Burch feels applies to all his works. *The Embryo Hunts in Secret* is marked, according to Burch, by "a raw, black-and-white 'crime magazine' style," from which some of the later films have moved away. (It is also incorrectly identified as the first Wakamatsu film to be shown in Europe.)[58] The primitive quality of Wakamatsu's work, and the look which distinguishes this film (and most of the rest of his oeuvre, contrary to Burch) stems in large measure from severe budget constraints. Wakamatsu's films typically fall below the ¥1,000,000 range (approximately, $5,000), which forces him to rely on all-location shooting, natural light, and single takes. *The Embryo Hunts in Secret* was shot completely indoors (save for a short opening scene), in basically two rooms and a hallway, preventing much extra lighting equipment even if it was affordable. Sato Tadao even attributes the "homely" features of the actresses to budgetary constraints as Wakamatsu cannot afford to hire better-known, more talented, and popular pink film stars.[59] These lesser-quality performers also account for the "flattening out" of emotional affect; the actors' inability to emote convincingly lends a Brechtian air to the films, which is aided by the deliberate politicizing of the motifs and Wakamatsu's refusal, as Burch has it, "to make concessions to the slick imagery of commercial erotica."[60]

The Brechtianism of *The Embryo Hunts in Secret* notwithstanding, the film is still disturbing to a Western viewer, the alienation effects insufficient to overcome our emotional distaste for the action. Rape and sadomasochism predominate in the pink film and *roman porno* as compared to American, and especially European "soft-core" films which feature lushly photographed, soft-focus, simulated lovemaking (as in the *Emmanuel* series). Ian Buruma (who translates the film's title as "When the Foetus Goes Poaching") finds that the film "becomes too unbearable to watch" (a man ties a woman up and tortures her throughout the bulk of the film).[61] The disturbing tone of the film is aided by a harpsichord playing vaguely classical pieces as underscoring, and by the fragmented editing style. The disjointed, fragmented feeling is increased by the hand-held camera (always disturbing in CinemaScope in the days before steadicams). A series of freeze-frames and flashbacks further fragments the action. It is difficult to believe that any audience can truly enjoy this film, which would certainly support the notion of its Brechtianism.

The flashbacks all revolve around images, memories, and fantasies of the man's mother. As he tortures the woman with a straight razor and a whip, he occasionally cries out for his mother, Wakamatsu offering up a complex series of cuts between the man, woman, flashbacks, and interpolated Christian imagery (the harpsichord music fits in this last aspect somehow). At one point, the man flashes back to an image of his father whipping his mother. In another mental image from the man's interior point of view, we see a stylized animation of an embryo in a womb, presumably the man's own intense desire to remember, to re-imagine, his time of greatest happiness (and an index to the film's allusive title). In another flashback/fantasy he imagines his own birth as he narrates in voiceover the end of his happiness. The man achieves something like happiness again when the woman finally frees herself from her bonds and stabs the man repeatedly with a knife. He happily calls out "Mother" and dies in her lap, curled up like a fetus.

Rape and torture are prevalent components in the pink films and the *roman porno*, as well as in other forms of Japanese erotica (magazines, comic books). There is no hard-core pornography in Japan (it is illegal) and there are certain censorship laws in general. Many Westerners find this ironic and disturbing in light of the fact that "rape, sadism, torture [are all] permissible in popular entertainment, but the official line is drawn at the showing of pubic hair."[62] It takes no staunch feminist to claim that pink films, which cater to overwhelmingly male audiences, fulfill repressed male desires to rape and torture women, especially if Buruma is right when he says that in these films " . . . women *always* fall in love with their rapists." Buruma also notes that typical targets of rape include "symbols of innocence: schoolgirls in uniform, nurses, just-married housewives. . . ."[63] After raping his victim, the rapist confesses his weakness and shame to her, at which point the woman's maternal instinct asserts itself.[64] On the surface, Wakamatsu does nothing to overturn these conventions. The man in

Embryo obviously desires his mother and substitutes this woman for her in a clear love/hate ritual enactment. In the later, even more disturbing, *Okasareta byakui* (*Violated Women in White*, 1967) the rapist/murderer attacks student nurses but at film's end is seen snuggling in the lap of the last surviving student. In *Embryo*, however, the woman kills her attacker and has never submitted willingly to his perversions. And while the man's death apparently makes him happy, the woman makes her escape.

In discussing *Violated Women in White*, Noel Burch rejects the equation between "unbridled sexual fulfillment [and] revolutionary politics" made by some "ultra-Lefitst groups in Japan," but he does feel that the film is political on the artistic plane as it demonstrates a convergence "between the ideology subtending and *fruitfully nourishing* [Burch's italics] this film, and certain literary speculations within a Marxist framework. . . ."[65] Later in his discussion of Wakamatsu and *Violated Women*, Burch again asserts that Wakamatsu denies causal connections between sexual alienation which leads to violence and ideological alienation from capitalism. Such connections are, in Waikamatsu's film *"put to work,"* [Burch's italics].[66]

The point to this film, and to many of Wakamatsu's works, is not that unbridled sexuality equals revolutionary politics, but that repressive politics goes hand in hand with repressive sexuality. Wakamatsu begins to explore the devastating effects of unfulfilled sexual drives in *Violated Women in White*. In what Burch calls a "prologue" to this film, we see "still images borrowed from the daily repertoire of commercial erotica." These images, Burch feels, situate "the hero's psychosis in social reality, to designate it as emblematic of social and political repression and revolt." However, this social contextualizinng does not justify the hero's later actions.[67] Such images, and the hero's reaction to them, are reflective of the image of women within the pink film. The hero (interestingly, portrayed by playwright Kara Juro, who appears as himself in Oshima's *Diary of a Shinjuku Thief*) responds to these images (drawings and posed photographs of nude women) by firing a pistol into the sea; his action is noted by Burch as a clear symbol for incest in terms of *mare nostrum* and "that the Chinese character used in Japanese to signify *the sea* contains within it a recognizable variant of the character for mother."[68] (Which might be stretching the point a bit; *part* of the character for "sea" resembles the character for mother *somewhat*, but then what are we to make of the action if not that?) This action is clearly a phallic rage directed at women whom he may not have but whom he desires, and to his mother whom he may also not have, but equally desires. His anger and his desire are clear indications of ambivalence, the same ambivalence which characterizes the image of women in the pink films. The reflexivity also extends to the motif of voyeurism, apparent in the next scene of the film.

Inside the student nurses' dormitory, two women make love, spied upon by another student (all the student nurses are women). It is only *after* this scene has begun that we see the boy spying on the women. The introduction of lesbian lovemaking (a common motif in heterosexual erotica) in this manner—we watch them making love before we watch him watching them—implicates us in the voyeuristic fantasy. The fantasy of implication is extended as the women virtually pull the boy inside to watch. The passivity of the male in this instance reflects the passivity of the males watching in the audience; entering the dormitory is like entering the world of the screen. But if the boy lives out one kind of fantasy for the audience, we are soon implicated in the other side of this fantasy, the dark side, where women who display themselves to men, while denying their physicality to those men, are punished for their behavior. The boy takes out his pistol and shoots one of the women.

The rest of the film has an ebb-and-flow structure (what Burch calls as "orgasmic structure"[69]). Particularly important sequences include one woman aggressively trying to seduce the boy following the shooting of a second student nurse. The boy begins to respond to her advances, but stops. She laughs at him and he imagines the remaining women also to be laughing at his impotence, expressed through close-ups in a style reminiscent of the "laughing faces" scene in Murnau's *Der Letze Mann* (1924). The humiliation of the male character is something of a recurring motif for Wakamatsu as many of his protagonists are shamed by sexually aggressive women, only to turn around and punish them, as the hero does here. Another important sequence finds the head nurse berating the boy. He ties her to a chair as he goes about killing a fourth student by tying her to a post and flaying her alive with a razor blade. (This takes place mostly offscreen after it is clear what he is doing.) When he shows the head nurse his handiwork, the woman tied to the post is shown in color, partially from the boy's point of view. One says "partially" in this instance because one is not exactly certain how the shot is to be taken. As Burch points out, "the sparing and startling insertions of color which suddenly theatricalize the violence serve to designate these crimes as fiction, exposing all that ominous black blood for what it really is: red paint."[70] The obvious theatricalizations are combined with Wakamatsu's fragmented editing style which refuses the eyeline match.

Fantasy (theatricalization, interior point of view) within the fiction again appears in the final sequences. The killer spares the youngest nurse, putting his gun aside and laying his head in her lap, in a shot reminiscent of the one in *Embryo*. She sings to him and he begins to make love to her. He imagines himself on the beach (as in the start) as she runs ahead of him, he playfully following behind, shown in slow motion. The sunset he sees is shown in color, followed by a color shot of the boy resting in the girl's lap, surrounded by the five dead bodies of the student nurses.[71] From here, Wakamatsu cuts to a color shot of a baby. From the baby, Wakamatsu cuts back to the scene of the dead bodies, except now the youngest nurse is absent from the shot. Then we see black-and-white stills (as in a crime magazine) of the police raid on the dormitory to arrest him. Possibly the youngest nurse called the police, her maternal instincts overcome by the horror of what the boy has done. Or perhaps there never was a sympathetic young nurse to mother the boy. In either instance, the wish-fulfillment fantasy of the (male) audience is clear and clearly ambivalent. The young nurse/mother betrayed the boy, as all women will betray men; or all men desire to be comforted and loved by their mothers, but their mothers are never really there.

   Yuke, yuke nidome no shojo (*Go, Go You Who Are a Virgin for the Second Time,* 1969) is by any standards a more interesting and less painful film to watch than the earlier films discussed. As before, Wakamatsu toys with presenting an explanation for the shocking sexual violence he presents by situating the film within a sociocultural moment in Japan and within a general milieu of violence and sexuality. As in *Violated Women,* Wakamatsu shows still images drawn from commercial exploitation forms, except in this later film, he shows them at the end, forcing a kind of retrospective understanding of the hero's motivations. This retrospective mode is also impacted by the gradual revelation, through flashbacks, of the boy's shocking crime and his motives for committing it, which prepares us for the crimes and suicide which end the film.

   There are two protagonists in this film, "a girl with a special proclivity for being gang-raped" and a boy who "turns out to have the corpse of a person he murdered in his room . . . ."[72] This description of the girl is basically accurate. At the start of the film she is raped by four boys as the hero watches off to the side, there is a flashback to her rape by two boys at the seashore, and later in the film she is raped again by one of the four boys who is helped by his girlfriend. The description of the male hero, however, is wrong. He has not one body, but four, and not in his room, but in the kitchen of the apartment in which he lives. We first see these bodies in a flash-cut, in color (the bulk of the film is in black and white) and gradually come to see how they got there in that bloody fashion. The four adults (two are his parents) had been engaged in an orgy. In one instance, they dragged the boy into the kitchen, tormented, and molested him; one woman humiliated him by urinating on the boy. It perhaps comes as no surprise, then, to learn that he brutally stabbed them all.

   The boy and girl form something of a friendship. They speak longingly of their parents, the boy even sings a plaintive song to his mother. A wistful, nostalgic feeling is often created by the use of music. At one point Gershwin's "Summertime" is heard, another time, in English, "Sometimes I Feel Like a Motherless Child" plays on the soundtrack. The desire for parents on their part and their innocent fun (they run laughing across the rooftop accompanied by a gentle flute solo *after* the boy has killed the four rapists and their three girlfriends) shows their essential childishness in contradistinction to the brutal events in which they are victims (until the boy turns to murder). Their innocence, their being caught in a web of circumstances, is made symbolically clear by their suicide at the end, a variation of the tradition of *shinju* reserved for lovers in the world of traditional theatre. (They matter of factly jump off the roof—their matter-of-factness in contrast to the *michiyuki*—the poetic, serious, sad final journey of the lovers—of Bumraku and Kabuki.) Before their suicide, while they are asleep, Wakamatsu delivers another montage of stills, among them images from Samurai *manqa* (comic books which are quite often graphically violent) and crime magazine photographs of Sharon Tate and Roman Polanski. At daybreak, we return to the rooftop, littered with dead bodies, as the boy and girl jump off.

The photographs of Sharon Tate are by themselves quite shocking, a clearly rhetorical move on Wakamatsu's part. *Go, Go You Who Are a Virgin . . .* was released in 1969; Sharon Tate and her friends were slain in August of that year. Just as Wakamatsu based *Violated Women* on the "notorious massacre of 'Chicago nurses,' "[73] here again he refers to a shocking real-life crime. A parallel between the crimes on view in this film and the Sharon Tate murder seems difficult to draw, especially since the so-called Manson Family involvement was not known until long after the film was made. But it is interesting that the Manson Family, in their psychopathic way, had vague "revolutionary" goals underlying their actions. The inability to equate political rebellion with spectacular sexual activity seems once again to be operative. On the other hand, we may understand that the hero has been brutalized by the adult world and tormented, in a way, by violent and sexually graphic images in the media. It is possible that Wakamatsu sides with those who feel that pornography has harmful effects, that the Brechtian devices he employs prevent our enjoyment of these images so that we understand the social implications of them. Lest Wakamatsu appear hypocritical (exploiting the pink film to condemn pornography), we should realize that he is condemning official (adult) hypocrisy. Adults engage in illicit activities, sex magazines encourage fantasies that may not be realized, crime magazines exploit violent impulses, all supported by a political regime which represses genuine individuality. The young are tormented and confused, encouraged to mistake spectacular sex for genuine political involvement.

The equation between unbridled sexuality and political revolution is the exact focus of *Tenshi no kokotsu* (*Angelic Orgasm*, 1970). One Japanese critic, seeing this film, was prompted to remark, "In *Angelic Orgasm*, sex weighs no weight. [Wakamatsu] is now more interested in stirring up a world revolution than in sex. He is no longer a pink film director."[74] And indeed, the film is more interested in left-wing radical politics than in sensational sex. Yet the portrayal of the leftists (a radical fringe, to be sure) hardly supports "world revolution." The main protagonists of *Angelic Orgasm* are the lowest-ranking cadres of an ultra-left paramilitary group called *Shiki-*

kyokai (Four Seasons Association). The protagonists belong to a troop known as *Jugatsu* (October), the code name of the troop leader. The rest of the troop go by the code names of Monday, Tuesday, Wednesday, and so on. Assigned to rob an arsenal at an American military base, Tuesday, Wednesday, and Thursday are killed, and October is blinded. The surviving members are assigned to other troops. They come to realize, however, that they were betrayed by the Association, which had become annoyed at the troop's undisciplined actions and their penchant for free expressions of sex. The survivors reform the troop and break away from the Association, dedicating themselves to anarchy, violence, and the free reign of sexuality. They take to bombing street corners to show their disdain for the ordinary world, determined to stick to the world of darkness, anarchy, and sexuality, until they are killed.

The betrayal of the youthful protagonists by their own organization recalls the sense of betrayal felt by the young Zengakuren leaders at the hands of the JCP during Ampo 1960. The Four Seasons Association does not betray the October group for political reasons, but rather for sexual ones. The October group was concerned with self-expression and self-knowledge, incompatible with the militaristically revolutionary aims of the Association. In this fashion, Wakamatsu castigates the far left for its hypocritical puritanism. This does not mean, once again, that he supports the actions of the October group in their sexual anarchy. Rather, he demonstrates that the youth are unable to find meaning in ultra-left politics, while they are equally alienated by mainstream society. Nihilism or extreme sensuality seem to be their only choices. One might understand their meaningless terrorism as a reflection of their desperation to find a sense of self, of identity. Their sexual expression and violence provide immediate gratification. As far back as Oshima's *Cruel Story of Youth*, the young soon came to substitute desire for political action or utopian dreams. Dreams are betrayed, politics can be corrupted. Only sex and violence provoke enough thrills to convince the young that they are alive.

The failure of left politics was conjoined with the failure of the educational system to provide youth with meaning in an extraordinarily perceptive and humorous film written and directed by Wakamatsu's sometime coscreenwriter Adachi Masao, called *Seiyugi* (*Sexual Play*, 1968). In this film, a group of ultra-leftist terrorists are figures of absurdist humor. Near the film's end, these bomb-making revolutionaries accidentally blow themselves up. Such an occurrence became all too familiar in the U.S. with the pathetic activities of the Weather Underground so that Adachi's perceptivity is something to be admired. The radicals appear as harmless lunatics without political viability.[75]

Juxtaposed to the college-student lunatic-radicals are a group of more typically alienated college students. Kenji and his four friends are first seen with two girls in a book-filled room playing at rape and reading erotic *manga*. As Kenji and his group go to class, we see students striking and picketing in front of graffiti-covered walls. (The fast production time of Wakamatsu and Adachi often found their films appearing while events they refer to are still on-going. Typical production time for Wakamatsu was sixteen days.[76]) Kenji and his cohorts grab a militant woman student, drag her into their car, and rape her in a campus gym. The woman, Taeko, falls in love with Kenji in typical pink film fashion, but he also falls in love with her. These college students, even Taeko, whose brother is one of the terrorists (the main bomb-maker, in fact), can find little meaning in organized protests. They play at sex in order to find something to believe in. After the ultra-leftists blow themselves up, for instance, Kenji's group holds an orgy. At one point, one of the group tears a picture of Mishima Yukio and his private army from a magazine and rips it up. The group put on Nazi uniforms and march around, shouting "Heil Hitler" in disdain for Mishima's activities. They head for the Diet building where a protest is being staged and begin to strip off their clothes. Only when Taeko announces that she is pregnant does their play come to a halt. When she confronts both Kenji's group and her brother's radical troop, the film switches to color cinematography. Taeko, wearing a kimono open to reveal that she is naked underneath, asks for a father for her baby. A flower covers her pubis, a double pun—the metaphorical "flower of womanhood" literalized to cover up the female genitalia, banned from the Japanese screen. Confronted by this female form, the radicals cower in fright. But Kenji comes forward to claim her and the two make love, an assertion of their disdain for violent politics, a reassertion of their sexuality. Sexual play as a healthy expression of vibrant youth is juxtaposed to the repression of sexuality in mainstream culture and the absurdity of terrorist bombings.

The question of identity, posed in an existential form by Teshigahara, in what might be called a racial form by Imamura, and in an overtly political form by Oshima, Wakamatsu, and Adachi, all relied in some fashion on women. The male protagonists in Teshigahara's film come to terms with, or lose their identity because of, women. For Imamura, women are central to the man's quest for his identity as he seeks it in contemporary family life or through the remnants of primitive culture. For Oshima, the question of identity is intimately linked to the relationship of sex and politics, expanded on by Wakamatsu and Adachi through conjoined images of sexual and political violence. The links between identity, politics, sexuality, and violence necessarily conflate with the image of women. As Richard Tucker notes about the New Wave films, "Violence is seen as a liberating force, as is the sexual act, yet the paradox remains that violence also oppresses and the sexual act can so easily oppress the female."[77] It is therefore to the female, to images of women, that we now turn.

CHAPTER FOUR

Insect Women

In an interview with Joan Mellen, actress Hidari Sachiko claimed, " . . . if you want to say something about Japan, you have to focus on women."[1] It is quite an interesting observation. The longevity of Japanese society and the nation's preoccuptation with its own history and sense of identity make an entry point into contemporary culture quite difficult. A focus on women can reveal most of Japan's inner tensions and contradictions. The changing roles of women in Japanese society and the changing nature of their image in myth, religion, and ideology provide a good index of Japan's cultural agenda at a given moment. Women in Japanese culture have occupied places of esteem, from the Sun Goddess from whom the Japanese claim descent to the highly cultured courtly society of the Heian period, when women gave voice to an entire aesthetic system, until the erosion of women's power under the increasingly Confucian-influenced ideology of feudalism. Japan's attempts to modernize during the Meiji era (1868–1912) included a focus not only on industrialization and technical education but, to some degree, on the emancipation of women. The Meiji era saw a resurgence of women writers, for instance. Again, in the Occupation period, Japan's restructuring and retooling for peace saw women's issues becoming paramount.

The image of women in Japanese society, as in many other cultures, is one of ambivalence. In Japanese high and popular culture one sees images of women ranging from the extremes of outright worship to hatred and fear. These extremes can be encapsulated as subscribing to the universal archetypes of Mother and Whore sifted through certain uniquely Japanese perspectives. These extremes, and the gradations in between, appear in various forms at various times. One must be careful, when dealing with artistic or popular cultural texts, to distinguish between the official cultural agenda and attempts to subvert its norms. And one must always be aware that even progressive attempts may be subject to certain ambivalences which can work through the text.

Richard Tucker has stated that the Japanese "have produced a substantially greater body of work about women than any other national cinema."[2] Considering Japan's film history, this might be something of a surprise, for Japanese films did not even feature women until the early 1920s. Before that, women's roles were taken by *onnagata* (*oyama*), the male actors trained in women's roles in the traditional theatres. While Japanese films, then, featured women's roles, women as women were absent. Actresses first made their appearance in cinema as part of an overall process of "Westernizing" the film industry. Just as the status of women would become part and parcel of postwar democratic reforms, so too, in the 1920s, women were perceived as "innovations" along with such others as "the introduction of long-, medium-, and close shots, together with editing principles; . . . "[3] Noel Burch notes the connection between these attempted formal innovations and a left-leaning political agenda: "The objectively progressive forces in Japan at this time [after World War I] identified their struggle with the introduction of the Hollywood codes and elimination of the benshi, *oyama* and other elements inherited from the traditional arts and culture."[4] The presence of women in women's roles was thus a political act. In fact, film actresses were first used in the *keiko eiga*, the tendency film, which itself had leftist connotations.[5]

Many of the tendency films focused on the urban working class, or lower class, and adopted a Marxist position. The majority of these films utilized women as central characters. This focus on women was unique to cinema, because the corresponding leftist movements in literature and theatre (the proletarian novels and the Shingeki theatre) did not manifest a similar focus. This link between women and the working, or other oppressed, classes, in the short-lived tendency films of the late '20s-early 30s, thus looks forward to the New Wave, which would find women a powerful metaphor for the situation of Japan's alienated groups in the postwar era.

As the worldwide depression hit Japan in the 1930s and the increasingly conservative drift of the population paved the way for the militarist era, movie audiences became less interested in Marxist views of the problems of urban and industrial Japan. The tendency film was replaced in the stream of Japanese film history by the "*feminisuto*" films, films produced by directors who have a feminist viewpoint. Sato Tadao maintains that many Japanese movies manifest this view, but it is best expressed in the works of Mizoguchi Kenji, Shindo Kaneto, and Imamura Shohei.[6] In their films, and the films of other *feminisuto* directors, one finds a politicized view of women. While the politicization of the image of women remains constant, the specific politics on view changes. One must be aware that when Sato calls Mizoguchi, Shindo, and Imamura *feminisutos* (from the Japanese pronunciation of feminist), he has something quite specific in mind. As Audie Bock points out, "This English loan word has nuances in Japan that differ considerably from its Western usage."[7] Sato's notion of feminism:

> The image of a woman suffering uncomplainingly can imbue us with admiration for a virtuous existence almost beyond our reach, rich in endurance and

courage. One can idealize her rather than merely pity her, and this can lead to what I call the worship of womanhood, a special Japanese brand of feminism.[8]

Sato believes that this Japanese feminism has its roots in the moral consciousness of the common people, which would indicate that the popular art of the cinema is a privileged place to examine the image of women in Japan.

Mizoguchi Kenji, Sato's first *feminisuto* director, may be taken as paradigmatic of the classical/transcendental image of women. As Keiko McDonald has noted, Mizoguchi's "most congenial subject matter [is] the fate of women held captive by feudal values,"[9] and it is the case that without exception Mizoguchi's most affecting films are those which focus on women. While Mizoguchi is clearly on women's side and clearly recognizes the oppression to which they have been subjected, his attitude is nevertheless both ambivalent and transcendental. Richard Tucker recognizes that while Mizoguchi's films focus on women, their main thematic purpose is their relationship to men. He believes that Mizoguchi's main theme is that "man is nothing without the love of a woman, that woman's love redeems an often harsh and cruel world."[10] Women are prized, therefore, for their value to men, a far cry from what we in the West consider feminist. Others similarly recognize the essentially ambivalent view held by Mizoguchi: "Fluid camera movement, superb long-shot, long-take photography and intricate use of sound and framing provide a veneer of aestheticism to an ambivalent attitude toward women and an enigmatic political stance toward oppression, poverty and even the Japanese family."[11] Mizoguchi fails to be explicitly condemnatory. As Andrew and Andrew point out, "His temperament continually drove him to a transhistorical meditation on culture that has alienated him from those viewers who dream of programmatic solutions to the problems of social life."[12] On the other hand, many critics have forgiven Mizoguchi his "transhistorical stance":

> Though his political views may have lacked sophistication and commitment, Mizoguchi's late films are suffused with a view of life that transcends politics. Even his ambivalent view of women and their oppression becomes acceptable because all is cast in an aestheticism bespeaking the ephemeral quality of human suffering.[13]

Such a statement will not suffice for a genuinely politically minded critic, any critic, that is, who seeks actively to change the status and image of women in the here and now, who rejects the transcendental ideology of the traditional culture. Joan Mellen is one such critic of a political slant who forthrightly defends Mizoguchi as a feminist in the Western sense of the term.

To esteem woman is only to keep her enslaved so much the longer. This is
the "feminism" endorsed by such Japanese critics as Tadao Sato, who con-
descend to the Japanese woman while pretending to sympathize with her.
Critics who lack Mizoguchi's appreciation of the need for Japanese women to
alter their conditions cannot help but misunderstand his films.[14]

Mellen quite clearly believes that Mizoguchi is explicitly condemnatory,
that he is clearly a political feminist. The very inability of critics to agree
on Mizoguchi's politics is the best indication of his essential ambivalence.

The ambivalent view of women held by Mizoguchi is expressed by the
archetypal images of women he has utilized. There are three distinct images
of women in Mizoguchi's cinema: "the prostitute," "the princess," and
"the priestess." These three archetypes are drawn from the canon of Japanese popular culture and from universal images of women. Previous writings on Mizoguchi have put forth two competing images of women used
by Mizoguchi. Bock describes these two types as the "long-suffering ideal
woman" and the "spiteful rebel."[15] Andrew and Andrew support this duali-
ty in Mizoguchi's image of women and see it as corresponding (with some
hesitation) to *jidai-geki* (period plays) and *gendai-geki* (modern plays): "In
the *gendai-geki* . . . his heroines are in revolt against a system in which they
are exploited, frequently without the aid of even the most fragile family
support, whereas the *jidai-geki* . . . become legends of women who suffer
for an idea of culture that the film clearly valorizes in the end."[16] The
spiteful rebel is "often a prostitute or geisha or similiar social outcast. . . . She resents the abuses of fathers, employers and men who buy
her and leave her, and attempts to lash back."[17] The *jidai-geki* woman is
Mizoguchi's idealized image, for she is "the one who can love." However,
this love is not a love between equals, but rather a matter of the woman's
"selfless devotion to a man in the traditional Japanese sense. [The woman]
becomes the spiritual guide, the moral and often financial support for a
husband, lover, brother or son."[18] Romantic love in Mizoguchi's films is
therefore closer to the classic mother-son relationship that critics of Japanese culture see as so crucial. Sato describes this love as indulgence on the
part of women toward their men. "The women . . . by having their men
rely on them to the ultimate degree, take this dependence to be the most
profound expression of love."[19] Ian Buruma thinks mother-love is Mizoguchi's ideal, one that clearly derives from a common image in Japanese culture. Buruma quotes a woman's magazine telling its readers that
"the most attractive women . . . are women full of maternal love. Women
without maternal love are the types men never . . . marry."[20]

The recognition that there are three distinct images of women competing
in Mizoguchi's cinema not only increases the recognition of Mizoguchi's
essential ambivalence, but increases our understanding of the political use
of women in the Japanese cinema. The three archetypes recur in various

forms throughout Japanese film history, their recurrence an index of the essential ambivalence the culture holds toward its women.

"The prostitute" archetype in Mizoguchi's cinema, as I have termed it, corresponds to an extent with the "spiteful rebel." Prostitutes abound in Mizoguchi's works and the major films which feature the rebellious prostitute include *Naniwa ereji* (*Osaka Elegy*, 1936), in which a woman turns to extortion and prostitution to rescue her family from disgrace only to be ostracized by the family for her efforts; *Gion no shimai* (*Sisters of the Gion*, 1936), which looks at two young geisha/prostitutes, one of whom hates men and the other is more traditionally subservient, but both are in different ways betrayed; *Yoru no onnatachi* (*Women of the Night*, 1948), which looks at three women forced into prostitution by postwar circumstances; and *Akasen Chitai* (*Redlight District*, 1956; aka *Street of Shame*), which focuses on five prostitutes who have entered the life for different reasons. In these four films some sort of social protest and rebellion comes to the fore. However, such actions are often mute and ineffectual. The women don't so much castigate the system; instead they "scream with their glance."[21]

Yet there is in these films a greater political dimension than many transhistorical interpretations of Mizoguchi's work might indicate. This political dimension may be found in these films through "an instinct for salvation through generosity toward fellow women in revolt against the city of men."[22] There is, in other words, a notion of sisterhood that Mizoguchi puts forth, of women banding together to fight male oppression. To make this notion of sisterhood stand out, Mizoguchi often literalizes it. The women are "sisters of the gion," not sisters by blood, but by profession and by sisterhood; the women of the night, in the film by that name, are actually related, two sisters and their sister-in-law. And if they can ultimately do little against male oppression, there is at least a touch of redemption to be found in sisterhood.

The opposite archetype of the prostitute is "the princess." This archetype appears in the famous *jidai-geki Saikaku ichidai onna* (*The Life of Oharu*, 1952) and *Sansho dayu* (*Sansho the Bailiff*, 1954). In these films, Mizoguchi focuses on aristocratic women brought low by tragic circumstances and forced into prostitution. For Mizoguchi, nobility of birth is an objective correlative for nobility of spirit. Unlike the prostitutes in the *gendai-geki*, these princesses do not become social rebels. They are too noble for that. It is their very nobility, in fact, which enables them, despite the degradations they experience, to come through somehow untouched. Such nobility is not available to all women brought low. To demonstrate this, Mizoguchi uses a modern version of the princess archetype in a trilogy of literary adaptations made in the years immediately preceding his classic period films.

Mizoguchi examines the destruction of the prewar class system and the new, postwar democratization via a focus on women in *Yuki fujin ezu* (*Pic-*

ture of Madam Yuki, 1950), an adaptation of a bestseller by Funahashi Seiichi; *Oyusama (Miss Oyu,* 1951), from Tanizaki's *"Ashikari";* and *Musashino Fujin (Lady of Musashino,* 1951), from Ooka Shohei's novel. And what he finds, especially in the first and last films of this trilogy, is that aristocracy of spirit is no match for the postwar values of economic ruthlessness. Whereas the heroines of *Oharu* and *Sansho the Bailiff* survive despite their loss of status and ensuing degradations, the heroines of *Picture of Madam Yuki* and *Lady from Musashino* kill themselves, unable to transcend the modern world of crass commercialism and exploitation. In this respect, Mizoguchi's women's inability to survive the commercial world contrasts with Imamura Shohei's heroines who thrive in it.

Neither the prostitute nor the princess represent Mizoguchi's ideal woman. That role falls to the priestess archetype. This archetype has much in common with the long-suffering mother-figure, and it transcends genre and period, appearing in both *jidai-* and *gendai-geki* and early and late in the director's career. The priestess archetype is alluded to by Buruma, who compares Mizoguchi's women to Chirst and to Kannon (the Buddhist goddess of mercy).[23] It is the function of women who fall into this category to inspire men. This woman is prized for her ability to help men find salvation and/or transcendence. This archetype figures prominently in *Taki no shiraito (White Threads of the Waterfall,* 1933), a *gendai-geki*; *Zangiku monogatari (Story of the Last Chrysanthemums,* 1939), a *Meiji-mono*; and *Ugetsu monogatari* (1953) and *Yokihi (Princess Yang Kwei Fei,* 1955) both *jidai-geki*. These films reach their considerable emotional heights when the heroines sacrifice themselves for their men. *Taki no shiraito* undergoes considerable hardship in order to send her lover to law school; Otoku, the servant girl-heroine of *Last Chrysanthemums* inspires the profligate son of a famous Kabuki actor to work hard at his art; Yang Kwei Fei brings happiness to the Emperor of China when he elevates her from kitchen maid to royal concubine. The ultimate image of the priestess is Miyagi of *Ugetsu,* who enables her potter-husband to come to terms with earthly existence and find solace in his family and his craft.

All three archetypal images of women are present in *Ugetsu*: the prostitute, in the form of Ohama, Genjuro's sister-in-law; the princess in the form of Lady Wakasa, the aristocratic ghost-lover, and the priestess, Miyagi, Genjuro's wife. The tragic power of the film derives from the fact that Genjuro initially mistakes Wakasa, the princess, for his priestess, not realizing, until it is almost too late (and too late for Miyagi) that his own wife was the true source of his salvation. Mizoguchi plays upon a number of important motifs. One is the eroticization inherent in certain roles. Miyagi, as the wife, represents the mundane, the ordinary, whereas the aristocratic other-worldly (literally) Wakasa is exotic and hence more erotic. Wakasa's exoticism is aided by the use of Noh-style makeup, costume, and movements. Her theatricalization is her eroticization. (This motif will be taken up and extended by Shinoda Masahiro in *Double Suicide*.) Another aspect of women that Mizoguchi brings forward is their inherent power. Ohama survives her fall into prostitution and browbeats her husband back to normalcy. Both Miyagi and Wakasa are able to transcend death in their efforts to win Genjuro. But it is Wakasa's *desire*, her own erotic needs, which brings her back from the grave, whereas Miyagi's power is directed toward Genjuro's well-being. It is easy to see Miyagi, Wakasa, and Ohama as three sides of womanhood. Wakasa is fearful when she places self-interest above altruism; Ohama is admirable when she forgives her husband and shows him the errors of his ways; Miyagi is to be worshipped when she sacrifices herself for her husband.

It is this altruistic, sacrificial power that makes the priestess the image of woman that Mizoguchi favors. Self-reflexivity is apparent in the following films: In *Story of the Last Chrysanthemums*, a woman inspires an actor, in *Utamaro o meguru gonin no onna* (*Utamaro and His Five Women*, 1946), various women inspire the famous woodblock artist, and in *Ugetsu*, a woman gives her inspiration to a potter. Mizoguchi wants to show that the priestess image is a medium between the prostitute and the princess. The prostitute comes to reject men, to rebel, while the princess is untouchable. The priestess is approachable and nourishing. And these priestesses are, as it were, available to all men, drawn as they are from the ranks of ordinary Japanese women: an actress, servant, village wife, working girl. Unfortunately, it is typically the case that in many of the films the priestess-figure must die in order to bring about the man's triumph and/or transcendence. In his recognition of the oppression of women, Mizoguchi is a genuine feminist, but in his love of women, his fear, admiration, and worship of them, he is a *feminisuto* who sees in women superior, ahistorical transcendent beings.

While Mizoguchi's image of women may be clearly related to the image of women in Japanese culture, it is also the case that Mizoguchi is a genuine auteur. The image of women on view is personal to Mizoguchi's canon in terms of how he works through his ambivalences. So that while Mizoguchi was engaged in refining his image of women (and his film style) in the postwar era, other significant changes in the culture appeared which influenced the treatment of women in society and in film. One such change, of course, was the Occupation. The Occupation affected filmmaking through direct censorship and script approval as well as by putting forth an overt cultural agenda for Japan. The Occupation authorities' intention was to support "democracy" and to oppose traditional Japanese ideology. One of the Occupation's key components in the democratizing process was the emancipation of women. Filmmakers were encouraged to show the "new woman" in action, a woman who could assert herself in society in political, social, and cultural realms. Thus we might say that if women were already politicized in the Japanese cinema when they appeared on movie screens in the 1920s, they were already politicized again in the postwar era.

This new politicization of women took many forms, from the sensationalistic, albeit superficial, introduction of kissing to Japanese cinema in films like *Aru yo no seppun* (*A Certain Night's Kiss*) and *Hatachi no seishun* (*Twenty-Year-Old Youth*) to more socially substantial films like *Joyu* (*Actress*) and *Joyu Sumako no koi* (*The Love of Sumako the Actress*), both films focusing on Matsui Sumako, Japan's first "emancipated" woman who rose to fame in the Shingeki theatre, and *Joseito to kyoshi* (*Girl Pupils and Teachers*) all made in 1946.[24]

The political use of women can be seen in the case of Kurosawa Akira, who made virtually his only films with women heroes in the immediate postwar era: *Asu o tsukuru hitobito* (*Those Who Make Tomorrow*, which he co-directed) and *Waga seishun ni kuinashi* (*No Regrets For Our Youth*), both made in 1946. *Those Who Make Tomorrow* seems as clearly calculated as any film to please the Occupation authorities. It deals with the benefits of labor unions, the emancipation of women, and the breaking down of class barriers, all within the context of a movie studio. *No Regrets For Our Youth* is far more satisfactory as a dramatic film for, based on a true story, it deals with the role of intellectuals in opposing the militarists. With Hara Setsuko in the leading role, the film clearly puts forth a genuinely heroic image of a woman, one who is actively engaged in a political struggle. Kurosawa would not continue the focus on women in his cinema, but two other important directors, Kinoshita Keisuke and Imai Tadashi, working in the postwar humanistic paradigm would.

Kinoshita Keisuke was very much influenced by his mentor, Shimazu Yasujiro, a master of the *shomin-geki* (drama of the common people). Kinoshita always maintained an interest in the common people, whether in the cities, towns, or farming villages, and whether he worked in *jidai-geki* or *gendai-geki*. And for Kinoshita, like Mizoguchi before him and Imamura Shohei after him, women represent the essence of the common people.

Two of Kinoshita's films clearly demonstrate the continued politicization of the image of women in Japanese cinema. *Nihon no higeki* (*A Japanese Tragedy*, 1953) and *Nijushi no hitomi* (*Twenty-Four Eyes*, 1954) represent the postwar liberal-humanist response to the war and to postwar ideology. *A Japanese Tragedy* is a *haha mono* (mother picture), an important Japanese genre. The film stars Mochizuki Yuko, who, before her death was known as *Nippon no haha*, the mother of Japan, for her numerous appearances in *haha mono*.[25] Mochizuki plays a war widow trying to please her son and daughter. Most of the film is set in Atami, a popular resort in Japan, and is somewhat reminiscent of Ozu's *Tokyo monogatari* (*Tokyo Story*) released that same year. (Ozu's film also uses Atami in a rhetorical manner in a memorable sequence focusing on the aging parents at an inn at the resort, where they have been sent by their children who do not wish to spend time with their parents.) In *A Japanese Tragedy*, when the children so firmly reject their mother, she commits suicide, unable to live in a world in which materialism has completely replaced familialism. The film is notable not only for the extreme sentiment it arouses, but also for its interesting stylistic devices, which include a complex time scheme of flashbacks, and the use of newspaper clippings and newsreel footage intercut with the dramatic action. The drama of the film is compared to historical incidents so that the cultural changes of the real Japan impact on the familial breakdown in this fictional tale. With its use of crosscutting and comparing historical events to personal events, *A Japanese Tragedy* must be seen as a precursor to Imamura's *Nihon Sengoshi* (*A History of Postwar Japan as Told by a Bar Hostess*, 1970).

Twenty-Four Eyes is even more clearly indicative of the relationship between women and politics than is *A Japanese Tragedy*, for here Kinoshita desires to make the basic decency of one woman stand in opposition to the entire militarist era in Japan. *Twenty-Four Eyes*, one of Kinoshita's best-loved films in Japan and perhaps his best-known in the U.S., focuses on Miss Oishi (Takamine Hideko), a young schoolteacher sent to a poor fishing village on Japan's Inland Sea. Her first assignment finds her in a one-room schoolhouse teaching five boys and seven girls—the twelve pupils possessing the twenty-four eyes of the title. The story begins in 1928 and continues until the immediate postwar era. Miss Oishi must first win over the students and their conservative parents, initially hard for her given her penchant for Western-style clothing, an index of her liberated or emancipated attitudes. As the militarists begin to take power and their ideology begins to infect the nation's institutions, Miss Oishi (she has since been promoted to the main school on the island) is seen as a rebel when she defends one of her colleagues who is accused of being a Communist. She marries a seaman from the village and raises a family with him. She quits her job as a protest against the encroaching militarist ideology and the Japanese system which perpetuates poverty and class, seen when one student must quit school to work in a noodle shop.

The war claims her husband and some of her male students. Left a widow with two children, she takes a teaching job after the war in the same schoolhouse in which she began. In the last scene, Miss Oishi has a reunion with the seven students who survived. The musical motif of the school song, heard periodically throughout the film, is heard once again as teacher and former pupils tearfully reminisce about the prewar days.

Miss Oishi is the essential Kinoshita woman, a sentimental reminder of Mizoguchi's Miyagi in *Ugetsu*. Miss Oishi's resignation from her teaching position is similar to the mother's suicide in *A Japanese Tragedy*, and is typical of the kind of action his heroines are prone to:

Kinoshita's women, the central figures in all of his tragedies, always know that war, political oppression, class distinctions and individual selfishness are evils. Their values always side with freedom of expression, love of family and, at the same time, romantic love. . . . What they do in situations where their values are threatened is endure, sometimes in silence and suffering, sometimes protesting, but in extremity they choose death rather than forfeit the purity of their emotion and commitment.[26]

Kinoshita's heroines have much in common with Mizoguchi's priestesses, lacking only, in most cases, the male figure to inspire. In this respect, Kinoshita is closer to Imamura, who finds women able to transcend male bonds and male society. Kinoshita may therefore be seen as something like a transitional figure between Mizoguchi and Imamura.

Imai Tadashi continued a different aspect of Mizoguchi's image of women, their oppression by feudalism. Imai's antifeudal sentiments are seen in his best-known film in the U.S., *Yoru no tsuzumi* (*Night Drum*, 1958), in which a husband wants to forgive his wife's adultery but social codes force him into killing his wife and her lover. His commitment to the relationship between the emerging postwar ideology of democracy and the emancipation of women may be seen in *Aoi sammyaku* (*Blue Mountains*, 1947). Described by Anderson and Richie as a youth film, *Blue Mountains* is more properly placed within the category of a woman's film. A young female high school teacher confronts an old-fashioned and distorted idea about male-female relationships. She tries to teach her students and the townspeople that healthy relationships are not shameful. The Japanese understood this film as addressing the issue of women's liberation and male-female equality.[27]

Imai's most interesting woman's film is unquestionably *Nigorie* (*Troubled Waters*, 1953).[28] *Nigorie* is an omnibus film consisting of three stories by Higuchi Ichiyo, who is generally acknowledged as the first, and still among the most important women writers of the modern era. She lived a life of poverty in the middle of the Meiji era and died at a very young age of tuberculosis. Robert Lyons Danly has encapsulated Ichiyo's major concerns: "She preferred to examine the people life had ambushed. She looked increasingly at women: prostitutes, concubines, women who had affairs with their boarders. Her final parcel of stories addressed society's relegation of half its members to an oppressed, cipherlike existence."[29] The stories in Imai's film are among Ichiyo's best. The first episode is based on "*Ju-san'ya*" ("The Thirteenth Night") and looks at an unhappily married woman who tells her parents that she no longer wants to live with her adulterous husband. Returning home by rickshaw, she discovers that her driver is an old school friend. After some emotional conversation, she returns home. The second story is adapted from "*Otsugomori*" ("On the Last Day of the Year"), the tale of a maid who needs money for her sick uncle. While the mistress and her two spoiled daughters spend money profligately, the maid cannot secure a loan from her employer. Finally, she resorts to theft, stealing the money from her mistress. She is saved by the wastrel son, who, having seen her commit the crime, takes the rest of the money out of the drawer, and claims to his mother that he took it all. The final episode is taken from the story "Nigorie" and tells of a courtesan of the Yoshiwara district who is murdered by a favored former patron who cannot give her up. After murdering her, he kills himself. The first story relies on the archetype of the princess, especially the princess who is unable to deal with the contemporary world. The third story focuses on a prostitute, one who is not so much a rebel as an innocent victim of male weakness. The middle story does not use the priestess archetype, save for the fact that the heroine is drawn from the ranks of the ordinary Japanese woman, and she does commit her crime out of filial duty. In some clear way, each woman in each story is held in thrall to feudalistic values, of patriarchy, of class, of male ego and only one woman is spared pain.

The underlying theme of the film might be said to be the failure of democracy to liberate women fully in the postwar era. Imai is drawing a parallel between the promise of democracy in the 1950s and the promise of reform in the Meiji era when Ichiyo wrote her stories. As Danly notes:

> There were many promises in the air in the Meiji period, and many hopes that went unfulfilled. Ichiyo's generation grew up in the heady days of the 1870's and 1880's, when Japan was giddy with Western liberalism and Christian brotherly love, only to discover in the reactionary 1890's that many of the enlightened notions to which they had been exposed—popular rights, intellectual freedom, feminism, the sanctity of the private self—were in point of fact unattainable.[30]

The shift from the classical/transcendental paradigm as represented by Mizoguchi, to the modern/psychological paradigm of Kinoshita and Imai was the shift from traditional to modern culture following World War II. The disillusionment with the postwar era, as expressed in *Nigorie*, looks forward to the dialectical attitude taken by the New Wave toward the traditional and the modern. Two directors, both crucial predecessors and contemporaries of the New Wave, who put forth a more probing image of women, are Masumura Yasuzo and Shindo Kaneto. We have seen Masumura's considerable influence on the youth film, and on Oshima, but he was equally committed to the image of women. The same year that he released *Kisses* (1957), Masumura directed *Danryu* (*Warm Current*), a remake of a 1939 hospital melodrama. The film's primary importance is that it helped Hidari Sachiko reach stardom with her first adult role. Too, the image of a crusading nurse would reappear in the much less melodramatic *Red Angel* in 1966.

Masumura favors two distinct images of women: One clearly corresponds to the priestess archetype favored by Mizoguchi, and the other, an extension of the prostitute and princess images, is combined in one horrific figure best expressed as the "spider woman." This latter image, the spider woman, appears most memorably in Masumura's adaptation of Tanizaki's *Shisei (Tattoo,* 1966).[31] The script by Shindo Kaneto merges Masumura's concerns with feminine psychology with Shindo's own concern with eroticism to tell the story of an innocent woman duped by men who becomes an amorous, man-hating killer. This change comes about when a tattoo artist paints a spider on her back and she is sold into prostitution. As portrayed by Wakao Ayako, whose persona is described by Sato Tadao as a sweet, virginal maiden,[32] the spider woman is both desirable and fearful.

The priestess archetype is best found in *Akai tenshi (Red Angel),* which also stars Wakao Ayako (who worked with Masumura on a number of films). This powerful film is at once an antiwar tract, an examination of irrepressible sexuality, and a tribute to the strength and vitality of women. *Red Angel* (in black-and-white CinemaScope, the lack of color possibly a blessing considering the graphic presentation of the war) is set in China in 1936 and opens at a hospital for combat veterans suffering from tuberculosis or war injuries. Wakao, who portrays Nurse Sakura Nishi, narrates the film so that the story is told in flashback. A head nurse warns her staff to be on the lookout for loafers. As soon as the soldiers are even remotely better, they are sent back to combat. Ohara (played by Kawazu Yusuke, the star of *Cruel Story of Youth)* remarks to Sakura that soldiers who have been injured are prevented from going home so that the public does not see them, lest they lose heart. The doctors and nurses operate under the most primitive conditions. Dead bodies lay in heaps; the dead soldiers' dog tags are unceremoniously cut off to be returned to their families. Only the officers receive blood transfusions in combat hospitals (reminiscent of a line of dialogue heard in *M*A*S*H* in which the command to use larger stitches is given if the soldier is an enlisted man). Amputations are the most common way of treating arm and leg wounds; the discarded limbs pile up in barrels.

Early in the film, Sakura is raped by a wounded soldier as his comrades look on. She does not report him. Later, in order to try and save an enlisted man, Sakura agrees to sleep with the head doctor of a hospital near the front if he will authorize a blood transfusion. The doctor agrees, but the soldier dies any way. The aura of despair grows ever stronger, and is deepened when Sakura agrees to make love to Ohara, whose hands have been amputated by Dr. Okabe. Ohara pleads with Sakura to help him sexually as, having no hands, he cannot even satisfy his needs by himself. After they make love, Ohara kills himself, feeling it will be the last time he can be with a woman. Following this, Sakura and Dr. Okabe are sent to a hospital closer to the front. Okabe is a morphine addict and he is

Akai tenshi (*Red Angel*)
Masumura Yasuzo, director. Kawakita/Japan Film Library Council

impotent. Sakura helps the doctor overcome his addiction and, the night before an impending attack, helps the doctor overcome his impotency, as well. In the attack, the entire command, doctors and nurses included, save for Sakura, is wiped out.

Sakura is the archetype of the healing woman, as a nurse and as a sexual partner. She heals men's bodies and souls, yet for all the good she does, the men she helps still die. Masumura's point is that the saving essence of woman is not enough in time of war. As Sato notes, Sakura's "zest for life is unable to save them because they are trapped within a social code that stresses glory on the battlefield and regards weakness with shame."[33] The feudalistic values that the militarists favored are subtly castigated when Masumura shows Dr. Okabe's corpse, the hands clutching a broken samurai sword. Even the priestess is unable to save men betrayed by the very system in which they live.

The dark side of feudal ideology is also apparent in the films directed by Shindo Kaneto, whom Sato puts forward as an exemplary *feminisuto*. Shindo, like Kinoshita, has been clearly influenced by Mizoguchi, and in his case quite overtly so. Shindo was an assistant to Mizoguchi in the period 1936–47, and has written of his mentor and made an interesting documentary film on the subject. His view of women seems almost a direct extension of Mizoguchi's. This is seen most specifically in the atmospheric horror film, *Onibaba* (1964). *Onibaba*, like *Ugetsu*, is set during Japan's period of civil wars before the Tokugawa Shogunate was established in 1600. Like *Ugetsu*, *Onibaba* focuses on the innocent victims of the war, especially women. And like *Ugetsu*, a supernatural element hovers around the film. However, *Onibaba* reveals what *Ugetsu* suppressed, namely, that women cling to life and survive by asserting their sexual essences, that women, more than men, can cope with times of terror. The two women in *Onibaba*, a woman and her daughter-in-law, survive by killing wounded samurai, stripping their bodies, and selling the armor for food. They live this way until a friend of the young woman's husband (whom the friend claims is dead) returns to the village to begin an intense sexual relationship with the daughter-in-law. The older woman is partially jealous, but even more concerned with her own survival should the daughter-in-law leave with the man. She tries to keep the younger woman from seeing the man by posing as a demon.

In a sense, the women in *Onibaba* fit into the spider woman category. But they have been forced into this role in order to survive. For all their murderous ways, the women in the film are objects of sympathy and understanding on Shindo's part. As he has said, "They are people totally abandoned, outside society's political protection. Among these outcasts I wanted to capture their immense energy for survival."[34] On this issue, Shindo agrees completely with Imamura.

Later in the '60s, Shindo turned to an even more overt focus on eroticism. *Honno* (*Lost Sex*, 1966) combines the erotic impulses of women, as seen in *Onibaba*, with the priestess archetype, as in *Red Angel*. This film tells of a man rendered impotent due to radiation exposure in Nagasaki who is restored to manhood by his housekeeper. Shindo, who was influential in bringing the issue of the atomic bomb to Japanese screens in the early 1950s, here tries to bring together all of the various strands of his political and social concerns: antiwar, women as exploited objects, women as erotic objects, and women as healing priestesses. The linking of women with antiwar motifs, as seen in Kinoshita's works, once again reminds us that the image of women in the Japanese cinema has been politicized. The New Wave directors would continue this image, extend it, and reflect upon it.

The women who work in the Japanese cinema are subject to the same ideology which oppresses them in the culture at large. There have been almost no women commercial filmmakers in Japan (major star Tanaka Kinuyo is an exception who comes to mind) and women studio executives are even rarer (Kawakita Kashiko and her daughter Kazuko are major figures in the commercial cinema outside the large production houses, while the equally remarkable Tomiyama Katsue is perhaps *the* major force for independent and experimental filmmaking in Japan). On the other hand, the star system has given women a public voice along with an image. Major women stars of the 1960s were Okada Mariko, Wakao Ayako, Yamamoto Fujiko, Asaoka Ruriko, Sakuma Yoshiko, and Yoshinaga Sayuri (an ingenue who has since made a successful transition to adult stardom), among others. For all their fame and adulation, many of these women were confined not only to one studio but to a certain genre, as well. Yet we should not underestimate the financial power these stars wielded, which can be seen in a unique aspect of the New Wave: many of the major filmmakers were (and still are) married to famous actresses.

Shindo Kaneto may be included in this group. His leading player in *Onibaba, Lost Sex*, and *Kuroneko* (1968) was Otowa Nobuko, his wife. Hani Susumu was married to Hidari Sachiko; Shinoda is married to Iwashita Shima; Yoshida Yoshishige is married to Okada Mariko (perhaps the biggest star connected with the New Wave); and Oshima Nagisa—who is not primarily a *feminisuto* director but has nevertheless focused on significant women in many of his films—is married to Koyama Akiko. Marriage to these actresses gave the directors a certain box-office potential when securing funds for independent projects, and one can safely say that being married to popular stars provided the directors with insights into the nature and desires of career women in today's Japan.

The New Wave director most often thought of as a *feminisuto*, and even a genuine feminist by some, is Imamura Shohei. If Mizoguchi often focused on women who fit into the princess archetype, Imamura is definitely the poet of the peasant. Almost without exception, Imamura's heroines are drawn from Japan's traditional village life. Ian Buruma notes that, "Imamura sees his heroines as symbols of Japanese life: the native, vital, one is almost tempted to say, innocent life to be found in the rural areas of Japan."[35] Sato Tadao thinks, further, that to Imamura "ordinary women realistically mirrored the conditions of the masses since they seldom rose to positions of leadership or became members of the ruling class."[36] Sato's notion of women as mirrors of the masses is quite correct albeit limiting, for women reflect the masses not in their powerlessness, but in their *essence*.

Imamura is very much concerned with essences, with seeking not merely underlying truths, but underlying forces which guide and shape his heroines. His characters, especially the women, are representative of Japan—not the Japan as it appears to Westerners, nor the Japan the Japanese would like to project to the world, but the Japan that persists despite modernization and Westernization. It is his interest in the nation's essence—or, more particularly, the tribal essence of the nation—that makes Imamuna's interest anthropological. It is this anthropological interest that has inspired Imamura toward documentary pursuits, like *Ningen johatsu* (*A Man Vanishes*, 1967) and the later *Nihon sengo-shi: Madamu onboro no seikatsu* (History of Postwar Japan as Told by a Bar Hostess, 1971) and *Karayuki-san* (1975). And this interest has led him to creating what might be called "case studies" of particular women, who though fictional, are clearly representative of the true Japanese woman.

Imamura claims that the women in his films are true to life. He tells us, "just look around you at Japanese women. They *are* strong, and they outlive men."[37] Their strength does not come from their willingness to sacrifice themselves for men. In fact, Imamura wishes explicitly to disassociate his heroines from the sort of image put forth by Mizoguchi: "Self-sacrificing women like the heroines of Naruse's *Floating Clouds* (*Ukigumo*) and Mizoguchi's *Life of Oharu* don't really exist."[38] Imamura's women do indeed achieve a kind of transcendence, but it comes not through self-sacrifice, but through coming to terms with themselves as sexual beings, through tapping into their "inexhaustible natures,"[39] and it is achieved in the here-and-now.

Imamura's world, even more forthrightly than Mizoguchi's, Imai's, and Shindo's, is characterized by power, and by economic, political, and sexual difference. But it is precisely within such a world that Imamura's heroines triumph. We saw the beginnings of the Imamura heroine in *Endless Desire* and the youth film, *Pigs and Battleships*. In the character of Haruko, girl-friend of the hapless gangster Kinta in *Pigs and Battleships*, Imamura showed how women will prove to be the tough ones, the survivors. While Kinta could not resist the easy allure of American culture with its promise of quick money, Haruko managed to keep herself emotionally separate from her actions. It is possible to understand Kinta's death because of his will-ingness (or his weakness in doing so) to shed his Japanese identity, to trade it in for American goods. But Haruko survives by remaining true to her essential Japanese self. This is not to say that Japan is better than the U.S. or that the essence of Japan must battle American encroachments. In *Pigs and Battleships*, the U.S. merely represents the so-called "modernization" of Japan, the surface change the nation is undergoing. It is therefore the woman's ability to keep hold of the deeper spirit that prevents her de-struction. This survival of the deeper spirit is always very much on Ima-mura's mind. In an interview with Audie Bock, he said that he seeks to uncover "the superstition and the irrationality that pervade the Japanese consciousness under the veneer of the business suits and advanced tech-nology."[40] And it is women who hold the key to understanding this. If Imamura is interested in the essence of the Japanese spirit, then *Nippon konchuki* (*The Insect Woman*, 1963) is the spiritual essence of Imamura's cine-ma.

In *The Insect Woman*, Imamura focuses on the life of a woman who is born in near-poverty in rural Tohoku some years before World War II. The film follows her through a series of events corresponding to the changes wrought in Japan by the war and postwar periods. The heroine, Tome (Hidari Sachiko), is always conscious of herself as a sexual being, first in her near-incestuous relationship with her slightly retarded stepfather, Chuji, then as a young woman at work in a factory who becomes her boss' lover. Eventually, Tome becomes a prostitute and a madam. Tome's development as a sexual being is a movement from innocence (the rural, tribal life), to sophistication (a factory worker and union organizer) to decadence (prostitution). Tome is alive, vital, and strong, at one with her sexuality and uncorrupted as long as she remains in the village. When she moves from the village to the factory, she grows up and discovers power which ultimately leads, when she moves to Tokyo, to her corruption, and she becomes not only a victim but a victimizer. In Tokyo, her sexuality, far from naturally expressing itself, becomes something to be bartered, sold in a marketplace, the marketplace which is postwar Japan.

If it is true that Tome stands for the essence of Japanese life, then we can claim that Tome's experiences are a microcosm for Japan's modern era. Tome begins life in a farming village as a member of an extended family (she lives with her mother, stepfather, grandparents, and her mother's lover, who may be her real father). But just as Japan was transformed from a rural nation to an urban one in the wake of industrialization, so too, Tome must leave her farming village for life as a factory worker. Tome's union activities while at the factory represent the promise of postwar democracy and freedom. Later, Tome's employment by a woman who lives with an American becomes an index of Japan's heavy reliance on the U.S. Tome's prostitution is a complex metaphor not only for the prostitution of Japan to the U.S., but also of the Japanese spirit for economic gain.

If Tome prostitutes herself, she never loses her essence. She is, first of all, a survivor—through hardships such as poverty, rape, economic, and physical exploitation, Tome endures. Her endurance is a function of her womanhood, her roots as a sexual being which is at some very deep level, uncorruptible. She tenaciously holds on to her roots in the premodern culture that is the essence of Japan. However, such tenacity tends to mythicize her, to remove her, to an extent, from the very historical situation she symbolizes. This idea is structured into the text in terms of a mythic pattern of life, growth, death, and rebirth. Tome is born in the village, grows to womanhood in the factory, experiences a kind of death in Tokyo (she goes to prison), and is reborn when she returns home. The mythic cycle is further strengthened by the character of Tome's daughter, Nobuko, whose life process mirrors, reproduces, her mother's.

Tome is the first of Imamura's fully realized women survivors. There is nothing romanticized, or aestheticized here, as in Mizoguchi or Kinoshita, and nothing of the healing woman of Masumura or Shindo. Tome is presented as a whole woman, her flaws intact, from the terrible poetry she writes in her diary, to the cruelty she inflicts upon the girls in the bordello. Far from inspiring men, she learns to use them as they wish to use her. Tome's image reappears not only in her daughter, Nobuko, but in the figure of Madam Omboro, in the impressionistic documentary, *History of Postwar Japan as Told by a Bar Hostess*. Japan's relationship to the U.S., alluded to in *Pigs and Battleships*, and the woman-as-survivor motif of *The Insect Woman*, are both literalized in this film.

Imamura's own presence is clearly felt in *History of Postwar Japan . . . ,* which consists of the filmmaker interviewing Madam Omboro (real name, Akaza Etsuko) while showing her newsreel footage of various events. Madam Omboro traces the course of her life in terms of Japan's modern experience. The macrocosm of Japan is compared to the microcosm of Omboro. And both macro- and microcosm are pervaded by the U.S. Omboro talks about the Emperor's speech which brought World War II to an end when she was fifteen; the American Occupation and the black market; the Korean War; the Anti-Security Pact events of 1959–60; the "Pueblo Incident" in which a U.S. patrol boat was captured by North Korea; the Vietnam War; protests surrounding the docking of U.S. nuclear submarines; and, always, the presence of U.S. servicemen. These political events are compared to events in her own life. She quit high school because she was a *burakumin* (or *eta*), a member of the pariah class without much prospect of making a good marriage or securing a good job. She therefore took a low-level job in a bank and married a policeman. He quit his job and left her for another woman. The increased U.S. presence in Japan during the Korean War brought her into closer contact with American sailors and inspired her to open a small bar in Yokosuka (the setting of *Pigs and Battleships*). She joined *Soka Gakkai*, one of Japan's so-called "New Religions." She took American sailors for lovers and had a child by one of them. At film's end, the now thirty-six-year-old woman marries a twenty-three-year-old sailor and moves to San Diego with him, knowing full well that she will shortly divorce him and probably open a bar in Texas.

Joan Mellen asserts that Imamura finds Omboro to be praiseworthy as a kind of repository of the strength of the Japanese people. Although she has been little better than a prostitute unapologetically living off American largesse, she has not been degraded:

> Her sense of values in some deepest sense has not been corrupted by her running a bar for foreigners, for her earthy nature has prevented her from becoming a sycophant of privilege and position; she had become involved only with rank-and-file sailors rather than officers who would try and control her.[41]

Such a fine distinction as this will not stand up. For while it is true that Madam Omboro is remarkably resilient, it is also true that she has been corrupted. This corruption is clear when we see her teenaged daughter playing up to U.S. servicemen in the bar, the bar this daughter will inherit; her corruption is clear in the manner in which she uses men to reach her goals, a reversal, it is true, of female oppression, but hardly an ethical system to put in its place. The cost of relying exclusively on U.S. largesse is a loss of steadfast moral values on Omboro's part, just as Japan's reliance on the U.S. is a loss of something deep within the Japanese spirit. This is not to say that Omboro and Japan are ruined. It is to say, however, that politics and economics do exert a corrupting force on the spirit, no matter how resilient that spirit proves to be.

Imamura's vision is less expansive, and hence more clearly focused, in *Akai satsui* (*Intentions of Murder*, 1964; aka *Unholy Desire*). The film looks at a somewhat slow-witted housewife who becomes the willing victim of a rapist. If it was the roots of the primitive that enabled Tome, the insect woman, to survive, and Madam Omboro to triumph over poverty, it is clearly her awakening to her essential sexuality that enables Sadako, the heroine of this film, to win a victory over patriarchy. Sadako, like Tome and Omboro, is an insect woman, a woman of little education living in a rural village, subject to staunch and deeply rooted social conditions and circumstances. Sadako is not legally married to the man she lives with, their child, a son, lives with the man's parents at their insistence. Unknown to her, Sadako is related to her common-law husband as she is a grand-daughter of his grandfather's mistress. This introduces the motif of incest so important to Imamura's conception of the Japanese as constituting a tribe, with women as the repository of the tribal essence. Sadako's first reaction to being raped is to commit suicide, but her essentially sensual nature intercedes and she, instead, sits down to a large meal. The rapist returns to her again and again, convinced that he loves her (a variation on the pink film in which the woman falls in love with the rapist). For the rapist, Sadako is a mother figure, in typical pink film fashion, except that Sadako intends to kill the man. She changes her mind, but the man dies any way, of a heart attack while they are making love. Meanwhile, her husband's mistress has gathered photographs of Sadako's relationship with the rapist, but she too, is killed. Even when the husband finds the pictures and confronts Sadako with the evidence, she denies it.

Through the rape and her burgeoning sexuality, which is to say, through her awakening to desire, Sadako gains strength and self-assurance. Some-thing primal has been awakened within her, a combination of sexual power and mother-love that proves overwhelming to her formerly over-bearing husband. She finds that she can now control him and she launches a fight to gain custody of her son. At film's end, Sadako has been established as a matriarchal ruler, the son more important to her than the husband. Sadako has been transformed into something like the priestess archetype of Mizoguchi's, but moves away from inspiring men to ruling over the tribe. She is now in essence like the ancient shamanesses of Japanese myth-ology.

Sato thinks this is true of all of Imamura's women: "Imamura views women as the priestesses of the old, common social body, the disintegration of which only produced smaller units that had existed from the beginning, the small family. Imamura clearly indicates that in this small social unit women, as in the past, continue to function as *miko*, priestess."[42] Dave Kehr sees Sadako's transformation into a *miko* through Imamura's symbolic use of a knitting machine that Sadako gradually learns to master. "At first she can't find her way around the arrangement of wires and yarn, but by the end of the film she has mastered the mechanical, back-and-forth movment. . . ." Kehr goes on to say that the "click-clack of the machine . . . becomes an amplified, indomitable heartbeat, pounding out the rhythm of her life. She seems to have invoked some primal force, something supernatural, with the incantation of her knitting machine."[43]

While women's function is not necessarily to inspire men, men nevertheless look to women for inspiration. While women turn out to be more resilient than men, they are also less free, for men force them into such priestess-like roles. This is evident in *The Profound Desire of the Gods*. The image of women in this film is quite clearly related to women's roles in the Shinto mythology. These myths find women as *miko* who rule the tribe, their sexuality and spirituality are above the laws of men, until such time as the men decide to rebel. The incest motif comes to the fore in terms of tribal identity, in which all members of the tribe are essentially all members of one family. Such an image is deeply held by the Japanese and explains much of the fascination incest holds for Imamura. The links between sexuality and the family are profound, as the discussion of *The Pornographers* revealed. The difficulty that *The Profound Desire of the Gods* poses for Westerners may lie in this area. The isolation of the Japanese from other cultures, it can be argued, mitigated against the need for women as exchange value, and the original *matriarchy* of Shinto would argue against the incest taboo as put forth by Freud in *Totem and Taboo*. Thus incest exerts a different mythic force in Imamura's films. Incest is tied up with Shinto and Shinto underlies the Japanese essence.[44]

However, in utilizing the Shinto mythos, Imamura unintentionally shares an image with the Buddhist-derived archetypes of Mizoguchi. Both directors see women as transcendent. In *The Profound Desire of the Gods*, Uma sails off into the sunset, never to land, never to be recovered; Toriko haunts the railroad tracks and the sugar-cane fields, an undying reminder of what modern Japan has lost. But this sense of loss is experienced by men, Kametaro and the engineer Kariya. Perhaps Imamura is saying that women in their essences can no longer survive in the modern world, except as a deeply felt need by men who are themselves uncertain about the value of modernity. Imamura's anthropological concerns have brought him full circle to Mizoguchi's aesthetic impulses. In searching for essences under the veneer of modernism, Imamura returns to transcendentalism.

Like Imamura, Hani Susumu has been concerned with exploring the essence of Japanese life through an examination of the essence of Japanese women. But if Imamura found that the true Japanese spirit is traceable to the roots of rural life, Hani's ordinary women live in the real Japan of today, Tokyo and its urban working-class neighborhoods.

Mitasareta seikatsu (*A Full Life*, 1962) is the first of Hani's important women's films, independently produced by Hani's own company and distributed by Shochiku. There is much of the documentary flavor and technique of his earlier *Bad Boys*, including black-and-white photography, post-dubbed dialogue, asynchronous sound and some handheld shots. The film's use of CinemaScope precluded some of the freewheeling style of the earlier film, while its subject matter endows it with much more of a mainstream appeal, aided by the presence of actress Arima Ineko. Arima stars as Asakura Junko, a former professional stage actress who has become dissatisfied with her marriage. Joan Mellen is convinced that Junko leaves her husband, Yoshioka, because he is "irresponsible and selfish," in other words, because he is a typical Japanese male.[45] This is much too harsh, a case of a critic reading into a film what she hopes will be there. Junko leaves the marriage primarily because she realizes that she has sacrificed her self-identity. She realizes that she has been trapped, as she says, in the "man-made snares" of marriage, romance, and consumerism geared to maintaining certain standards of "femininity." She wonders, "How can I get myself back once I've let go?" The beginning of an answer comes with her divorce. As she tells her friend Harumi, "I left him [my husband] and I awoke from my dream." Later in the film, having learned even more about herself, Junko tells Harumi, "Just being loved isn't enough for me. We must love ourselves."

Awakening from her dream, Junko must face reality, a reality fraught with economic peril and uncertainty. She rejoins the acting troupe she left three years previously. The troupe is under the direction of Ishiguro, whom she and the rest of the members call "sensei" (teacher, a term of respect in general). She makes very little money acting and so takes a job as a handler in a dog show; she also moves to a small apartment in a working-class neighborhood. Along with economic peril has come emotional peril, as well. One interesting scene finds her ex-husband at her apartment. Close-ups of his body as he washes himself reveal Junko's sexual desire asserting itself. She remarks to Yoshioka how hard her life is now, but she is certainly not bitter. Her husband apologizes to her and treats her as an adult equal. He offers her money and he offers to make love to her. She refuses his offerings, but again without bitterness.

With each decision she makes, with each hardship she faces, Junko begins to mature. Aiding her maturation is her exposure not only to the difficult world of the theatre, and to economic hardship, but also to political realities. For *A Full Life* carefully integrates the foreground of Junko's rise to selfhood with the background of May–June 1960 and the Ampo demonstrations. In this sense, Hani clearly links Junko's maturation to Japan's own coming of age. Junko's first lesson in politics comes from Karashima, a Zengakuren activist who lives next door. He asks Junko to keep some books and papers in her apartment to hide them from potential police searches. Later in the film, as the Anti-Security Treaty protests heat up, Junko bandages Karashima who has been injured in a riot. This incident, among others, inspires her to take a more active role in the protests. Junko also comes to understand the relationship between art and politics. Many members of the acting troupe feel that Ishiguro is placing too much emphasis on the demonstrations at the expense of the play they are rehearsing. But Ishiguro feels that art and politics are inextricably linked, as are politics and individual relationships. Junko comes to understand this, too.

When Ishiguro is injured in a demonstration, Junko goes to the hospital to see him. The news of Kanba Michiko's death (heard on a radio in the hospital room) throws a dark cloud over the protests. The signing of the pact is a further defeat. Yet Junko finds a space for herself in this political reality, literalized in the final scene as Junko sits near Ishiguro while many of the actors and political figures argue the next course of action. Junko and Ishiguro have decided to marry, despite their respective past failures at it. They recognize that their marriage won't erase the past, but they can come together as equals. Whereas earlier in the film, Junko had to borrow money from Ishiguro, later in the film she pays it back. Junko resisted the temptation to return to her husband, and she resisted the offer of marriage made by Uda, a fellow actor whose wife had died and who needed a mother for his little girl. Junko rejected the chance to *play* wife and mother in favor of a marriage of equals. It might be easy to see in Junko's sewing Ishiguro's shirt while the men discuss politics just one more example of a woman finding happiness in domesticity and service to men. Joan Mellen, however, suggests (and here I agree with her) that Junko represents a great leap forward from earlier portrayals of women: "Like Mizoguchi's, Hani's women are stronger than men because of this capacity to live on behalf of others. It is a far cry from the traditional resignation and self-sacrifice expected of the Japanese woman because it is freely chosen."[46]

This idea of the woman's *choice*, of Junko's coming to terms in a realistic manner with her options in the contemporary world, is a clear thematic undercurrent in the film. Junko is juxtaposed to two other women. One of them is a fellow actress who also works at the dog show. This woman holds a utilitarian view of marriage: Get to know what it is like in order to be able to portray it better on the stage, and then get out of it entirely. This same woman also does not believe in political action. In a sense, to abandon personal relationships is also to abandon politics. On the other side of the coin is Junko's friend, Harumi, who clearly represents the woman completely caught in the web of social strictures which bind women in contemporary Japan. Harumi is a widow who dotes on her son. She lives in fear of her mother-in-law—when Harumi's husband died he left his money and property to his mother. Harumi is having an affair with a married man, one of those typical Japanese affairs in which the forces of *giri* completely conflict with the needs of *ninjo*. Harumi attempts suicide when her mother-in-law, having found a packet of letters from Harumi's lover, takes her son away and banishes her from the house. Harumi is a traditionally helpless victim of Japan's oppressive patriarchal structure, a fate Junko avoids by becoming her own true, full self.

Kanojo to kare (*She and He*, 1963) is also about self-discovery, but on a slightly less global scale. Junko in *A Full Life* came to discover her wholeness as a result of the Anti-Security Pact protests. Naoko (Hidari Sachiko) experiences disillusionment and something like a struggle for self within the context of more typical day-to-day activities. Mellen claims that "through this ordinary woman Hani wishes to expose how Confucian relationships are still demanded of the Japanese wife in the 1960s."[47] Once again, Mellen overreads the film's portrayal of male-dominated society. What Naoko really confronts is not Confucian ideology, but the covert, subtle manifestations of power and prejudice. For Naoko's husband (Okada Eiji, the star of Resnais' *Hiroshima Mon Amour* and Teshigahara's *Woman in the Dunes*) neither treats her poorly nor cruelly. In fact, Hani shows that her husband, Eiichi, is basically a good, caring husband, caught up in class and status consciousness that he expects (but does not impose upon) his wife to share.

She and He is even more firmly a slice-of-life drama than *A Full Life*. The film's primary location is a typical Tokyo housing development, home to Naoko and Eiichi. Nearby their project (a complex of buildings surrounding a courtyard) is a shantytown which is home to Ikona, a former classmate of Eiichi's, now a ragpicker. Ikona cares for Hanako, a blind girl abandoned by her parents. Naoko offers scraps of kindness to Ikona, and scraps of food to Ikona's dog, Kuma. At one point, Naoko ministers to Hanako when she becomes ill, allowing the girl to stay in her apartment. When Eiichi returns from a business trip and sees the girl, he calls a charity hospital to take the child. Eiichi, however, does try to find Ikona a more suitable job, but Ikona refuses his help. Eiichi is somewhat antagonistic to Ikona, doubtless because he is a former classmate brought low. But the vast majority of the apartment dwellers are more overtly hostile and prejudiced against him and all the shantytown dwellers. In fact, the apartment tenants raise money to build a fence around the courtyard. Eventually, the shantytown is torn down and (in a bit of heavy-handed symbolism, perhaps) a golf course is put in its place.

Naoko's kindness is not confined to Ikona, Hanako, and Kuma, the dog. She is also friendly to the neighborhood laundry boy who comes to her for advice and, even when he moves to the country, continues to write to her. Naoko also looks after the welfare of her neighbors. When a neighbor is sick, Naoko cares for the woman's child. Hani attributes Naoko's kindness to her childhood in Manchuria where she was orphaned during the war and then repatriated to Japan. Mellen feels this background is an index of Naoko's experience of "the dark side of life," an index of her suffering.[48] More precisely, her Manchurian background has subjected Naoko to prejudice and she therefore has sympathy with other victims of middle-class narrow-mindedness: the working-class laundry boy, the handicapped girl, and the poverty-stricken ragpicker.

In another use of heavy-handed symbolism, perhaps, Hani contrasts Naoko to her neighbors. Late one night, after the residents have been evicted from the shantytown save for Ikona who refuses to leave, someone steals Kuma. From her bedroom, Naoko can hear Ikona's pitiable shouts for the dog. Naoko dresses to go help Ikona find him. Eiichi tries to prevent her, but Naoko insists that "the dog's important to him." Naoko eventually finds the dog dead. The senseless cruelty of this act is obviously a metaphor for the uncaring and callous treatment of the other residents of the housing development. Only Naoko felt sympathy and compassion.

The ending of the film is somewhat ambiguous. Mellen is once again quite sure that the film condemns Eiichi's attitude as Naoko is forced to capitulate to her husband.[49] In fact, Naoko's final gesture (which Mellen conveniently missed), touching her sleeping husband next to her in bed, reveals her tenderness for him and her slight sense of loss; in other words, as Richard Tucker perceives, a feeling "close to *mono no aware*. The essential difference here is that Naoko has acted as a free individual and has attempted to cut across the traditional responses and change a situation. . . . [I]t suggests to the viewer that there is a value in individual identity."[50] Naoko has achieved her selfhood by defying middle-class conventions. Thus she may stay with her husband, not in bondage, nor as a child living in a dollhouse, but as a self-assertive individual whose discontent can be put to positive use.

From the search by women for self-identity and fulfillment, Hani turned to the question of Japanese identity in two fairly well-known films, *Bwana Toshi no uta* (*The Song of Bwana Toshi*, 1965) and *Andes no hanayome* (*Bride of the Andes*, 1966). Both films focus on Japanese people outside of Japan, the former in Africa, the latter in Peru. In *Bride of the Andes*, Hani looks at Japaneseness through the figure of the woman (Hidari Sachiko again). Hani's main point, as Joan Mellen says, is "that one avenue for the liberation of the Japanese from a neofeudal social order may lie precisely through communication with other cultures." Mellen goes on to say that "if Naoko in *She and He* could find no outlet for her impulses of compassion, the woman of *Bride of the Andes* locates means of expressing similar needs among the Indians of South America, free of the insularity of the Japanese archipelago."[51] And once she asserts herself and her inner compassion, once she finds what Donald Richie calls her "combination of toughness, trust and trying again and again,"[52] she finds herself an object of respect and admiration by her husband.

Less concerned with the essence of Japaneseness than either Imamura or Hani but perhaps even more concerned with the plight of women in today's Japan is Yoshida Yoshishige. Yoshida, as much as any other Japanese director, including Mizoguchi, deserves the appellation *feminisuto*. In a canon which consists of sixteen feature films made between 1960 and 1973, fully half are devoted to women; and all save one of his most important and successful works fall into the category of a woman's film. (The exception is clearly *Martial Law*.) Yoshida worked primarily in melodrama, an interest which may be easily traced to his marriage to Okada Mariko, considered by many to be among the most beautiful of Japan's actresses and, as we have noted, the biggest star of the New Wave cinema. Her career and persona were established at Toho in the late 1950s; at Shochiku she became even more clearly associated with strong-willed, sexually potent women. To star Okada in a film is already to imbue it with strong *feminisuto* overtones. Yoshida, like Douglas Sirk before him, takes a dialectical stance toward his material, seen through camera angles and movements which disavow the manifest content of the shot. However, pictorial beauty as such, is an integral part of his cinema.

Yoshida finds that the beauty of women stems from the fact that they embody all the virtues that men lack. One ideal subscribed to by the heroine in *Akitsu Springs*, his first important *feminisuto* film, is self-negation. The heroine falls in love with with a boy during the war and she remains true to him over the years despite his evident profligacy. *Akitsu Springs* is quite clearly a variation on the standard melodrama featuring a beautiful heroine and an undeserving *nimaime* male. While the boy, Shusaku, slowly grows more cynical and bitter, Shinko continues to hold out hope for him and for their relationship. In the final sequence, Shinko suggests *shinju*, traditional lovers' suicide, but Shusaku refuses, saying, "We've outgrown that. Pondering life/death is a thing of the past." Shinko, to demonstrate that some still retain idealism even in the face of defeat, slashes her wrists and dies.

The film spans seventeen years, during which time Shinko waits for Shusaku to make a commitment to her, even when Shusaku lives with another woman. *Akitsu Springs* is reminiscent of a popular American melodrama, *Back Street* (based on Fannie Hurst's novel and filmed under this title three separate times), the story of a woman who is in love with a man fate prevented her from marrying. She nevertheless devotes her life to him, living on the back street, as it were, of his life. Her devotion to him is so complete that when news of his death reaches her, she too expires. In *Akitsu Springs*, Shinko early tells Shusaku, "I'll be ready to die whenever word reaches me of your death." And in both films, the issue is raised as to what, exactly, the strong woman sees in the weak male. But while such a question may be a flaw in the Hollywood versions, it is the very mythic structure of the Japanese tale. It is precisely the man's weakness and the

Akitsu Onsen (*Akitsu Hot Springs*)
Yoshida Yoshishige, director. Shochiku Co., Ltd.

woman's sacrifice for him, that makes her noble. And in *Akitsu Springs*, it is Shinko's death that makes her tragic, sacrificing herself for a man who will not even die with her.

If *Akitsu Springs* is basically a stylish version of the Hollywood and Japanese melodrama, it takes its place in the New Wave by its insistence on linking historical events with individual lives. A comparison between historical events and the life of a woman is a motif used by Imamura in *The Insect Woman* and *History of Postwar Japan as Told by a Bar Hostess*. In fact, Yoshida's film, like Imamura's, shows us the heroine's direct response to the Emperor's radio broadcast which ended World War II and disavowed his divinity. Whereas Imamura's Tome made love during the speech, thereby reasserting her essential sexual identity which remains unaffected by the Emperor, Shinko experiences the defeat as a death and simultaneous rebirth. She is both the old Japan and the new, saddened by the war, but optimistic over the future. Her slow turn to disillusionment and despair as she watches Shusaku lose all his ideals, is compared to the gradual erosion of postwar reforms. Shusaku thus represents Japan's turn away from its postwar promise, Shinko the essential spirit of Japan brought low by this failure. Woman is the standard-bearer of the lost hope, she retains her ideals while all around her others abandon theirs.

From the image of a woman brought gradually to despair, Yoshida's following *feminisuto* films focus on women already in its throes. Sato describes these woman by noting

the heroine . . . continues to languish while searching for sexual fulfillment. She is usually a proud woman, and the more pride she has the less she can bear the thought of having sexual relations with a worthless man and surrendering to him psychologically. At the same time, however, she needs men to liberate herself from the insecurity and loneliness of a strong ego. Through such a woman Yoshida relates the dilemma of individual autonomy and the need for social bonds. . . .[53]

Yoshida's focus on women revolves around the dialectic between freedom vs. male-female relationships. Freedom seems to be incompatible with relationships with men as such relations typically demand self-negation on the woman's part. The idealized images that women nevertheless hold of romantic love are inevitably defeated when women assert themselves as whole, individualized beings. The new woman in Yoshida's films must deal with her own disillusionment while at the same time she is subject to male desires, to men's idealized images of women. The clearest and unquestionably most stylish examination of this dilemma is to be found in *Mizu de kakareta monogatari* (*A Story Written with Water*, 1965). The heroine of this film, Shizuka, like Shinko in *Akitsu Springs* (both are played by Okada Mariko), is driven to suicide by the emptiness of her existence, primarily the emptiness of her erotic existence. The eroticism of *A Story Written with Water* is more profound than in the earlier film, and more complex, tied as it is to incest.

The film focuses on Shizuka's relationship to her son, Shizuo. Shizuka, a widow, is the mistress of Hashimoto Denzo, a well-to-do banker, while Shizuo is married to his daughter, Yumiko. Shizuka's relationship to Denzo provides her with no sexual satisfaction, while Shizuo's relations with Yumiko are similarly unsatisfactory. Mother and son are seen to share the most profound erotic compulsion toward each other, which manifests itself first in a series of flashbacks. Shizuo remembers bathing with his mother; playing by a stream with friends when his mother calls him from a bridge; following his mother to the small house where she carries on her liaison with Denzo (thus telling us that this affair began before his father's death from tuberculosis); his parents kissing in his father's hospital bed. Shizuka remembers many of these scenes as well, in addition to her memory of her husband's final moments: He lay in bed as she removed her clothes to give him one final kiss before he died. The erotic compulsion felt by mother and son climaxes when Shizuo goes into his mother's bedroom carrying a bottle of sleeping pills and talks to her of *shinju*, lovers' suicide. He lays his head on her breast; she throws her head back in a swoon of ecstasy, the camera rocking back and forth like a pendulum. A fade to black hides the next activity (including the possibility of incest and then double suicide). The next morning we see that mother and son did not commit suicide as Shizuka and Denzo take a drive to the country in his car. The car is discovered later, crashed into a tree, Denzo dead at the wheel. Shizuka has drowned in the lake, her shoes and umbrella floating on the surface of the water. Shizuo, meanwhile, following the (implied) incest with his mother, has drawn closer to Yumiko. The film's final shot shows Shizuo clinging tight to Yumiko as they search for Shizuka's body.

The intense aura of eroticism in the film stems not only from the motif of incest, but from the motif of water. As Ian Buruma notes, "Sensual experience in Japan is often associated with water, the most maternal of symbols." (Buruma also notes that love scenes are called *nureba*, "wet scenes.")[54] This is a recurring symbol in many films and erotic stories in Japan, used especially often by Yoshida. Shinko's suicide in *Akitsu Springs* takes place by a stream while Shizuka, in this film, drowns herself in a lake. Shizuo's memory of bathing with his mother in a large pool is a recurring image, finalized when his father looks into a mirror and suddenly coughs up blood. (The Oedipal overtones are perhaps too precise to ignore.)

The erotic aura is offset by Yoshida's film style which clearly shows the influence of Antonioni, especially his classic trilogy of alienation, *L'Avventura* (1960), *La Notte* (1961), and *L'Eclisse* (1962). Black-and-white cinematography emphasizes the starkness of the interior settings, fragmented camera angles and camera movements unmotivated by character point of view objectively reveal the emotional sterility and alienation of the characters, and elliptical narration, combined with a complex chronology and a surrealistic dream sequence, deemphasize plot and causality. *A Story Written with Water* is thus a melodrama the way *L'Eclisse* is a melodrama; the basic elements are sifted through an overtly modernist sensibility.

A Story Written with Water was Yoshida's first film away from Shochiku studios as a contract director. Following this film, he made five more melodramas starring his wife, all of which explore the relationship between erotic love and marriage. *Onna no mizuumi* (*Woman of the Lake*, 1966) was the first film produced by Yoshida's and Okada's own company, *Gendai eiga-sha*, which became their permanent production house (sometimes in partnership with the ATG). *Woman of the Lake* turns Kawabata Yasunari's impressionistic, elliptical novel of a man's erotic musings about the women in his life (including his mother and a beautiful cousin) into a rather conventionally plotted melodrama. The film is interesting mainly for its revelation of the power that idealizations about love have over actual relationships. The heroine, Miyako, is married to Yuzo, but develops a passionate fascination for Kitano. She allows him to take nude pictures of her that Ginpei (the novel's central figure) secures. He becomes obsessed with Miyako. When Miyako learns that Kitano is engaged to be married, she agrees to meet Ginpei at the lakeshore, where they make love. Miyako makes a halfhearted attempt to kill Ginpei, but fails. Ginpei, meanwhile, realizes that he is really in love with Miyako's image (as in the pictures) and not the real woman. All of the protagonists are seen to be victims of their own interior musings, their romanticized inner longings. This makes the film an accurate adaptation of the novel, but the obligation to exteriorize the novel's internal monologues through the heavily plotted melodrama, tends to obscure this point. Too, the book focuses on Ginpei while Yoshida tried to shift the emphasis to Miyako. A certain obligation to the book (Kawabata is possibly Japan's most respected novelist) meant a lessening of Yoshida's primary interest in the figure of the modern woman.

Joen (The Affair, 1967) is somewhat better as a woman's film. Here, Okada Mariko plays Oriko, who is unhappily married to Furuhata. She married him primarily to disassociate herself from the life led by her mother, who had many affairs. Furuhata has taken a mistress because Oriko has grown so cold toward him. However, Oriko's attempts to disavow her sexuality dissolve when she sees her sister-in-law making love to a laborer. This laborer, as it happens, was her mother's lover before she died in a traffic accident. Oriko tries to resist the erotic longings the laborer inspires in her, but she cannot. Later, she meets Mitsuharu, a sculptor who was another of her mother's lovers. Furuhata thinks that Oriko is having an affair with Mitsuharu. When she tells her husband about the laborer, he quickly divorces her, at which point she begins an affair with the sculptor. In the best melodramatic fashion, Mitsuharu is seriously injured when one of his sculptures falls on him, rendering him paralyzed from the waist down. On her way to visit Mitsuharu in the hospital, one day, Oriko sees the laborer. Faced with a choice, she opts for Mitsuharu, believing that to care for him is better than being with a man she does not love (her husband) or being with a man who provides merely erotic thrills.

The Affair is interesting both for the choices the woman is confronted with and her ultimate decision. The three men in her life clearly represent different realms: the economic/material world of her husband; the physical, sensual side of life offered by the laborer (the realm of the senses); and the artistic, emotional sphere of the sculptor. Selecting the sculptor, the artist, is hardly a surprising choice on the woman's part (considering that a male director made the film). But the melodramatic twist of rendering him asexual, and her decision to care for him nevertheless, transforms that film from a woman's quest for erotic satisfaction to a woman's realization that she is happiest in the traditional Japanese context of mother. In this sense, *The Affair* is both New Wave and traditional—the New Woman is allowed to assert herself, but she ultimately chooses to return to the traditional role desired by men, the role of mother, the self-sacrificing priestess archetype of Mizoguchi.

Honoo to onna (Impasse; the title translates as the more poetic "Flame and

Woman" neatly rendered in the French title, *La Femme et la Flamme*) made the same year as *The Affair* (whose Japanese title more poetically translates as "Flame of Feeling"), concerns the inability of a woman to find satisfaction in her traditional family structure. The heroine, Ritsuko, is married to Shingo, a design engineer. Shingo is unable to father a child so Ritsuko is artificially inseminated. The birth of a son, Takashi, however, does not help marital relations between husband and wife. When Sakaguchi, a doctor having marital problems with his wife, Shina, is revealed as the sperm donor, Ritsuko develops a passion for the doctor. Eventually, following other complications (Shina kidnaps Takashi and she tries to seduce Shingo), Ritsuko, Shingo, and Takashi are reunited.

Ritsuko's inability to feel erotic attraction toward her husband is literalized by his sterility. This sterility is a metaphor for the modern woman's alienation from the roles she is expected to play—dutiful wife and devoted mother. Oriko's own mother in *The Affair* rejected this role in favor of erotic self-fulfillment, while Oriko herself explored erotic self-fulfillment only to opt for the role of mother. In *Impasse*, Ritsuko was not satisfied to be a wife and mother, initially rejecting it in pursuit of the potent man, Sakaguchi. The ending of the film, while it may seem like an attempt at reintegration of the woman to her "proper" male-bound role of wife and mother, is actually ambiguous. Ritsuko's self-assertion, once made, is not so easily repressed. As in Hani's *She and He*, once the woman finds herself (her self) she is not likely to let it go.

Yoshida followed these two interesting 1967 films with two less interesting films in 1968: *Juhyo no yorumeki* (*Affair in the Snow*) and *Saraba natsu no hikari* (*Farewell to the Summer Light*). In the former film (whose Japanese title translates as "Flicker of the Silver Thaw") Okada Mariko is the object of rivalry between two men, one of whom kills himself, thus resolving the situation; in the latter work, Okada portrays a businesswoman who falls in love with a student while in Europe. She leaves her husband for the younger man. The younger man, however, soon discovers that he, too, will be unable to keep the now-emancipated woman.

With this group of six films made between 1965 and 1968, Yoshida produced an enviable series of melodramas concerning the personal liberation of women. In 1969 he turned his attention to more global concerns, producing his trilogy of twentieth-century Japan, beginning with *Eros plus Massacre*. This film, unquestionably his finest achievement to date, presents his most complex image of women and returns women to an overtly politicized image. (The film will be the primary subject of Chapter 7.) He interrupted his trilogy in 1971 to make one more woman's film, *Kokuhakuteki joyu-ron* (*Confessions among Actresses*). This film, in keeping with the deliberately modernistic and highly self-reflexive films in the trilogy, continually points out the nature of film and film acting. In this fashion, Yoshida extends his exploration of the discrepancy between reality and idealized fantasy images of romance. Three actresses who are making a film together reflect on their lives, while the film reflects on the "mask" of the actor. To Burch the film posits "an implicit moral condemnation of the 'masks' that modern society makes us wear." While this is not a bad idea for Burch, the film is ultimately too "literary."[55] Whatever such a critique might mean, perhaps Burch overlooks the various levels through which Yoshida is operating. The three actresses are played by three important stars, Okada Mariko, Asaoka Ruriko (Yumiko in *A Story Written with Water*) and Arima Ineko (the star of Hani's *A Full Life*). All have personae of sexually potent, liberated women. Yoshida can rely on three levels of characterization: the actresses as stars, the characters they play in this film, and the characters they play in the film they are making (the film within the film). This mise-en-abîme structure is particularly cinematic, and bears comparison to Bergman's *Persona*, even if it is derivative of the Japanese melodrama.

Yoshida went into temporary retirement in 1973, a year when the achievements and advancements of the New Wave were already retreating into respectability. Of all the major New Wave directors, only Shinoda Masahiro maintained a consistent output through the 1970s and into the '80s, averaging almost a film a year. Never as radical as Oshima, nor as consistent as Yoshida, and certainly never as satirical as Imamura, Shinoda, on the other hand, is unquestionably the most versatile of the New Wave directors. He made an interesting, confusing, but ultimately standard Samurai film, *Sarutobi (Samurai Spy,* 1967), but also produced the extremely deconstructive *Ansatsu (Assassination,* 1964). He adapted works from the classical theatrical canon of Chikamatsu, but worked closely on a number of films with New Wave playwright Terayama Shuji. He has made films set in a variety of periods: the second century, the twelfth century, the seventeenth century, the nineteenth century, and the twentieth century. He even made a documentary (on the 1972 Winter Olympics in Sapporo). But there is a recurring interest of his, a motif which transcends genres and periods: an interest in women.

Many critics feel that Shinoda's basic view of women derives from Mizoguchi. Audie Bock has it that " . . . those who suffer most from political injustice are the women in (Shinoda's) films. . . . These long-suffering women bear an uncanny resemblance to many a Kenji Mizoguchi heroine. . . ."[56] Early in his career, Shinoda tried to politicize the image of women within the context of the melodramatic stories to which he was assigned. Of the three central protagonists of *Dry Lake* it is the woman who emerges as the true hero. She is the one who breaks away from the feudal past and the nihilistic present to work for a better future as a participant in the Ampo demonstrations. In *Watakushi-tachi no kekkon (Our Marriage,* 1962), Shinoda combines the story of two young women who experience romantic difficulties with the issue of water pollution which has affected the seaweed industry. However, Shinoda did not really reach a maturity

Ansatsu (*Assassination*)
Shinoda Masahiro, director. Shochiku Co., Ltd.

of vision and style until *Kawaita hana* (*Pale Flower*, 1963), his ninth film. *Pale Flower* is based on a story by Ishihara Shintaro, who, as we have seen, was the virtual spokesman for the newly identified generation of alienated youth in the postwar era. It is, in fact, Shinoda's particular contribution to the politicized image of women to link his female figures with these "youth" images. Where Imamura and Hani link women to the essence of premodern Japan and with groups who have been discriminated against, and Yoshida sees women as representative of, and alienated from, the Japanese family system, Shinoda links women to youth and gives them many of the same characteristics; alienation from family, business, and friends; rebellion; thrill-seeking; sexual experimentation. However, if Shinoda tended to side rather straightforwardly with his youth characters, in the later women's films there is, as in Mizoguchi, an ambivalence present in his attitude. And nowhere is this more powerfully presented than in *Pale Flower*.

This *yakuza* film, which begins to deconstruct the genre at the genre's very point of origin, contains a powerful sub-plot involving the killer-hero and an enigmatic young woman. The hero, newly released from prison, finds that the *yakuza* world has changed so that now his only satisfaction in performing his job is the thrill of the kill. He becomes fatally attracted

Kawaita hana (*Pale Flower*)
Shinoda Masahiro, director
Shochiku Co., Ltd.

to a woman (Kaga Mariko) whom he meets at a high-stakes gambling den. As their odd relationship progresses, he allows the woman to accompany him on an assignment. This introduces an undercurrent of sadomasochism, which is carried further when the hero goes to jail out of love for the woman only to learn that she has become a drug addict at the hands of an equally mysterious Chinese assassin. Kaga's characterization of the woman has much in it of the spider-woman motif, albeit in an almost unconscious manner on the woman's part. Shinoda's heroine becomes a destructive force when she gives in to her feelings of desire. Like the young people in the youth films, she gives vent to her vague restlessness and feelings of alienation and so unleashes elemental forces, forces destructive to men.

This interpretation of woman's power is reinforced by Shinoda's adaptation of Kawabata's novel *Utsukushisa to kanashimi to* (*With Beauty and Sorrow*, 1965; Howard Hibbett's English translation of the novel renders the title as *Beauty and Sadness*). Kaga Mariko again stars (rare instances in which Shinoda does not star his wife, Iwashita Shima), here playing a young painter who loves her mentor, an older woman who was once the lover of a famous novelist. Kaga's character seeks revenge for her teacher who was abandoned by the writer when she was pregnant. She first seduces the older man, then seduces his son and then (we infer) arranges a boating accident in which the younger man is killed. The lesbian motif, explicit in the novel, is less explicit in the film version, but the spider-woman motif is as clear, perhaps clearer. (The novel, in typical Kawabata fashion, is mainly told through the musings of the male figure.) Kaga's youthful vitality and sexuality seduces all the characters with whom she interacts. Kawabata felt that Shinoda's film was the best adaptation of all his works.[57] Donald Richie feels that the film demonstrates Shinoda's admiration for Mizoguchi with its concern for "the aesthetics of Japanese life and the overtones of emotions within Japanese settings. . . ."[58] The links to Kawabata and Mizoguchi bring forth the transcendental paradigm. One critic feels Kawabata's novel "is a meditation not only on love, loneliness, and loss but also upon the nature of Time itself, expressing Kawabata's recurrent theme of beauty's close links with sadness, the traditional association that he has identified as the very heart of Japanese poetic sense (the feeling of *aware*)."[59] The introduction of the spider-woman image works against the transcendental, *aware*-inducing aspects of the film, throwing them into highlight.

The spider-woman complex also recurs in a later, minor film, *Sakura no mori no mankai no shita* (*Under the Cherry Blossoms*, 1975). Here Shinoda strays into *Ugetsu* and *Onibaba* territory in this bizarre story of a hunter (Wakayama Tomisaburo of the memorable "Sword of Vengeance" series) uncontrollably attracted to a noblewoman (Iwashita Shima) who has him commit numerous murders for her pleasure.

A more interesting woman's film of the later period presents a more victimized and politicized image of women. *Hanare goze Orin* (*Banished Orin*, 1977; aka *Melody in Grey*) recalls Shinoda's earlier *Akanegumo* (*Clouds at Sunset*, 1967). Both films deal with a deserter from the Japanese army who meets a lower-class woman and has a short-lived, tragic relationship with her. *Clouds at Sunset* takes place in 1937; *Banished Orin* during the Russo-Japanese war in the early part of this century (although the film tells its story in flashbacks which span a number of years). Orin (Iwashita Shima) is a blind shamisen player. She travels the country with a group of roaming entertainers subject to severe restrictions, the main one being a vow of chastity. As a member of a disgraced lower caste, Orin has, in fact, very few human privileges and dignities. She is a symbol not only of the place of women under feudalism, but of all Japanese rigidly bound by *giri*. The concept of *giri* is compounded by the male figure, an army deserter—the army a metaphor for the whole of Japanese society from which desertion is the ultimate sin. Two outcasts, two disgraced people, are drawn together, eventually giving themselves over to the force of *ninjo*, human feelings which threaten to disrupt the imposed harmony of Japanese society. Things end badly for Orin and her lover. The setting in the past both a strategy of displacement and a hope for a better future.

Shinoda's last genuinely radical film was also his most complex statement about, and use of, the image of women. *Himiko* (1974) has much in common with Imamura as it explores the roots of Japanese society and identity.

Iwashita Shima, in the title role, encompasses all the archetypal images of women as she plays a peasant-princess-priestess of the Tomb Period. The film's fragmented narrative style, presentational acting, and daring ending combine with a provocative thematic suggestion that all the religious and mythic elements in today's Japanese psyche have their roots in the Emperor system, which is revealed to be political and ideological in origin.

The character of Himiko feels herself torn between the archetype of the priestess and a genuine sexual being. She is a prophet by day to her tribe, the direct spokeswoman of the Sun Goddess. At night, Himiko's powerful sexual urges must be satisfied by male slaves.[60] Himiko thus is presented, on the one hand, as a priestess and a demon. But on the other hand, it is revealed that she is very much a woman under patriarchy, for despite her seeming power as the shamaness, the *miko* of the tribe, she is really the political pawn of the conquering Emperor, who is trying to displace the more primitive tribes who inhabit Japan's central plain, the Yamato region of the deepest myths. Himiko's political fortunes crumble when she becomes sexually obsessed by her half-brother. The incest motif, so important to Imamura, is again revealed as a fundamental tribal essence. Another politico-religious faction dethrones Himiko, who had cruelly punished her half-brother for rejecting her, and replaces her by another woman (also to be called Himiko). Shinoda is hereby saying that the priestess archetype was a mere creation of politically minded men; that even the traditional shamanesses were mere ideological screens for the perpetuation of the patriarchal Emperor system.

The connection between these second-century political maneuverings and the current system in which the Emperor still occupies a significant symbolic place is brilliantly drawn by a high angle shot at the film's conclusion. Shinoda's camera follows the priest Nashime through a forest. The angle changes and Nashime looks up to see a helicopter hovering overhead. The helicopter raises up and the point of view shifts to reveal the distinctive keyhole-shaped tombs that give this period in Japanese history its name. Many of these tombs remain unopened, silent monuments to the sanctity of the Emperor system. Implicit in this shot is Shinoda's call to open these tombs to demythicize the Emperor system. From the point of view of the next chapter, it is interesting that Shinoda feels that a direct link to the Emperor can be traced back to Korea.[61] This Korean connection at the dawn of Japanese civilization provides an important transition between the politicization of the image of women and the politicization of Koreans (among other outcasts) in the New Wave cinema.

As we have seen, the concern with women manifested by the New Wave filmmakers is in many ways a continuation of the *feminisuto* tradition established by Mizoguchi. A basic sympathy for women and an understanding of how ideology and social customs conspire to keep women in a certain place through the use of recurring archetypes has been characteristic of the Japanese cinema since the 1920s. To an extent, the *feminisuto* directors of the New Wave, Imamura, Hani, Yoshida and Shinoda, merely extended this tradition into the volatile 1960s. The genre conventions of the commercial cinema necessitated a dialectical stance toward women's images. The needs of political progressivism must be balanced against the basically conservative nature of mass-market cinema. The recognition by the New Wave filmmakers that the image of women was already politicized within commercial restrictions (rebellion vs. melodrama, so to speak) necessitated a self-conscious approach to women's issues, a deliberate highlighting, even a deconstruction. Just as the Japanese cinema already possesses a radical formal component in its traditional features, so, too, the use of women was already radicalized. In order to make film style and the image of women genuinely political, genuinely progressive, a repositioning of traditional archetypes was required.

One such repositioning, such highlighting, was in the use of the archetype of the priestess. The New Wave directors realized a crucial link in the Japanese psyche between women and identity. The priestess functioned not only to inspire men, to be their savior, but also as the repository of premodern, prelogical values. The priestess archetype in the New Wave often took the form of the mother, as in the traditional use of the image, but to this was added the motif of incest. This woman was now the mother of invention as it were (the inspirer of men), but also the Mother of Japan, the essence of the Japanese spirit. The already eroticized image of the mother in Japanese culture was strengthened in the New Wave by further linking the prostitute archetype to this mother-figure. David Goodman sees the priestess and the prostitute as already linked in Shinto mythology: "Just as the *miko* is the sacred manifestation of female sexuality, prostitutes are its profane manifestation."[62] The collapsing together of the priestess and prostitute archetypes is therefore the conflation of the sacred and profane realms. This is one way in which the transcendental and humanistic paradigms of the earlier generations are avoided. This strategy, combined with the dialectical stance toward genre conventions, has the effect of making these films tentative, of refusing easy emotional involvement and release. An overt Brechtianism emerges which effects the re-politicization of the image of women.

The re-politicization can be seen in the works of Oshima Nagisa. Oshima is not typically thought of as a *feminisuto* director in the manner of Imamura or Yoshida. But he is, of course, thought of as an overtly political filmmaker. Audie Bock feels that "The abuse of power and the oppression of individuals and whole segments of the population have been his themes. . . ."[63] It is the case in that in the majority of his political films (that is, the majority of his films) women have played prominent roles. (This is also true of Jean-Luc Godard's films, to which Oshima's are often, if not always correctly, compared.) In films which overtly deal with significant New Wave motifs—the alienation of youth, sexuality and identity, discrimination—women occupy an important symbolic place. In *Cruel Story of Youth*, *The Sun's Burial*, and *Gishiki* (*The Ceremony*, 1971), Oshima links the alienation and disillusionment of youth with the alienation and disillusionment of women. The image of the woman in *The Sun's Burial* is similar to Imamura's heroine in *Pigs and Battleships*; in *The Ceremony* the woman-as-priestess archetype is central to the film along with the motif of incest. In *Violence at Noon*, the failure of the woman to act as a true priestess (from the man's point of view) leads to his sociopathy. In *Koshikei* (*Death by Hanging*, 1968), Oshima establishes a connection between women and oppressed classes, as well as continuing the association between women and national identity. Thus we see that in the films of Oshima Nagisa, the paradigmatic canon of the New Wave cinema, women are conspicuous by their presence, linked in some form to all of the political, social, cultural, and aesthetic issues of the movement.

CHAPTER FIVE

Forest of Pressure

There is virtually no tradition of the "social problem" film in Japan. To be sure, there have been cycles of film devoted to certain overt political issues, such as the *keiko eiga* (tendency films) of the 1930s and a string of anti-war films in the late '50s. But if we define the social problem film as dealing with issues of a transpolitical and/or continuing historical nature, the Japanese cinema can boast of no such tradition.

This might come as something of a surprise. The generic nature of the mainstream Japanese cinema would seem to encourage a film form both socially and commercially viable. The Hollywood cinema, for instance, has a long tradition of the social problem film. Cycles of anti-racist films, for example, appeared in the '40s, the '50s and then again in the late '60s. Films focusing on problems like anti-Semitism, drug addiction, alcoholism, poverty, and the like have appeared at various times. One may question the efficacy of such films in dealing with these issues, or the ideological underpinnings of the films, but their existence is an undeniable fact. Yet the genre-bound Japanese cinema, which boasts of Samurai films, *yakuza* (gangster) films, *shomin-geki* (townspeople dramas), *haha mono* (mother films), mysteries, melodramas, pink movies, and *roman poruno* (and even Westerns), seems to have ignored the social problem genre.

Explaining the lack of the social problem tradition in the Japanese cinema is not easy, for a number of factors must be considered. One can say that the Hollywood industry turned to the social problem film partly as a result of veiled censorship threats. The notion that films put forth a system of values at odds with the dominant culture was used to put pressure on early filmmakers, many of whom were not, in fact, especially sympathetic to those values. The threat of government regulation led to periodic content changes, rules and guidelines for the major films to adopt. The social problem film could also be used as a positive force to prove cinema's "moral" or education value.

One can claim, too, that Hollywood turned to the social problem film out of a sense of inferiority to the older arts of literature and theatre. The idea that film was "just entertainment," suitable merely for children and immigrants, could be countered by films which seemed to engage the pressing issues of its day. One reason that the Japanese cinema has not felt the pressure to deal with social *content* was that the cinema was almost immediately respected as a valid artistic medium at the level of its *form*.

Perhaps the main reason for the lack of a social problem tradition however, is ideological: the myth that Japan has no social problems. The social problem film obviously relies upon overt, current and much-discussed issues. American's multiracial, multi-ethnic makeup has led to a variety of racial and ethnic conflicts. The Hollywood cinema, to a small extent, has acknowledged this. The Japanese claim, on the other hand, and few would argue, that they are a remarkably homogeneous people. Racial issues do not pose problems, it seems,and religious rivalries have not been common. Most Japanese do not consider themselves especially religious, basically subscribing to certain tenets of Shinto and Buddhism, which ever since the sixth century have found a way to co-exist with remarkably little friction.

Christianity has certainly had an impact in Japan and there was even a period at the beginning of the Tokugoawa era when the newly converted Japanese Christians were severely persecuted and some Jesuit missionaries martyred (seen in Shinoda's unexceptional film version of Endo Shusaku's *Silence*). Today only a small percentage of Japanese consider themselves Christians, and those who do are not subject to persecution or prejudice of any kind. On the placid surface that the Japanese like to put forth, things do indeed seem calm. Yet there are within the culture certain disgraced classes and certain people from non-Japanese backgrounds who have been (and still are) the objects of racial, ethnic, or cultural scorn. The appearance that such classes do not exist marks the repression of such conflicts.

There are two major groups which have for quite some time consistently experienced prejudice and discrimination: the *burakumin* (or *eta*) and Koreans. Discrimination against the *burakumin* has a lengthy history. The origins of this caste (which has something in common with India's "untouchables") go back to the Japanese middle ages when firm Buddhistic strictures against slaughtering animals, working with animal skins (tanning, hiding), and handling corpses created the need for a class of people who would perform these necessary but distasteful chores. Those who took these chores upon themselves (or were forced into assuming them) passed on their lot to their descendants. It soon became nearly impossible for a *burakumin* to marry outside the caste, thus insuring that *burakumin* married *burakumin*.

The reforms associated with the Meiji Restoration in 1868 officially did away with the Japanese class system, from the Samurai at the top to *burakumin* at the bottom. But just as the former members of the Samurai class found themselves continuing as the ruling elite of Japan, *burakumin* found their lot substantially unimproved. In fact, the late Meiji era contains a number of instances in which *burakumin* settlements were viciously attacked by rioting citizens whose disgust at the *burakumin*'s existence erupted periodically. One would not want to claim that an actual conspiracy exists to keep the *burakumin* plight out of the public eye, but there is little in literature and the arts that deals with the problem, especially before World War II.

The plight of Koreans drew virtually no public attention until well after the war, although there are more complex, if obvious, reasons for this. Japan had annexed Korea in 1910, representing the culmination of nearly four hundred years of Japanese intentions toward that nation. Between 1910 and the end of World War II, Japan had expropriated Korean land and conscripted Koreans into industrial and military service. In fact, in 1945–46, 1.5 million Koreans and ethnic Koreans were voluntarily repatriated. The Japanese attitude toward Koreans in general found a more sinister corollary in their attitude toward Korean women. " . . . in 1941, the Japanese authorities actually conscripted Korean women into a corps of 'entertainers' to 'comfort' the Japanese troops in Manchuria. With the beginning of the Pacific War, from 50,000 to 70,000 Korean girls and women were drafted and sent to the front to 'entertain' the Japanese troops."[1]

The annexation of Korea in 1910 was the culmination not only of long-held designs on Korea, but on the widely held dream of the Meiji Restoration: Japan's emergence as a "modern" (Western) nation. The immediate goals of Meiji were industrialization and Westernization to avoid colonization and exploitation by European nations (as the case of China frighteningly revealed to the Japanese) and to compete with those nations for markets. Such watershed events to the Meiji ruling class as Japan's victory in the Sino-Japanese war, which represented Japan's emergence as the most powerful Asian nation, and its victory in the Russo-Japanese war, which represented Japan's ability to compete with Western Europe, were preludes to becoming an actual colonial power. There seems to have been little protest in Japan over its Korean intentions. By the 1930s and throughout the war years, of course, little protest over foreign policy would have been tolerated so that the "Korean problem" was not even an issue until after the war years. In fact, the problem was both exacerbated and postponed as a Japanese social issue by the Korean War at the beginning of the 1950s as Japanese anti-communism and its support for the U.S. as a military protector and ally made all discussion of Korea a moot point until that war's end.

In the 1950s, the issue of discrimination and prejudice against *burakumin* and Koreans was kept from public consciousness by Japan's concern for its economic miracle. As the standard of living for the vast majority of Japan's people, especially the urban classes, rose spectacularly, social problems were repressed, only to appear later, in the '60s and into the '70s (much like the U.S. 1950s, whose ideological maneuverings directly led to the 1960s eruptions). An index of greater social awareness on the part of the Japanese as the fifties came to an end is reported by Mikiso Hane. "In 1960, a controversy ensued when employment officers of two major firms in Kyoto indicated that their companies had a policy of not hiring *burakumin* and Koreans."[2] In addition, the Komatsugawa Incident in which a young Korean was sentenced to die for the murder of a Japanese high school student brought the Korean problem to the fore.

The *burakumin* issue had been introduced into Japanese literature with Shimazaki Toson's *Hakai* (*The Broken Commandment*), which had been published near the end of the Meiji era in 1906. It was not adapted into film until the postwar era, when there were two adaptations. The first was by Kinoshita Kesiuke in 1948, known in English as *Apostasy*. Kinoshita's version, as befitting a film made under the occupation, concentrates on the theme of equality and anti-prejudice. The novel was remade in 1962 by Ichikawa Kon (the English title of this film version is *The Outcast*). As one might expect from Ichikawa, and from a a film made in the '60s, this adaptation is much darker and more pessimistic than either the original novel or the 1948 film. Discrimination against the *burakumin* was also taken up by Imai Tadashi, who produced the two-part *Hashi ga nai kawa* (*River Without a Bridge*, 1969–70).

The New Wave filmmakers were not overly concerned with the plight of the *burakumin*, per se, except insofar as they condemned discrimination based on class or race, an issue seen as early as Oshima's *A Town of Love and Hope* in 1959, in which the alienated youth is discriminated against because of his poverty-stricken background. Imamura Shohei addressed the issue directly in *History of Postwar Japan as Told by a Bar Hostess*. Etsuko (Madam Omboro) mentions in one of her talks with Imamura that she is of *eta* origin. She tells the director that her mother insisted to her that she could never "wipe out my background." This hopeless certainty caused her to quit school, believing that she would always be an outcast. Etsuko attributes her turn to prostitution (especially serving U.S. servicemen) to the knowledge that "no well-brought up guy would take me."[3] Imamura is careful to draw our attention to the irony of Etsuko's situation when she becomes pregnant with the child of a U.S. Navy man. Her own parents are appalled. Etsuko's parents are not alone in their prejudice. Such children in Japan are called "half-breeds" and are frequently the victims of discrimination and prejudice. Yet, as Joan Mellen points out, "Omboro refuses to have the abortion insisted upon by her father. . . . Her act is one of defiance against the Japanese racism that had been so cruelly directed toward her in her youth."[4] Etsuko, as we noted in Chapter 4, leaves Japan for the U.S. and, like the hero in Toson's *The Broken Commandment*, heads for Texas.

Imamura produced another documentary film which, while not centrally about the *burakumin* issue, at least addresses it in a direct way. *Karayuki-san* (1975), made as part of a series of documentary films for television focusing on Japanese who did not choose to return home after World War II, is the story of a seventy-four-year-old woman living in Malaysia. She had been sold into prostitution as a young woman to serve the Japanese army in Southeast Asia. (Her story is more familiar to U.S. viewers through Kumai Kei's Academy-award nominated *Sandakan #8*). The woman, reminiscing to Imamura, recalls that she was a member of the *eta* caste and recalls how "one of her brothers, a merchant, was physically handicapped and his customers demanded that he hand them his merchandise with chopsticks so as not to touch him."[5] The prejudice experienced by her brother also points to Japanese attitudes toward the handicapped, the subject of some other important documentary films of the New Wave. The kayaruki-san herself has been conveniently forgotten by Japan, not because of her *burakumin* status but Japan's desire to forget the more than 10,000 such women who volunteered, were kidnapped, or sold into prostitution for the imperial army's pleasure.

Discrimination against the children of U.S. servicemen, alluded to by Imamura's *History of Postwar Japan* . . . , was the subject of Imai Tadashi's *Kiku to Isamu* (Kiku and Isamu, 1959). The problems of these children is compounded by the fact that not only was their father a U.S. soldier, but that he was black. In Japan, where many Japanese felt that all foreigners were somehow inferior, blacks were considered more inferior than whites. Imai's film is a definite condemnation of the racist responses the children elicit. As in Toson's novel about a *burakumin*, one of the children, Isamu, leaves Japan for the U.S. when he is adopted by a black family. Joan Mellen, never satisfied with any of Imai's films, finds fault with this one as well, maintaining that somehow Imai "absolves" his audience "of the task of even seeking a remedy for . . . racism" while he refuses "to confront the audience . . . with the fact of its own racism."[6] Yet the ending of the film, in which Kiku decides to become a farmer, friendless in the village, her brother gone to America, must strike any Japanese not as "uplifting" (as Mellen says it is) but as tinged with pathos, for to be alone in Japan, as Kiku is and will surely remain, is the ultimate misery.

The Korean question would prove more significant to the New Wave than the issue of discrimination against the *burakumin*. Imamura broached the subject in *Nianchan* in 1959, and it was taken up in a similar fashion by Imamura's assistant director on that film, Urayama Kiriro in *Kyupora no aru machi* (*A Street of Cupolas*, 1962). Urayama's film is closer in spirit to the films of Kinoshita and Imai than to Imamura's mature works. The story follows a family whose father loses his job. The film links together an examination of poor working conditions, unfair educational opportunities, discrimination against factory workers, and discrimination against Koreans. Today the film is more notable for the presence of then-rising ingenue star Yoshinaga Sayuri (in the 1980s one of Japan's biggest stars) than for its social problem revelations. Another film which roped social problems together without a clear focus was Kumai Kei's *Chi no mure* (*The Swarming Earth*, 1970), which looked at prejudice against not only Koreans and *bura-*

kumin, but also *hibakusha*, victims of the atomic bomb blasts at Hiroshima and Nagasaki. A more direct and focused examination of the Korean problem (though it is certainly not the primary focus of the film) can be found in Teshigahara's *The Face of Another*. A point in common between the faceless hero and Japan's Koreans is well expressed by the following passage from the novel:

> I had clearly taken into consideration that the restaurant was Korean and that there would be Korean customers. Of course, I had unconsciously reckoned that even if there were still some crudeness about the mask, Koreans would probably take no notice of it, and moreover I felt it would be easier to associate with them. Or perhaps, seeking points of similarity between myself who had lost my face and Koreans who were frequently the objects of prejudice, I had without realizing it, come to have a feeling of closeness with them.[7]

This feeling of solidarity with the Koreans in Japan is extended later in the novel to include American blacks whom the protagonist sees on television rioting in U.S. streets:

> Of course, I had almost nothing in common with the Negroes, except for being an object of prejudice. The Negroes were comrades bound in the same cause, but I was quite alone. Even though the Negro question might be a grave social problem, my own case could never go beyond the limits of the personal.[8]

This recognition on the hero's part that his problem is "personal" is precisely why *The Face of Another* is an existentialist parable and not a social problem film. What is signficant, however, is that the feeling of alienation from the Japanese mainstream manifested by the hero is shared by those denied entry into the mainstream. And it is this feeling of alienation on the part of the New Wave directors that made them sensitive to the Korean problem.

Oshima Nagisa made the Korean question a particularly strong motif in his oeuvre, devoting four films to the issue. However, as something of a prelude to his focus on discrimination against Koreans in Japan, Oshima made *The Catch*. In addition to its focus on youth and the legacy of the militarist era, this story of a downed black American pilot captured by a small village, is also a tale of prejudice. Oshima is quite clear about the symbolic significance of the black soldier:

> War is never waged against people who are thought to be superior and the Second World War is, in that sense, somewhat of a continuation of the earlier Sino-Japanese war. If the American were a white man, a Japanese would feel some kind of admiration or respect, whereas physically they could detest the negro because he is physically very different and, they feel, inferior to them, whereas they subconsciously consider the white man superior.[9]

Shiiku (*The Catch*)
Oshima Nagisa, director. Kawakita/Japan Film Library Council

The black man is profoundly *other* to the villagers who come to project onto him their innermost fears or resentments. A woman whose husband is having an affair spits on the soldier; a man whose son runs away to avoid the draft claims that the airman bewitched the boy, another man whose son is killed in the war claims that his son died while the village was caring for the black man. When the black man is murdered by them, the villagers rewrite the events surrounding his death. As Ian Cameron notes, the villagers undertake a process "of adjusting the facts to get off the hook and avoid any guilt or responsibility. In microcosm we are observing the Japanese nation coming to terms—false ones—with its militarist record, wartime atrocities and eventual defeat, thus achieving a spurious peace of mind."[10] It is the very otherness of the black soldier which allows them to be so free with the facts. Oshima realizes that this same dynamic in which the discriminated subject loses his/her own integrity and becomes merely a sign applies to the Japanese treatment of Koreans.

"*Yunbogi no nikki*" ("Diary of Yunbogi Boy," 1965), the first of four films Oshima made on the Korean issue, set the militant tone for the rest of the films which followed. "Diary of Yunbogi Boy" is based on a book by Yi Yunbogi and arose out of Oshima's trip to Korea to make a television documentary, *Seishun no hi* (*A Tomb for Youth*, 1964). While in Korea, he took black-and-white photographs of poor children living in the streets of large cities. "Diary of Yunbogi Boy" focuses on one ten-year-old-boy living in poverty on the streeets of Taegu, South Korea. His story is told by Oshima's remarkable series of stills, combined with poetic narration, voice-over dialogue, and music. The narrator, using slogans, repetition, and poetic metaphor, describes Yunbogi's poverty and situates it within the context of Japan's exploitation of Korea and the hopes for rebellion and revolution. Yunbogi is the oldest of three boys and a girl, Sunna, eight years old. Their mother left them and the father is ill. Yunbogi tries to support his brothers and sister, first as a gum peddler in the streets, then as a goatherd, a shoeshine boy, and a newspaper seller. Periodically, the juvenile authorities take him, and other streets urchins, to a boys' home, the ironically named "Garden of Hope," from which they soon escape or are released. The narration informs us that there are 50,000 war orphans on the streets of Korea's cities, and the song, in English, "Sometimes I Feel Like a Motherless Child," plays on the soundtrack. Sunna tells Yunbogi that she wants to leave school to work to help support the family. Yunbogi forbids her, but she later leaves home to a future in which she will doubtless turn to prostitution.

This description of "Diary of Yunbogi Boy" may call to mind the classics of the Italian Neo-Realist cinema, especially (and perhaps obviously) *Sciuscia* (*Shoeshine*, 1946). The street existence of the young boys, innocent victims of war, the dissolution of their families under postwar economic conditions, the banding together of the youngsters, even the job of shoeshine boy and the threat of the boys' home, gives this film many points in common with De Sica's classic. But Oshima, unlike De Sica, does not blame conditions on war and social customs (such as the "Mafia code" in *Shoeshine*, which prevents informing on a friend or relative). The systematic cycle of poverty, uncaring bureaucracy, destruction of the Korean family system, and the exploitation of the young are the direct results of Japanese and U.S. imperialism. Unlike *Shoeshine*, "Diary of Yunbogi Boy" is not a call for social understanding and humanistic sympathizing. The film is a direct call to revolution. At one point in the film, Oshima shows images of the celebration of August 15, Korean Independence Day. Yunbogi reveals his admiration for Yukansan, who died in 1919, a martyr in Korea's struggle against "thirty-six years of horrid Japanese rule" according to the film. Still photographs of the massive student demonstrations against the rule of President Syngman Rhee prompts the narrator to ask, "Yunbogi, will you be throwing stones one day?" To which the narrator replies, "Yunbogi, you will be throwing stones one day!"

The film is like a protest song, a feeling aided by the use of a poetic litany recited in full or in part throughout the film. The first two lines of this seventeen-line hymn to revolution are most often repeated: "Yunbogi! You are a 10-year-old boy!/Yunbogi! You are a 10-year-old Korean boy!" This line recurs each time Yunbogi changes jobs and is heard following the direct call for revolution issued during the shots of the student demonstrations. They are heard again at film's end. These lines of the refrain not only situate Yunbogi in a dramatic context (a small boy with all those responsibilities and hardships), but, by their repetition, take on a defining, even insistent placing of Yunbogi within a revolutionary context. The narrator specifies Yunbogi not simply as a ten-year-old boy, but a ten-year-old *Korean* boy, thus historicizing him. Yunbogi is given a sense of mission which is strengthened by two more lines of the refrain, also frequently recurring. These lines compare the exploited, mistreated Koreans to red peppers and wheat: "Boiled red peppers get hotter!/Beaten wheat sprouts anew!" These lines are heard, for instance, during the images of Korean Independence Day and the student demonstrations. At the end of the film, the narrator makes Yunbogi a symbol of all the street youths, saying, "Yunbogi! You are all Korean boys/You are all looking for your mother/You are all looking for your sister" and then proclaims that "Yunbogi! You are a boiled red pepper too!/Yunbogi! You are a sheaf of beaten wheat that will sprout anew!" This overt call to revolution finalizes our image of the ten-year-old Yunbogi as a revolutionary *manque* and thus functions as a warning and a prediction by Oshima that such poverty and systematic exploitation must inevitably lead to rebellion.

Koshikei (*Death by Hanging*, 1968) might be said to show one form such rebellion might take. In the Komatsugawa Incident, Oshima found a perfect metaphor for Japan's mistreatment of Korea and of Koreans living in Japan. The seemingly senseless murder of a Japanese high school girl was seen as the inevitable culmination of the systematic prejudice, discrimination, and exploitation of ethnic Koreans living in Japan.

On one level, *Death by Hanging* is part of Oshima's exploration of the linked drives of sexuality and violence, and like *Violence at Noon* earlier and *Diary of a Shinjuku Thief* later, they are revealed to have a specifically political dimension. In this, one of his most famous and critically acclaimed films, Oshima, relying heavily on the objective facts of the Komatsugawa Incident, launches a virtual tour-de-force against Japanese attitudes toward Koreans. The film basically concerns the efforts of Japanese officialdom— the prison warden, education department chief, prosecutor, priest, doctor, and security chief—to execute the prisoner, R, for the murder of a high school girl. Sentenced to die by hanging, "the body of the condemned man, R, refuses to die." The officials are then at a loss, for R at first refuses to accept being R and hence, in their eyes, may not now be executed for R's crime. R must be re-educated to himself, re-turned into a young Korean boy who will eventually kill a Japanese girl student at Komatsugawa High. And this aspect of this highly theatricalized and stylized black comedy is crucial to Oshima's point: that R was always already predetermined to commit such a crime. *Death by Hanging*, as Dana Polan notes, "deals explicitly with the question of the social definition of the human subject. [The film] shows the definition of that subject in bourgeois thought and its contradiction by an historically open definition, one that pinpoints how each human being's identity is in great part an effect of social codings."[11] Crime is thus a matter of social, that is, political, perspective.

To demonstrate the political nature of R's crime, Oshima recreates R's life within the walls of the prison. This strategy on the film's part has many ramifications, one of which is to show an essential hypocrisy in the bureaucratic attitudes toward R's crime and the crimes of all Rs. Through the mostly comic recreations of R's childhood, we learn of R's alcoholic father, deaf mother, and his many younger brothers and sisters, living together in a small house. This view of R's youth is not necessarily to be taken literally, for although there is doubtless a core of fact to it, it also represents the clichéd image of the poor held by bourgeois Japan. In fact, R himself acknowledges this basically reductionist, stereotypical view of his circumstances when he concludes from their theatrical presentation: "There was this poor Korean from a bad family; therefore he killed a girl. Then he was condemned." This is also a brilliant autocritique of the film's basic narrative line. Oshima wants to insure that we come away from the film with more than that sentiment in mind.

As the playacting continues, this time with R taking on a role himself, the role of R, we come to learn of R's intelligence, sensitivity, and imagination. At one point, R fantasizes a family trip to the zoo in Ueno Park only to have the education officer put a stop to this inner journey as it is not part of the official record. Thus there is the constant attempt to make R conform to a model of R, as there is in the greater society to make Koreans conform to a model of Koreans, a model which predetermines their failure in Japanese society as if to confirm the official record.

The image of R and of R's crime held by the Japanese officials, whom we may call the "orthodox right," is counterbalanced in the film by the figure of R's "sister," who represents the views of the "orthodox left." In her view, R is not guilty of any crime; that the real crime belongs to the Japanese for their imperialism and treatment of Koreans in Japan. The sister's sloganeering also has the effect of distancing R from her, of reducing R to another political cliché, a cliché of the left, which makes Joan Mellen conclude that Oshima is hostile to her character.[12] While it is true that Oshima has no love of the orthodox left, R's basic sympathy with, and physical attraction to, the woman cannot be overlooked. R reveals his inner self to her as he never has before. Instead of merely seeing R's childhood imposed upon him in the playacting by the officials, we see still images from R's interior point of view, not only of these theatricalized scenes, but shots of young Korean children taken from "Diary of Yunbogi Boy" thus returning the theme of this film to Oshima's ominous warnings at the end of the 1965 short. It is at this point that "R accepts being R for the sake of all Rs." And R, while denying the right of a nation to execute an individual—if he has been wrong in killing a girl, it is wrong to kill him—and denying, too, the very concept of nation, accepts his place on the gallows. As the trapdoor beneath the noose opens, R disappears. The voice-over which began the film now concludes the film by thanking the witnesses for their participation, and thanking the film audience as well—thanking them (us) individually: "Thank you, and you, and you, and you . . . ," the famous *anata mo* which gave Stephen Heath the title of his memorable article.[13]

Death by Hanging, as we have mentioned, is based on the Komatsugawa Incident. On September 1, 1958, Li Jin Wu was arrested and accused of the murder of Ota Yoshie, a student at Komatsugawa High School. A number of sensational trials and appeals followed, attracting much attention in the press; the event climaxed on November 16, 1962, when Li, aged twenty-two, was hanged at Miyagi Prison. Between the first trial and Li's execution, much was uncovered and commentators of all political persuasions had their say. Li was born of Korean parents in Tokyo in 1940, the third child of nine. His father was a day laborer; his mother was a deaf-mute due to a childhood accident. The family lived in a number of slum neighborhoods throughout Li's childhood. What most attracted Li to the attention of Japan's political elite was the intelligence and promise he had shown as a youth. Li had been active in student governments in elementary and junior high school. Poverty prevented him from attending regular high school, but he made an attempt to secure a good secondary education by attending Komatsugawa at night. While attending school, Li sought work with major electronic companies, but was turned down because he was Korean. He was able to find work in various smaller companies but found such work unsatisfactory and inevitably left after a short time. This contributed to the impression by the courts that he was unable to hold down a job because he was "anti-social."

Li's trial began on November 15, 1958, and he was soon found guilty. The prosecution demanded the death penalty, which was handed down on February 27, 1959. In December of that year, the Tokyo High Court upheld the decision. The case was then taken to the Supreme Court, which heard the appeal beginning in April 1961; in August the appeal was denied, and in November 1962 the execution was carried out.

The defense tried to make the case that Li had been systematically denied his heritage as a Korean yet denied access to economic and social advancement because he was Korean. It was this double-bind that the defense tried to use as grounds for clemency, and it was this double-bind that intellectuals were quick to point out. To many Japanese critics of the courts, it seemed hypocritical, at least, to discriminate against someone of a different ethnic background while at the same time to expect him to act like a member of the dominant society. Japanese theatre critic Tsuno Kaitaro understands

Li's crime as "the crime of a Korean—no, rather the crime of one who had been dispossessed of his nationality at birth. His parents, along with hundreds of thousands of others had been brought to Japan during the thirty-odd years before World War II. They were stripped of their language and given new Japanized names."[14] The systematic nature of Japanese imperialism and discrimination doomed Li from birth.

The Supreme Court recognized this aspect to Li's crime, but repressed the social aspect in favor of an "environmental" one, but still somehow managed to maintain that Li was individually at fault:

> . . . [E]ven though the influence of the home environment upon the formation of the defendant's character cannot be denied, his crime derives primarily from the weakness of his own moral and ethical sense as demonstrated by his lack of a sense of personal responsibility as a member of society, by his lack of awareness of the seriousness of his crime, and by his inability to exercise independent judgement regarding his actions. It is consequently impossible to interpret as grounds for extenuation the argument that the defendant's crime was due to abnormal character formation caused by his home environment.[15]

To critics of the Japanese establishment, Li's character formation was precisely *not* "abnormal" given the systematic discrimination and prejudice meted out to Koreans. In the face of such hostility:

> Those whose identities have been irreparably damaged by society attempt to challenge that society in its totality by violating its most sacred taboos. The victim of this sort of crime is a hostage representing the entire community. The Japanese community, however, has consistently disposed of these challenges with judiciary methods and sentimentalism. Without ever asking who the criminal is, the Japanese have consistently reduced every crime to the proportions of the private individual and have dealt with it in those terms alone.[16]

While this might sound something like the "orthodox left" represented by R's sister in *Death by Hanging*, and one of the officials in the film even calculates how many Japanese would die if every Korean took this attitude, there can be no doubt that Oshima is in fundamental agreement with this statement. Oshima has consistently demonstrated that crime is a symbolic act against the state, against a set of circumstances, and against a system judged a priori to be unfair, discriminating, and hopelessly constricting.

Japanese leftists, in basic sympathy with Li and other Koreans, nevertheless recognize their own complicity in maintaining the system. Tsuno commented: "We enter into [Li's] crime but we are denied participation. We belong to the side that placed the rope around his neck; we find within ourselves 'the nation,' Japan, which called his act a crime and killed him for it."[17] In other words, Tsuno blames himself, and you, and you, and you . . .

The act of implicating his spectators in the death of Li is balanced by two of Oshima's other films which highlight the Korean question. In *Nihon shunka-ko* (*A Treatise on Japanese Bawdy Song*, 1967), a group of high school students imagine themselves in the place of Koreans dominated by Japanese imperialism. They seek revenge in a *Death by Hanging*-like merger of sex and violence. The idea of taking the place of Koreans is even more strongly on view in *Kaette kita yopparai* (*Three Resurrected Drunkards*, 1968), in which three students are mistaken for Koreans and chased by the police as illegal immigrants. The film is notorious for Oshima's strategy of starting the film all over again in the middle. Eventually we see that the events change later on, but audiences' first instinct upon seeing the film is to think that a mistake has been made in projecting (perhaps in much the same way a first viewing encourages one to think the film starts to burn in Bergman's *Persona*). This starting again is a brilliant demonstration of the political problem of "repetition." "Whereas, as Marx suggests . . . past historical understanding was mere repetition no matter how political its content, the practice of cinema *as practice* [Polan's italics], as production, can break through repetition and reification."[18] The past in this film that repeats is the past of this film, and like Marx's notion in *The Eighteenth Brumaire of Louis Bonaparte*, the second time through the events degenerate into farce.

The use of repetition in *Three Resurrected Drunkards* is similar to the use of repetition in *Death by Hanging*. R has committed a crime (before the film begins) which will be repeated in the film; the film opens with a hanging which is repeated at the end. The second time through, the repetitions in these films are farcical (as is most of *Death by Hanging* in general), intending to show the essentially *ideological* nature of the events in history in the first place. At the same time, repetitions in the films (in the case of *Three Resurrected Drunkards*, the repetition *of* the film) is intended to show the essentially ideological nature of the cinematic institution. Noel Burch insists that *Death by Hanging* is

perhaps the first Japanese film which makes explicit the affinities between the national cinema's chief historical tendencies and a Marxist concept of a *reflexively critical representation*, first given theoretical form by Brecht and now, in the West and in Japan, central to the issue of the relationship of the performing arts to the class struggle.[19]

What should be noted is that it is precisely in *Death by Hanging* (as well as *Three Resurrected Drunkards*, made in the same year) that the most evidently Brechtian use of film form occurs, that is, precisely in those films with an overt political *content*, a content derived from the Korean question, a question of class and ethnic struggle within the culture at large.

What we have been calling the Korean problem and the continued discrimination against the *burakumin* do not qualify as necessarily major concerns of the New Wave. But if we link the documentary films of Ogawa Shinsuke and Tsuchimoto Noriaki to the group of primarily fiction filmmakers, the concept of prejudice and discrimination can be extended to a wider scope of issues. In this I take my lead from Sato Tadao who calls Ogawa and Tsuchimoto "cinematic guerrillas [who] drew attention to the existence of alienated minorites by independently producing and showing documentaries of their struggles."[20]

The films of Ogawa and Tsuchimoto (for whom Ogawa has acted as producer and mentor) mirror in their development those concerns which define the New Wave: a focus on youth, alienation and the quest for Japanese identity, women, and the problem of prejudice. For Ogawa and Tsuchimoto, the oppressed people are the weak people, people who are pressured by the state and by the culture at large. Ogawa and Tsuchimoto explicitly side with, and feel a part of, the weak.

Ogawa's first film, *"Seinen no umi"* ("Sea of Youth," 1966), concerns four correspondence students trying to earn a college degree. This inaugurates Ogawa's concern with youth and with discrimination. The film (about thirty minutes long) begins with shots of the students (three men and a woman) picketing and carrying signs. This is intercut with shots of uniformed college students playing football. The crosscutting has the effect of comparing the plight of the correspondence students, who have turned to activism out of necessity, to their classmates who have time for fun and games. Through voice-over narration (a common technique in Ogawa's films) we learn that there are 60,000 young people who attend Japanese colleges as correspondence students. Most of their number are working-class kids who hold down full-time jobs. These students are, of course, required to have the same number of credit hours for graduation as all other students. The issue at hand is the government's attempt to enforce a time limit in which those credit hours may be earned. Such a constraint would make earning a degree virtually impossible given the correspondence students' circumstances. To fight this proposed legislation, these four students have formed a committee to organize a protest campaign. This strategy upsets some of the faculty who discuss abandoning the entire correspondence system, and it alienates many of the full-time students who refuse to march in support of their part-time classmates. The correspondence students, despite this hostility, continue the struggle. "Sea of Youth" overtly supports the correspondence students in their cause and thus gives voice to a near-voiceless, powerless minority.

Ogawa is equally partisan in his next film, *Assatsu no mori* (*Forest of Pressure*, 1967; aka *The Oppressed Students*). The subject of this film is the massive student protests at Takaseki University. Japan at this time was experiencing waves of student demonstrations across the country, but most of the media attention was given to events at the more prestigous universities, such as Todai (Tokyo University), Kyodai (Kyoto University) and Waseda. Ogawa is thus giving voice to a group of students not only oppressed by their own administration but also also by the media who implicitly relegate these students of a less prestigious college to a second-class status.

The protests began in the university over outrage at the admission of unqualified or underqualified students. Middle- and working-class students were upset by the preferential treatment accorded to the sons of industrial or political leaders. The highly competitive entrance exams to all colleges, and the relatively few high school graduates who attend four-year colleges and universities, make admission to any school a significant achievement. Thus the understandable outrage at admissions based on political or economic favoritism. The protests blossomed into a nearly full-fledged revolt against the school authorities who, in typical administration shortsightedness, felt a crackdown on students was better than negotiation. The bulk of *Forest of Pressure* revolves around the radical students' efforts to form an independent community in Student Hall. The students inside the dormitory attempt to declare their facility off limits to faculty and administration. The police are eventually called in and many of the students evacuate the hall. But a large group remains inside, behind barricades.

Ogawa shows the types of pressure brought to bear against these student protestors. Not only does the campus administration try to force them out, but the students' parents also try to talk them out of their protest. As in "Sea of Youth," we also see fellow students reject the central figures. Ogawa attempts to put the protests at Takaseki into the larger context of the burgeoning student movements of the middle '60s. Ogawa also shows demonstrations at Sunagawa Air Base against the Japanese Self Defense Force, for instance.

Ogawa spent a year making *Forest of Pressure* and it became, perhaps unsurprisingly, a big hit among Japanese students in the '60s. Of course, this film, like most of the works of Ogawa and Tsuchimoto, is denied commercial distribution, not out of overt political maneuverings necessarily, but within the same industrial context that keeps documentaries out of American theatres. In fact, as we will see later, the distribution/exhibition of Ogawa's and Tsuchimoto's films must be taken into consideration in an understanding of the radical nature of their work.

After completing *Forest of Pressure*, Ogawa continued his focus on the student protest movement with *Gennin hokokusho* (*Eyewitness Report—The Chronicle of the Haneda Struggle*, 1967; aka *Report from Haneda*). Joan Mellen describes this film as a "news-style documentary dealing with the confrontation between students and riot police on the occasion of then Premier

Eisaku Sato's visit to the United States."[21] Haneda was the site of a large Anti-Security Treaty Protest in 1960; in November 1967, helmeted students armed with staves and rocks clashed with police as they tried to prevent Sato's departure for South Vietnam on a trip which would eventually take him to the U.S. There was one fatality among the protestors, six hundred injuries, and fifty-eight arrests.[22] The police and the government tried to blame the protestor's death on the riot itself, but Ogawa, through footage he had shot, demonstrated convincingly that the police overreacted to the situation. Ogawa's interest in the student riot at Haneda may be seen as a natural progression to an interest in the burgeoning protest movements against the building of a new airport at Narita. And just as the massive activities against Narita would make the Haneda Incident pale in comparison, so too Ogawa's film record of the affair would make an exponential leap of scope and commitment.

Haneda Airport, for years the only air thoroughfare in and out of Tokyo, was proving woefully inadequate for the city's, and the country's, needs by the middle of the 1960s. The government determined that the only solution was to build a new airport. For reasons that are still obscure, a site more than an hour's automobile travel from Tokyo was selected. The area near Narita in the village of Sanrizuka was prime farmland, owned in alleged perpetuity according to land-reform decrees in the immediate postwar period. The attempt by the national government to force the farm families to sell their land struck a raw nerve not only among the peasants themselves, but among a number of ever-increasingly militant groups. Apter and Sawa note that "to one degree or another Sanrizuka became important for all the militant groups who had mobilized for Ampo 1960. In Sanrizuka the state (or its surrogate, the airport) could be attacked directly, and the principle of class struggle against imperialism could be raised. Forming a coalition of workers and peasants against the state became the first objective."[23] This seemingly Marxist-oriented alliance was transcended when the building of the massive airport conjoined with the anti-pollution and anti-nuclear movements. The government was then further confronted with the Hiroshima Peace Marchers, the Minamata Group, and various factions of the New Left, including the Zenkyoto (*Zenkoku kyoto kaigi*, the All-Student Joint Struggle Conference, which "evolved out of the university struggle of 1968–9"[24]), and Beheiren (Citizens League for Peace in Vietnam). This last-mentioned group typifies the interrelationship of all the groups in Sanrizuka; how anti-pollution, anti-nuclear, anti-war, and farming groups see themselves as oppressed by the ruling government. Apter and Sawa note that Beheiren was

a citizen protest movement organized specifically to oppose the Vietnam war. . . . The airport at Sanrizuka was considered by Beheiren to be an extension of U.S. military needs because of the war. . . . Beheiren, originally formed out of the "silent majority" groups organized more or less spontaneously at the time of the Ampo Diet demonstrations in 1960, first really asserted itself as an organization independent of all political groups in 1965. Its first demonstration was a protest march over the February bombing of North Vietnam. Among its original members were several figures important in the Ampo demonstrations [including] Shinoda Masahiro. . . . [25]

That Ogawa would be attracted to the protest movement at Sanrizuka, combining as it did a variety of groups who opposed oppression, was inevitable.

Out of the protests at Sanrizuka, which still go on into the '80s to oppose further planned expansion, Ogawa produced an almost unprecedented series of films. From 1968 to 1973, Ogawa and his small crew committed themselves completely to documenting the complex protests, demonstrations, and shifting strategies undertaken by the peasants and their supporters to prevent the building of the airport. What Noel Burch has called "one long 'work in progress' "[26] is a group of films known collectively as the "Sanrizuka series." The series consists of *Nihon kaiho sensen—Sanrizuka* (*Japan Liberation Front—Summer in Sanrizuka*, 1968, and *Winter in Sanrizuka*, 1970); *Daisanji kyosei sokuryo soshi toso* (*The Third Struggle against Forced Surveying*, 1970; aka *The Three-Day War in Narita*); *Daini toride no hitobito* (*Peasants of the Second Fortress*, 1971); *Iwayama ni tetsuto ga dekita* (*The Building of Iwayama Tower*, 1972); and *Heta buraku* (*Heta Village*, 1973). This series is much too complex to discuss in this context. The films pose numerous problems for non-Japanese viewers, although David Apter's comment that "it probably won't appeal to American audiences since there are long mystifying silences and slow periods,"[27] smacks a bit too much of reverse cultural elitism. Even Noel Burch, however, is forced to call the first film, at least, "a rather indigestible assemblage . . . with an over-emphasis on the spectacular student battles with the police."[28] Ogawa's strategy of providing little background information in favor of the process of the protests forces one's attention away from the objective facts and onto what Burch calls the "material" behavior and discourse of the main protagonists. As in his earlier films, Ogawa is unabashedly on the side of his subjects so that he literally allows them to speak for themselves.

In making the Sanrizuka series, Ogawa began to develop a sense of how revolution in Japan may spring out of traditional roots, which gives him much in common with Imamura, that other poet of the peasants. Through the Sanrizuka protests Ogawa became intimately familiar with the life of rural Japan and came to believe that modern Japan's essential roots lie in its agricultural areas. Ogawa points out that in the Meiji era most Japanese were farmers; today, less than 20 percent of the population is employed in farm labor. This is only one of the changes with which contemporary Japan has had to deal. Ogawa states that in the 1940s and '50s farmers never would have dreamed that their land could be sold. Yet, by the 1960s, the sale of farmland was a relatively common occurrence. By the time of the Sanrizuka protests, Ogawa felt it was most interesting to learn why some farmers would *not* sell. The relationship Ogawa discovered between peasant and land provided him with his first glimpse of the *religious* nature of the farmers' lives. To the urban dweller, land equals real estate; to the farmer, land means soil, the soil in which things grow. What also grows out of the soil, besides rice (the essence of Japanese farming), is the family and the village.[29] And out of such roots can come revolution, revolution in a Japanese context.

Before embarking on his most radical course of action as a filmmaker, Ogawa made another film focusing on forgotten and weak people in today's Japan, *Dokkoi ningen bushi* (*A Song of Common Humanity*, 1974). The film features conversations with a group of day laborers who work the Yokohama docks. This film recalls, thematically at least, another social problem film by Imai Tadashi, *Dokkoi ikiteiru* (*And Yet We Live*, 1951). Imai's film shows the influence of Italian Neo-Realism in both its film style and its leftist slant.[30] Ogawa's film, on the contrary, is typically New Wave with its indirect method of giving factual information and the long-takes which preserve the integrity of each scene and show the filmmaker's willingness to let events and characters appear both before and after any dramatic moments which may (or may not) occur. Unfortunately, the lack of contextualizing within the film (the lack of factual information about the characters) makes the long, rambling monologues by these mostly sickly, alcoholic, alienated workers sometimes tedious to watch. The film primarily consists of the workers' direct address to the camera, usually in response to questions from Ogawa (offscreen), but the heavily accented Japanese, which necessitated the use of subtitles *in Japanese*, makes the film a quite specialized process. Ogawa's intention was once again to give voice to a voiceless minority by allowing them to speak for themselves, but it is difficult to say how many of us are equipped to listen.

Before turning to Ogawa's crowning achievement as a political documentary filmmaker, we should discuss some of the films of Ogawa's colleague, Tsuchimoto Noriaki. Tsuchimoto's films have much in common with his mentor's, beginning with his first effort, produced under Ogawa's production banner, *Paruchizan zenshi* (*Pre-history of the Partisan Party*, 1969). This film is perhaps the best documentary made anywhere about the student protests of the '60s. Tsuchimoto was the only filmmaker or journalist allowed to witness the secret workings of an ultra-radical splinter group at prestigious Kyoto University (alma mater of Oshima Nagisa). As Ogawa had done in making *Forest of Pressure*, Tsuchimoto virtually lived with his subjects during the course of the filming. Tsuchimoto, however, emerges as more evenhanded than Ogawa toward his subjects, more dispassionate as a filmmaker. This is probably a function of the Partisan group's overt desire for direct, violent confrontation with the authorities. While Tsuchimoto himself does not necessarily share his subjects' views on the efficacy of violence, he does convey the honesty and intensity of the group members themselves. This is seen most compellingly in a Flaherty-like sequence in which one of the radicals painstakingly makes a number of Molotov cocktails. This sequence, perhaps understandably enough, was excised by the Italian censors when the film was shown at the Venice Film Festival in 1970 (to my knowledge the only European showing of the film; it has never been seen in the U.S.).

Pre-history of the Partisan Party (its title an index that the students would later form a group outside of the university), mainly gives glimpses into what might be called the "dailiness" of revolutionary activity in the '60s. The endless meetings to discuss ideology and strategy, the preparations for demonstrations, the building of barricades, and so on, all build to a dramatic climax at the major demonstration. (The relatively small number of Partisans-to-be prevented their achieving any great destructive ends.) This group of ultra-radicals has been influenced by Lenin and Mao with a touch of Rosa Luxemburg added in, and they are in opposition to the more "traditional" Communist groups and they also conflict with the methods and ideology of the anti-Communist Zengakuren activists. While this does tend to make things a little confusing, as the various groups compete for media attention, it perfectly captures the student activities. The film is even more fascinating considering the posthistory of the film's subjects. Professor Takita, the Marxist Economics professor who was the ideological mentor of the group, went underground for ten years until he was arrested and sentenced to prison for two years. One student was later jailed under the conspiracy laws aimed at curbing student demonstrations. Another of the Partisans, who quotes Franz Fanon during an on-camera interview, is today in the Middle East (allegedly), while another member was killed during his participation in an airline hijacking in Kuala Lumpur.[31]

Tsuchimoto's major achievement thus far, for which he is justifiably internationally acclaimed, is his heartrending documentary *Minamata: kanja-sans to sono sekai* (*Minamata: The Victims and Their World*, 1972). Tsuchimoto in fact dedicated a good deal of his life to exploring and exposing the deadly pollution of mercury spilled into the waters of Minamata Bay. He has produced a lengthy series of medical films and a medical textbook on Minamata Disease, as well as a number of shorter films on the victims' protests. He has been actively involved in exposing similar cases of industrial-environmental pollution in other parts of the world. Minamata for Tsuchimoto, like Sanrizuka for Ogawa, became not simply the subject for an impressive series of films, but a cause to which the filmmaker became completely and utterly dedicated. As Burch notes in passing, the work of both filmmakers stands as "good examples of an attack on the notion of films as separate entities. . . ."[32]

Minamata Disease is not, strictly speaking, a disease but rather a poisoning caused by man-made environmental pollution. The origin of Minamata Disease stands as one of the most tragic instances of ecological near-disaster brought about by uncontrolled dumping of industrial waste. The Japanese maintain a precarious balance with nature in terms of the fishing waters off its coasts and its relatively small amount of arable land compared to its massive population. These practical considerations have also given rise to certain aesthetic considerations—the well-known poetic sense the Japanese have toward their natural surroundings. The concept of pollution, therefore, has quite deep reverberations throughout the national psyche, especially when the results of such pollution can be so clearly and tragically seen as in Minamata.

Minamata Disease was discovered in 1956 and its causes proven in 1959. Minamata Bay, located in the Shiranui Sea off the coast of Kyushu, provided the major source of food and revenue for the villagers of Kogoshima and Kumamoto prefectures. Another source of revenue was the Chisso Chemical Corporation's Minamata factory, which began production of acetaldehyde in 1932. No one thought much about the drainage channel of the factory which led into the northeast depth of Minamata Bay; at least not until 1952–53 when, first, fish floated on the surface of the sea, shellfish frequently perished, and sea birds began dropping out of the sky. Then, when cats (mostly, but some dogs and pigs, too) began to go mad and die, things looked more serious. The villagers called this syndrome which struck their cats "dancing disease" as the animals would stagger about as if drunk, go into convulsions, whirl about in violent circles, and then die. According to residents, so many cats died in this way that there were virtually none to be found in Minamata by 1958.

In April 1956, a six-year-old girl was taken to the pediatrics department of the factory hospital with severe brain damage symptoms. Within a few weeks it was discovered that her younger sister and members of a neighboring family had similar symptoms. Soon after, some thirty more cases were discovered. The Minamata Disease Research Group of Kumamoto University Medical School was formed. Almost immediately, they found a causal connection between the eating of fish and shellfish caught in the bay and the disease. At that time it was felt that until the precise cause of the poisoning could be isolated, the government should ban fishing and temporarily halt production at Chisso's factory. Neither measure was taken.

At the end of 1958, the researchers began to suspect that the specific culprit was methyl-mercury. Cats fed methyl-mercury by itself developed the same symptoms as cats with Minamata Disease, cats which had been fed fish caught in the bay. Fish and shellfish caught in the bay showed high concentrations of mercury and the internal organs of people who had died of Minamata Disease were similarly polluted. Chisso, however, maintained that it was *organic* mercury which caused the poisoning and that their chemical wastes included only inorganic mercury. Therefore, they could not be the source of poisoning. At the time the mercury theory was made public, Chisso refused the research group access to its waste water. However, in 1962, a researcher using water left over from earlier experiments, demonstrated that in the process of making acetaldehyde, the inorganic mercury used as a catalyst is methylated (i.e., turned into organic mercury). It was now clear that the dumping of waste water into the bay polluted the seaweed with methyl-mercury, thus starting a chain of methyl-mercury poisoning spreading from the seaweed, to the fish, the shellfish, and the residents. The ecological nightmare took an even more grim turn when it was discovered that Minamata Disease could be present in newborns. The researchers were now confronted with congenital (fetal) Minamata Disease.

All of these facts are revealed in Tsuchimoto's documentary. But there is a more human side to the disease. We learn that in the '50s and '60s, many sufferers of Minamata Disease were shunned. At first it was thought that the disease was communicable via casual contact. Women stricken with the disease were abandoned by their husbands, sent back to their families in disgrace, and those already stricken with the disease could certainly not expect to find a marriage partner, except perhaps, among those already stricken (although this would only apply to those with a mild case of the poisoning). There is much in the dynamics of these responses that compares to the *burakumin* issue. Even when Minamata Disease was demonstrated to be incommunicable and its cause clearly isolated, victims still found themselves shunned. This shunning of the innocent victims is also reminiscent of the reactions to *hibakusha*, radiation victims of Hiroshima and Nagasaki. Such persons are a stigma; in the case of the Hiroshima and Nagasaki a reminder of the ignominy of having been attacked with nuclear weapons, in the case of Minamata of having been poisoned by Japan's industrial might.

Minamata: The Victims and Their World can be divided into three parts. The first section presents the facts concerning the isolation of Minamata Disease by the medical research group and the efforts to discover a cure. (There is none.) The second part finds Tsuchimoto examining the lives of many victims of the poisoning, concentrating for the most part on the children stricken by congenital Minamata Disease. The symptoms of these children include cortical damage to the cerebellum and damage to the peripheral nerves causing many cases of mental retardation, loss of muscle control resembling symptoms of muscular dystrophy or cerebral palsy, blindness, deafness, and personality disorders. Many of the children are cared for in hospital wards, a few of the victims live with their families. One young boy who lives with his parents showed a charming and delightful personality, philosophically answering questions posed by the offscreen filmmakers. When the boy suddenly becomes tired and depressed, he kindly but forcefully asks the camera crew to leave.[33] Memorable, too, is the young boy who is deaf, dumb, and blind, but who loves the *feel* of music, the vibrations as they come through two large stereo speakers that his poor family has bought for him to give him some sort of human pleasure.

The third section of the film details the victims' confrontation with the board members of the Chisso company at their stockholders meeting. The question of compensation for the victims and the villagers is argued, but what strikes the Western viewer most is the issue raised about responsibility. Here the most memorable moment is when an angry middle-aged woman asks the head of the company if he or his executives would be willing to die as an expression of their guilt and atonement. While obviously such a death would be symbolic, it is precisely the symbolic acknowledgment of company guilt that many sought, perhaps in addition to substantial monetary payments, perhaps even in substitution for such payments. The confrontation between the victims and the company executives responsible for their plight provides a fitting climax to this story of corporate insensitivity and ecological disaster.

The protests of the victims might strike the Western viewer as the most natural and appropriate action to take. Compensation from the chemical company which dumped the waste into the bay and from the government which refused to intervene when the immediate cause of the poisoning was isolated should reasonably be expected from the victims and their families. But as Joan Mellen aptly points out, protesting against the company and/or the government (one and the same in the eyes of the more radical activists) is not an easy action in the face of Japanese tradition which makes questioning one's "superiors" an almost unthinkable proposition.[34] It is this aspect of citizen protest against the establishment which links Minamata with Sanrizuka—the idea of ordinary people, the descendents of the Japanese peasant, actively confronting their rulers. The roots of rebellion spring forth from the seat of the most ancient social structures: the family and the village.

There were other filmmakers in the late '60s and early '70s independently producing a variety of documentaries on the student struggles and other issues, such as the increasing militarization of Okinawa. But no other filmmakers matched the dedication and commitment of Ogawa and Tsuchimoto. Of the two, Burch feels "Ogawa's enterprise is no doubt the more theoretically and aesthetically important, while Tsuchimoto's films are no doubt more relevant to the actualities of class struggle in Japan."[35] One is inclined to agree with Burch (without necessarily possessing his certainty), especially given Ogawa's activities since the end of the New Wave in which he, more than any other filmmaker in the world perhaps, has tried to change the terms of filmmaking.

In a screening of *Heta Village* in 1973 before a farming community in

Kaminoyama in rural, mountainous Yamagata prefecture, Ogawa and his company were taught a valuable lesson. The farmers confronted Ogawa's crew with its failure to express properly the realities of farming life. While Ogawa had certainly captured the heated battles between peasants and police, his insights into farm life were superficial. The farmers told Ogawa that the only way to understand farm life was to experience it, and they offered Ogawa a field and farmhouse for his use. Amidst some trepidation, as the field was located at the foot of the Zao Mountain range (notable for its very cold winters), Ogawa accepted the offer. The issue for Ogawa soon became less one of film theory and more one of basic survival.

Ogawa's philosophy of filmmaking had always been that "documentary films get below the surface to the truth: through living with the villagers we learn what they suffer. What is hard and what is sad for them."[36] In 1974, Ogawa and his film production company set up a communal farm on 2400 square meters of rice paddies at Magino in Kaminoyama. At first they determined to experiment with rice growing; Filmmaking was temporarily abandoned in favor of the scientific study of rice. One reason for this attitude was practical: to become self-sufficient. But something happened during the first three years of their rice farming. While making scientific charts and performing experiments with soil, Ogawa gradually came to understand the deep relationship with the land that he perceived in the peasants at Sanrizuka. Ogawa came to believe that rice is not merely a grain, but the link to the hundreds of years of Japanese history.

In 1980, after six years of successful farming, Ogawa's communal company experienced a great amount of crop damage due to an unseasonably cold summer. This inspired them to undertake further scientific experiments devoted to understanding the affects of temperature changes on the rice crop. To do this, they chose a mountainous village resting some four hundred meters above sea level on the west side of Mt. Funahiki in the Zao range. Their initial intention was to chart the village's geographical features using topographical models and then to determine how the weather patterns affected the rice. However, the village and the villagers themselves soon came to occupy Ogawa's emotional interest. For here was a village suffering from the inevitable changes of time. Over the last decade the population had fallen from eighteen households to seven; only the elders remained. Ogawa saw in this village a microcosm of twentieth-century Japan.

Nippon-koku: Furuyashiki-mura (*A Japanese Village: Furuyashiki-mura*, 1982) is Ogawa's 210-minute tribute to the village, the villagers, and the continuity of life in rural Japan. The film is divided into three sections: "Rice," "Village Life," and "World War II." The structure of the film matches the evolution of Ogawa's involvement: First, he was concerned with rice growing; then, with the village; then, as he got to know the people, with their memories and feelings about their lives.

The "Rice" section of *Furuyashiki-mura* is one-hour long and is a painstaking recreation of Ogawa's scientific experiments involving climate, temperature, soil, and their effects on the rice crop. From an analysis of the weather above ground, and a discussion of the minerals below ground, Ogawa turns to details of life on the surface. In "Village Life," the villagers recall the old days. One woman, now past seventy, remembers finding a fossil high on the mountain trail when she was a young girl. The woman also reminisces about the brigade of women firefighters who protected the village when the men went to work in the mountains. An elderly man talks about his dream of seeing a road constructed which would connect Furuyashiki with the larger village of Kaminoyama, a road which would help bring about modernization. Instead, the road, when built, merely provided young villagers with easy access away from home. In this middle section, Ogawa compares the epochal transitions of nature (terrain, weather, soil—the fossil the woman found indicates that this mountain range was once below sea level) with the more fleeting lives of men. The movement from "Rice" to "Village Life" is a movement from the general to the particular, and from the timeless to the transitory.

This movement is mirrored in the change from "Village Life" to "World War II." This last section details a most specific period of village life, the most transitory. The impact of World War II, the deaths of many village men, for instance, and the changes wrought since the war, brings forth from the villagers a profound sense of ambivalence, which Ogawa shares. However, instead of allowing the film audience to experience this ambivalence in the form of *mono no aware*, Ogawa wants to show how this village, these villagers, have been forgotten about, abandoned by the state like the correspondence students in "Sea of Youth." Ogawa has found the similarity between protesting students and ordinary rural dwellers, has found a way to demonstrate how the state manages to wield power by picking on small groups, segregating them and thereby oppressing them. Students protesting against discrimination and against war, peasants protesting against their land being taken away from them, or ordinary villagers caught in the gap between the traditional and the modern all have something in common: voicelessness. Ogawa has given voice to them.

Ogawa not only opposes the state in its efforts to oppress voiceless minorities, he opposes the de facto existence of an oppressing class in the film world. Joan Mellen has pointed out that the films of Ogawa, Tsuchimoto, and other radical documentarists have never been released commercially. These filmmakers "must personally show [their] films before community organizations or student groups and at union meetings. The political act of showing films thus completes the political impulse from which they were originally made."[37] Indeed, it was one such showing in a farming community, as we have seen, which inspired Ogawa to become a farmer himself to better understand farming life.

We can compare Ogawa's sentiments vis-à-vis film production and exhibition with those expressed by the organizers of the *États Généraux du Cinéma Français* (EGC) in 1968. The EGC aimed at revolutionizing the French film industry as well as the "production and consumption" of films by attempting to break down the barriers between film "producers" and film "consumers." The idealists of the EGC felt that films should be shown in "factories and firms, schools and universities, youth clubs and cultural centers, ships, trains, aeroplanes and other means of transport, and mobile projection units created in suburban and country areas." Sylvia Harvey uncovers the revolutionary impulse behind this search for non-traditional projection sites, saying that it represents "the desire to produce a new kind of context for the reception of a particular film, and thereby also a new sort of relationship between audience and spectacle."[38]

Ogawa Shinsuke, finding that commercial sources were typically denied him, traveled about Japan with *Furuyashiki-mura*, showing it in precisely the kinds of locations remarked upon by the EGC. But Ogawa discovered something else, something even more revolutionary—he found "that a film can be stopped in the middle or shown again and again. We can be present to talk about it after the showing, or even stop it in the middle to talk." So much contemporary film theory seems devoted to proving a so-called "psychoanalytic" model of film based around film's inviolable unreeling and its relationship to dream states and "the imaginary." But Ogawa completely denies that films must be presented in any such fashion. Ogawa says simply, "Filmmaking does not stop when you stop the camera."[39] Political filmmaking extends beyond the detailing of politically charged subject matter and beyond, too, the concept of politically progressive form. Political filmmaking extends to the circumstances involved in researching a film, in getting to know one's subject. It extends to showing the film, to defending it in person as a part of the film. Political filmmaking, in essence, extends to one's life.

The overt social problem film as we have discussed it here, does not occupy a necessarily major place within the New Wave movement. In their attempts to engage the entirety of Japanese culture, the New Wave filmmakers sought for more global concerns, sought to elucidate the "gaps" in Japanese society as it affected major segments of the population, the young and women, primarily. (Koreans, although severely discriminated against, comprised only .5 percent of the total population in the late '60s.) Most interesting about many of the social problem films is that they are documentaries. Even Oshima's *Death by Hanging* functions partly as a "docudrama" based as it is on an actual incident. Moreover, the film begins as a documentary on prison executions. Burch: "the absence of people, the editing and off-screen narration of [the] opening, mark it first as 'neutral documentary' *on* capital punishment. . . ."[40] It is almost as if, in the face of such real problems in the culture at large, filmmakers eschewed fictionalizing in favor of the real thing.

Of course, the notion of "the real thing" is fraught with theoretical peril. And even if one could claim an intentional objectivity on the part of some documentary filmmakers, the films of Imamura, Ogawa, and Tsuchimoto are clearly partisan efforts. This is to say that the documentary films are overtly political and stand as committed works of film art in much the same way as the politically oriented fiction films of the New Wave. In fact, with the anti-commercial nature of these films and their situation outside the mainstream of film distribution, these documentary films occupy a more overtly oppositional role. The turn to independent production by Yoshida, Shinoda, and Oshima, for instance, is carried much further by Ogawa and Tsuchimoto who, unlike their fiction-film counterparts, stand resolutely outside the traditional exhibition circuits. In the case of the documentary filmmakers, this turns out to be an ironic match between subject and medium—films about weak and oppressed groups outside the Japanese mainstream are themselves powerless to gain acceptance.

CHAPTER SIX

Shinjuku Thieves

Near the end of *To the Distant Observer*, Noel Burch makes the claim that the "distribution and amplification of the *theatrical sign* . . . is an essential dimension of the modern Japanese cinema."[1] According to Jindrich Honzl the theatre's unique aesthetic dimension derives from the possibility that elements which make up the theatre (sets, props, actors, etc.) may transfer functions. Dominant cinema may not tolerate such "theatrical signs," except in special instances (the musical is given as an example of a special instance).[2] The Japanese New Wave cinema makes a radical break from dominant cinema (though not from Japanese cinema) in its use of the theatrical sign. It will be the work of this chapter to demonstrate the various uses of the theatre, and of the theatrical sign, in the New Wave cinema in an attempt to understand not only the project of the New Wave in general, but its divergence from mainstream Japanese aesthetics in particular; and how the New Wave sets off the cinema *against* the traditional theatre in an effort to highlight aspects of the traditional culture.

It is a commonplace in criticism of the Japanese cinema, in English as well as in Japanese, to discuss the links between Japanese film and theatre. In many respects, such links are crucial. They range from overt adaptations of classic plays in the Kabuki and Bunraku (puppet) canon, such as the numerous versions of *Chushingura* (*The Loyal Forty-Seven Ronin*), to the use of certain overt techniques, such as the use of Noh theatre in Kurosawa's *Kumonosu-jo* (*Throne of Blood*, 1957), to basic aesthetic similarities between the two modes which, when defined by Burch, for instance, underwrite his project in *To the Distant Observer*. However, in too many instances, the differences between film and theatre are effaced, which has the effect of "flattening out" the cinema, of denying it any integrity, especially a potential political integrity. In seeking to make *traditional* Japanese theatre *already* radical (by Western standards), a radical film practice can merely be an extension of the already given. If we wish to claim here a particular relationship between the New Wave cinema and Japanese theatre, we must allow the New Wave directors their attempts to radicalize (or re-radicalize) their own traditions. Burch has tried to make this claim, as we noted in Chapter 1, but in fact radicalism was not achieved by merely extending the traditional practices, but by trying to break with it, by trying to re-position it within a completely new context.

The New Wave filmmakers responded to their situation as postwar, post-humanist, alienated artists by attempting a thematic and technical assault on previous film practice in an attempt to reveal and overthrow the retro-grade tendencies of Japanese culture. They souqht themes and techniques which would uncover and condemn the materialistic, anti-individualistic, corrupt, hypocritical values becoming more and more firmly entrenched as the '60s wore on. They were not alone in their struggle on the aesthetic front. A remarkable New Wave of Japanese theatre directors and writers arose who were contemporary with the New Wave, tangential to it, and often in direct cooperation with it. The New Wave they inaugurated in the theatre has been termed the "post-Shingeki theatre" and has links to the worldwide avant-garde radical experimental theatre which became preva-lent in the '60s. "Post-Shingeki" is to be understood in two connected ways: It is a theatrical movement which arose out of Shingeki, the Western-derived modern theatre meant to break away from *Shimpa* and Kabuki; and it is a movement which is a response to Shingeki. Shingeki attempted a movement away from the traditional past represented by Kabuki, the most popular of the institutionalized "official" theatres of Japan. Shingeki was a product of modernization and modernism, but to the playwrights of the post-Shingeki movement, it had itself become institutionalized and thus incapable of launching a critique against the dominant culture.

One's attention is drawn to a comparison between the New Wave film-makers and the post-Shingeki playwrights for a number of reasons. In Chapter 1, we compared the Shingeki theatre to the postwar modern/psy-chological cinema, equating the two as subscribing to the same dominant paradigm. In a sense, then, the filmmakers and playwrights of these New Wave movements were rebelling against the same mode of thought. More-over, the origins of the post-Shingeki theatre are attributable to the same historical moment as the New Wave cinema: 1960. Not only did many younger playwrights, directors, and actors reject an alliance with the U.S. in terms of its imperialist policies in Asia, but they rejected, too, the Old Left, old-guard Japan Communist party (JCP). David G. Goodman, an authority on the post-Shingeki theatre whose writings and translations will be relied upon strongly in this chapter, explains the origins of the post-Shingeki movement:

Suzuki Tadashi, an important figure in the post-Shingeki movement who was a st dent at Waseda University at the time, has summarized the younger generation's perspective on the Security Treaty issue. According to Suzuki, the national debate over the 1960 renewal . . . concerned whether or not Japan should ally itself with the West by continuing to allow U.S. military bases on Japanese soil. From the younger generation's point of view, the alternative posed by the Old Left, principally the Japanese Comnunist Party (JCP), merely substituted an alliance with the Soviet Union for the existing relationship with the West. The young activists found the prospect of an alliance with the Soviet Bloc at least as repugnant as the alliance with the West. . . .[3]

Leftist theatre groups rallied around the Anti-Security Treaty cause and here, too, dissatisfaction with the Old Left arose. Kanze Hideo, "the rebellious scion of an important family of Noh actors," traces the origins of the Youth Art Theatre (*Seigei—Seinen geijutsu gekijo*), which had allied itself with Zengakuren against the JCP, to the dissatisfactions of young activists who were initially part of the Conference of Modern Theatre Artists (*Shingeki-jin kaigi*) formed to participate in the demonstrations. Kanze believes these youngsters "were frustrated because of the way the demonstrations were being organized and conducted by the old guard. As soon as things started getting serious, we were always told to disperse and go home."[4]

The cross-fertilization between the New Wave cinema and theatre also draws our attention to the two movements. The dominant post-Shingeki playwrights appear to be Satoh Makoto, Kara Juro, and Terayama Shuji. Kara appeared in Wakamatsu's *Violated Women in White* and (as himself) in Oshima's *Diary of a Shinjuku Thief*; Terayama was, as noted earlier, the screenwriter on a number of Shinoda Masahiro's early films, as well as the writer of *Buraikan* (1970) and Hani Susumu's *Hatsukoi jigokuhen* (*The Inferno of First Love*, 1968). Terayama himself became a film director who,although he shared many of the themes of the New Wave directors, approached cinema almost strictly as a non-commercial, avant-garde filmmaker. And as we will see shortly, New Wave filmmakers and playwrights were drawn to the same images, situations, and historical figures.

Unlike the New Wave film directors, the post-Shingeki playwrights could situate themselves in a long tradition of Japanese theatre. They had the past, not only of Shingeki, a twentieth-century theatrical movement, but also the preceding hundreds of years of Noh, Kabuki, and Bunraku, not to mention the roots of these theatres in religious rituals and court dances, and in the chanted narratives sung by traveling entertainers. College-educated like their New Wave film counterparts (but a bit younger), they were exposed to a long tradition, as well, of serious theatrical criticism drawn from Japanese and Western sources. While a number of New Wave directors, such as Imamura and Shinoda, were theatre majors in university, there was no such thing as a program of Cinema Studies. The post-Shingeki playwrights could position themselves within an ongoing discourse about theatre and its relationship to culture, and could utilize and demonstrate an awareness of their movement within this context.

In rejecting Shingeki, the post-Shingeki theatre rejected realism as a theatrical mode, and the ideology which underlies it. To the younger generation of theatre people," 'realism' was not simply one style of theatre among many but a pernicious and exclusive ideology that actively sought to repress all heterodox tendencies. . . ."[5] In rejecting realism, they could have turned (returned) to their own theatrical tradition, the essentially non-realistic theatres of Noh, Kabuki, and Bunraku. But these theatres, like Shingeki, were part of the official culture, institutionalized, part of the dominant ideology's aesthetic practice. They searched instead for a new paradigm in the *roots* of the old, "the Kabuki and Noh which grew out of the magical carnival chaos of folk art."[6] They turned as well to Bertolt Brecht who had radicalized European theatre by turning to traditional Japanese theatre. The post-Shingeki movement intended a break from the present and the past by a dialectical return to the pre-modern past. They wished

> to use the pre-modern popular imagination as a negating force to transcend the modern . . . although Shingeki's break with classical Noh and Kabuki was both justified and inevitable, it nonetheless cut us off from the sources of our traditions and trapped us within the restrictive confines of a static, bourgeois institution. Today we are seeking to reaffirm our tradition, but not as our predecessors did in the years leading up to the war. . . . Our hope is that by harnessing the energy of the Japanese popular imagination we can at once transcend the enervating cliches of modern drama and revolutionize what it means to be Japanese.[7]

The New Wave film directors may have attempted to deny their part in a "movement," but the post-Shingeki theatre, as the above quotation demonstrates, issued a virtual manifesto.

The link between theatre and desire was an important component of the "return" to the premodern popular imagination. Hirosue Tamotsu maintains in this context that "the acting and stylized beauty of Kabuki cannot be separated from illicit sex, nor can illicit sex be condemned as an inartistic, and thus inessential, aspect of Kabuki, for the art of Kabuki was the art of theatre and sex inseparably linked."[8] Tsuno Kaitaro contends that Kabuki was basically "cleaned up" after the Meiji Restoration by theatre producers and actors. In an effort to make their theatre "palatable to the period's wielders of power—the bourgeois and the bureaucrat"—they chose "to eradicate the irrational, the violent and the erotic from Kabuki."[9] For the post-Shingeki playwrights, as for many of the New Wave directors, sexuality was seen as inextricably linked to the premodern popular imagination, that is, to the essence of Japanese identity.

An interest in the premodern imagination is a characteristic, as we have noted, of Imamura Shohei, who majored in theatre at Waseda University in the late '40s and whose first film, *Stolen Desire*, focused on a traveling theatrical troupe. Imamura, like many in the post-Shingeki movement, sought to uncover the underpinnings of modern Japan in its ancient, shamanistic roots. Similarly, Shinoda Masahiro, another theatre major at Waseda, demonstrated an interest in folkloristic beginnings in *Himiko*. Shinoda took a particular interest in Kabuki and Bunraku, along with Noh, and came to discover that "the popular theatrical forms that had given rise to Noh drama had been invented by lowly outcasts who had been taken in by the military leaders of the fourteenth century."[10] Shinoda would also have discovered the roots of Kabuki in the so-called *kowara kojiki* (riverbank beggars), the image of theatre used to describe Kara Juro's Situation Theatre (*Jokyo gekijo*—named for Jean-Paul Sartre's essay "For a Theatre of Situations"[11]): "They [*Jokyo gekijo*] are performing 'beggar's theatre' and causing the local police, public health officials, and elementary school teachers to knit their brows in dismay."[12] Shinoda's college studies merged with his career in the Japanese New Wave cinema in the production of two important films crucially linked to both the traditional and post-Shingeki theatres of Japan.

In 1969, Shinoda produced a film version of a famous Bunraku play by Chikamatsu Monzaemon (1653–1724), Japan's most important premodern playwright. Chikamatsu's *Shinju ten no Amijima* (*The Love Suicide at Amijima*) originally appeared at Osaka's Puppet Theatre in 1720, and was one of a number of plays written about the popular theme of *shinju*, lovers' suicide. Such stories were designed to appeal to the newly emergent (and economically dominant) merchant class, whose cultural center was Osaka, then, as now, Japan's business center. The theme of *shinju* was intimately linked to the tension between *giri* and *ninjo* (duty and human desires). The lovers are forced into suicide because of monetary constraints, familial ties, or other failures to live up to expectations and obligations. The idea of *giri* was hegemonically imposed on the merchant class by the samurai, whose ideology dominated Japan until (and possibly into) the modern period. The merchants could experience the sweet-sadness (*aware*) of seeing their like caught in the trap of *giri* without hope of earthly release. Committing *shinju*, however, was also an implicit rebellion from the samurai code, for even if the lovers were unable to give free rein to their sensual desires, they nevertheless broke free of the bonds of *giri* in choosing to die. And, according to the Buddhist vision of life worked into these plays (and part of the religious heritage of samurai and merchant), the lovers could hope to attain togetherness in Amida's Western paradise.

In transferring *Double Suicide* (as the film is known in English) to the screen, Shinoda kept many of the crucial identifying aspects of the Bunraku and Kabuki (Chikamatsu's Bunraku play has also entered the Kabuki canon). Period music predominates although Takemitsu Toru, composer and co-scenarist, has added modern electronic motifs to parts of the composition. Narration in the classical style introduces the "play" to us, and an offscreen narrator occasionally interjects ominiscient point-of-view commentary. And Shinoda preserves the appearance of the *kuroko*, who figure prominently in many scenes, sometimes performing roles similar to that in the theatre (e.g., changing a set, delivering a prop), and sometimes appearing at the edge of the action as if they somehow were in control. Not preserved from the Bunraku theatre, however, are the puppets. Instead of using puppets, Shinoda substitutes live actors.

The appearance of the *kuroko* prominently declares the film's theatricality. However, Shinoda is interested in a dialectical view of the theatre compared to cinema, a tension introduced by the film's opening scene. Amidst preparations backstage at the Bunraku theatre, we hear Shinoda on the telephone talking to co-writer Tomioka Taeko. He tells her he has found a location for the final scene, the scene of the *shinju*. It will take place in a cemetery which, he tells Ms. Tomioka, "smacks of infinite space." Shinoda thus "gives away the ending." Of course, to the Japanese the ending of the play is already well known. Even to a Western audience it is clearly implied by the title. To the Japanese audience the ending of a play is rarely important in any case, since its attention is occupied by the aesthetic process, the spectacle, acting, and the inevitability of the plot. However, the introduction of the idea of "infinite space" will be a major motif in the dialectic of theatre/film—a dialectic which is the film's ultimate importance for our discussion.

The theatricality of the film is again declared even before the story starts by a matched cut from the heads of the leading puppets—the courtesan character and the *nimaime* male lead—to a close-up of the face of the leading character, Jihei, the love-obsessed merchant, made up in the style of the puppet. Thus a link is established between the puppets and the live actors a link which declares this film's indebtedness to the Bunraku (and not just to the basic story, or even the Kabuki version, although, it should be admitted, Nakamura Kichiemon is a well-known Kabuki actor. However, his performance is far from Kabuki-like, closer in spirit to film acting, albeit of a non-realistic sort). Jihei is seen walking on a curved bridge. His path crosses that of a group of white-clad traveling monks, their white robes signifying death, and then he stops in the middle of the bridge. He looks down and sees two bodies, a man and a woman, side-by-side on a mat, surrounded by the black-clad (*kuroko*) stagehands. A bridge often signifies the passage from one realm to another, typically the realm between life and death. But it also signifies the crossing over of the space between theatre and film, and film and life.

The settings of *Double Suicide* also declare the film's theatricality. The pleasure quarter to which Jihei proceeds, his path illuminated by a candle-bearing *kuroko*, is an artistic amalgamation of painted screens in imitation of *ukiyo-e* (pictures of the floating world) woodblock prints, among the Edo period's most significant artistic form. Many of the screens also feature ink-blot drawings in an Abstract-Expressionist style (nonrepresentational as opposed to the abstracted drawn-from-life style of the *ukiyo-e* screens). The silk-screen and ink-blot drawings on the sets are also recalled in the characters in a striking image of a *yakuza* with an elaborate tattoo on his back (the sign that he is a *yakuza*) kneeling in front of a courtesan, whose kimino has been pulled down to reveal her breasts. This is the "theatrical sign" as such—sets and characters equated through graphic matches, even more clearly seen in the introduction of Koharu, the courtesan with whom Jihei is in love. She is first shown standing in front of a large screen which boasts a picture of a courtesan.

The use of obviously stylized theatrical settings, the *kuroko* of the traditional theatre and the "graphic" presentation of the characters (the resemblance between Jihei and the doll and between the pictures on the screen and the live actors), is further refracted through Shinoda's casting of his wife, Iwashita Shima, in the dual role of Koharu, the courtesan, and Osan, Jihei's wife. The use of one actor in two roles is actually common in the Kabuki tradition, as Shinoda himself has noted. (He also claims, probably facetiously, that he cast his wife in the two roles to save money.[13]) The actor in a dual role in Kabuki has at least two aesthetic functions: the actor demonstrates his range of performance capabilities; and as part of the spectacle of the show, the so-called *hayagawari* (quick change of costume).[14] The use of actors in dual, or multiple roles, is fairly common in the West, from the many films in which actors play their exact doubles to the tour-de-force feats of Alec Guinness in *Kind Hearts and Coronets* (1949) and of Peter Sellers in *Dr. Strangelove . . .* (1963). However, in *Double Suicide* there is no spectacle involved in Iwashita's dual role—the two women never appear together in the same frame (compare this to the opening scene of Kurosawa's *Kagemusha*, 1980), nor do we ever see the "quick change" of costume. Nor is the resemblance between Koharu and Osan commented upon in the film and the disparity in their makeup and costume deemphasizes their resemblance. But that is the point. Shinoda is commenting upon the significance of roles and signs in society. Cast in the role of courtesan, Iwashita becomes eroticized; cast in the role of wife, Iwashita becomes de-eroticized. Set in the world of *ukiyo-e*, Iwashita-as-Koharu becomes part of an artistic/erotic amalgam; set in the world of lattice windows and checked walls, Iwashita-as-Osan merely represents *giri*.[15] Osan's de-eroticizaton is further reinforced by the blackening of her teeth, a social, not theatrical, custom, popular for a time in the Tokugawa period not only to mark women as married, but to deliberately make them less attractive to men. Shinoda is hereby commenting on the force of signs and convention in culture. And the very conventions that make Koharu an object of desire and Osan an index of obligation are the ones that inevitably drive Jihei to suicide.

The struggle between *giri* and *ninjo* which structures the story is manifested in the separation of Iwashita's image into two roles. The wife and prostitute are opposites, but they are also inextricably linked (like *giri/ninjo*). They are two sides of woman, one side compensates for the other. The wife is dominated by her sense of morality and obligation, but she also feels desire. The wife's desire is substituted for, transferred to, her double, the prostitute. Yet the prostitute also shows a strong moral/ethical sense. Early in the film, Osan sent a letter to Koharu asking her to release Jihei from his pledge to commit suicide not for her (Osan's) sake, but for his. Later in the film, Koharu asks Jihei to abandon her, not for her (Koharu's) sake, nor for his necessarily, but for Osan's. The two women, the socially acceptable but mundane and the erotically desirable but denied, both have altruistic and moral tendencies.

The bulk of *Double Suicide* is situated within the space of the theatrical. Jihei is thus literally and figuratively bound by conventions—the conventions of the theatre and by conventional morality. Near the end of the film, Jihei and Koharu walk through the pleasure quarter in the traditional *michiyuki*, the lovers' journey to death. Their *michiyuki* ends in a cemetery, the very one alluded to during the telephone conversation of the opening scene. Here, in this scene which "smacks of infinite space," Shinoda "opens up" the film. The "infinite space" is the space of the cinema as opposed to the closed, rigid, bound-in space of the theatre. In this cemetery, Jihei and Koharu make love, an obvious but effective conflation of sex and death. Also worth noting here is the demonstration of the cinema's ability to compact time within unrestricted space, as opposed to theatre which restricts space and, within each scene, is obliged to work in real time. While the lovers eventually return, as it were, to the realm of the theatrical (mainly at the "insistence" of the *kuroko*, who hand Jihei a sword with which he stabs Koharu and then help him hang himself from a *torii* gate) they taste a bit of freedom first—symbolized as they stand on a bridge and cut their hair.[16] It was the very rigidity of the theatre and its roles which forced them into the suicide, promised, in any case, by the title.

The use of theatrical conventions within the cinematic context "defamiliarizes" both theatre and cinema and highlights them. The effect of this strategy is to "make strange" the manner in which social roles and socially defined habits exert an ideological force on the individual. Once Jihei and Koharu leave the realm of the theatre, they are free, they are in infinite space, no longer literally confined by the theatrical settings. Yet they still commit *shinju* and are still surrounded by the *kuroko*, who insist that they perform their assigned roles. Yet even when they perform according to the script, the script of the play and the play of ideology, they are denied their ultimate reward. At film's end, instead of being placed side by side (as the couple in the opening live-action sequence), they are lined up head-to-foot, denied their togetherness in the land beyond. The omnipresent *kuroko* surround them still—perhaps *giri*, theatre, conventions know no bounds.

A dialectic between theatre and cinema, and the use of the theatrical sign (including an actor playing a dual role) are not without precedent in the cinema preceding Shinoda's film. Donald Kirihara has written an article which seeks to elucidate the tensions between theatre and cinema as expressed in Mizoguchi Kenji's *Zangiku monogatari* (*The Story of the Last Chrysanthemums*, 1939). Perhaps the most interesting angle he develops is that, in a film in which the average shot length is about one-minute, the interpolated theatrical sequences (performances of a Kabuki play) use *more* editing than the rest of the film (a point also made by Burch[17]). Burch finds this apparent paradox "remarkably significant of Mizoguchi's 'dialectical sense' that it should be precisely and solely to provide a framework for this eminently presentational art that he should have seen fit to abandon utterly his own presentational systemics in favour of the Western editing codes."[18] Kirihara sees the same paradox at work, but adds that the importance of this paradox may well provide an opportunity to compare the "representation . . . and the mode being represented."[19]

Another important antecedent may be found in Ichikawa Kon's playful version of *Yukinojo henge* (*An Actor's Revenge*, 1963). Hasegawa Kazuo (in this, his *three hundredth* film) plays two roles, that of an *onnagata* Kabuki actor out for revenge against the people responsible for his family's destruction, and as a notorious Edo thief. Noel Burch is struck by Hasegawa's role as Yukinojo, who is an *onnagata* (*oyama* is the alternate term utilized by Burch) offstage as well as on. He also notes "the way the diegesis proper . . . shifts from one level of 'realism' to another" in the shifting of spatial planes and representations.[20] One should also point out that the dual role played by Hasegawa is used for a source of distancing humor, a kind of "in" joke. The thief, Yamitaro, says he feels a certain "brotherliness" to Yukinojo. Similarly, a woman character comments on the resemblance between the thief and the actor. Ichikawa plays with cinema's creative geography as he is careful to show, via crosscutting, Yamitaro's witnessing every instance of Yukinojo's revenge, thus demonstrating a set of possibilities contained only by the cinema.

The film's overt theatricality is aided by a brilliant handling of Cinema-Scope framing. The Kabuki stage is an essentially horizontal one, with the exception of the *hanamichi*, a raised ramp which runs from the back of the auditorium onto the stage, which is used only occasionally in the course of a play. *An Actor's Revenge* emphasizes the horizontality of the CinemaScope frame by eschewing composition in depth. In addition, a number of crucial and spectacular scenes are filmed in front of a low, long wall which stretches across the boundaries of the frame, left to right. The action filmed in front of this wall similarly plays out horizontally, the depth of the frame constrained by the wall in the rear and a constant camera-to-subject ratio.

The use of color in the film is equally spectacular, given over to the kind of colorful display which characterizes the Kabuki itself. The use of color and CinemaScope in *An Actor's Revenge* contrasts strongly with Shinoda's choice to shoot *Double Suicide* in black and white, flat. Shinoda says that the choice of black and white was motivated by his conception of *Double Suicide* as, at heart, a kind of family drama, a *shomin-geki*, as compared to the spectacle of Kabuki.[21] The black-and-white cinematography of the film also has the function of deemphasizing the human characters, reducing them, as much of the set design was intended, to their graphic elements. In addition, one can imagine the appearance of the *kuroko* being much less disturbing in color as behind their partially transparent veils one could detect flesh tones, which would serve to humanize these silent harbingers of death. Moreover, the artistic (graphic) patterns of both the pleasure quarter and the paper shop (the lattice work) are much clearer without the distraction of color. One perceives that in a film so concerned with *giri* and *ninjo*, black and white is clearly symbolic—nothingness and death, a predetermined end to characters who are like puppets on a string.

The use of *kuroko* in the modern plays of the post-Shingeki playwrights demonstrates similar thematic concerns. Terayama Shuji utilizes *kuroko* in *Inugami* (*Dog God*, 1969), in which they act as a chorus, and in a manner similar to that of Bunraku.[22] In *Jashumon* (*Gate of Heretics*, 1971), the *kuroko* "pull" the main actors to the stage by miming the motions of puppeteers. Thematically, *Gate of Heretics* recalls *Double Suicide* and *Buraikan*:

> Rather than emphasizing the eternal Japanese conflict between *ninjo* and *giri* . . . Terayama points out the ways in which our moral choices have been conditioned by society. He depicts his characters as puppets whose actions are literally controlled by the whims of authoritarian puppetmasters. The play's conclusion celebrates the victory of free individuals over the constraints of dictatorial elements of society . . . .[23]

The familiar (to the Japanese) image of the *kuroko* within the context of a live-action play in which they act as puppet operators nevertheless, imbues them with a malevolence necessarily lacking in the Bunraku theatre. The theme of Terayama's play, save for the hopeful ending, is precisely the same as Shinoda's transformation of Chikamatsu's Edo-period original.

Satoh Makoto's *Onna-goroshi abura no jigoku* (*Murder in Oil Hell*, 1969), based loosely on Chikamatsu's play,[24] also features a variation on the image of the *kuroko*. Satoh utilizes characters referred to as Another Character A and B, who appear at different times throughout the play, "omnipresent" in David Goodman's term.[25] Goodman interprets Another Character A and B as *tengu*, or at least related to *tengu* in that they are "half-man and half-birds," associated with "perilous, ambivalent, non-moral forces" which inhabit Japanese unconsciousness.[26] However, it is also clear that they are *kuroko*, not only for their omnipresence, as in Shinoda's film and the Bunraku theatre (out of necessity, of course), but because they "establish outlines . . . within which the [characters] operate. In the introductory scene of the play, they appear with a piece of chalk to draw on the floor and

Buraikan (Release Title, *The Scandalous Adventures of Buraikan*)
Shinoda Masahiro, director. Kawakita/Japan Film Library Council

walls, to describe literally the patterns within which the action will take
place . . . at the end of the play . . . Another Character A and B reappear
to erase these forms. . . ."[27] The constraints placed upon actors in the
traditional theatre, especially in the Bunraku where the "actors" are literally
puppets, was a metaphor too powerful to be ignored by Shinoda, Terayama, and Satoh.

The other side of theatre, however, the liberating side, was also of interest
to Shinoda and to the playwrights of the post-Shingeki theatre. Shinoda's
collaboration with Terayama on *Buraikan* (sometimes known in the West
as *The Scandalous Adventures of Buraikan*) is a good example of a film which
celebrates the play side of theatre, the side of the premodern imagination.
The dialectic in *Buraikan* is not between theatre and cinema, as in *Double
Suicide*, but between theatre-as-revolution and theatre-as-institution. *Buraikan* is a film about rebellion—from parents, from government, from *giri*,
from mainstream culture through a celebration of play, of acting, sexuality,
and violence. Although the ultimate vision of the possibility of revolution
seems grim, play is defeated, the dominant ideology reasserts itself, *Buraikan* nevertheless sides with the forces of *ninjo*, of desire as a necessary
counterbalance to the stultifying forces of convention.

Buraikan is a free adaptation of a Kabuki play written by Kawatake Mokuami (1816–93) in the late Edo period. The play, *Kumo ni mago ueno no hatsuhana* (*Naozamurai*, 1874) is part of the Kabuki genre of *sewa-mono*, dramas of contemporary life.[28] However, it also has elements of the *shiranami-mono* (robber plays), for which Mokuami is best known. The robber plays centered on social outcasts—thieves, prostitutes, drifters, those who populated the pleasure quarters (*ukiyo*) of the period. To the post-Shingeki playwrights and the New Wave filmmakers, such figures held a great deal of attraction in terms of their alienation and outsider status. Shinoda and Terayama add to Mokuami's original the explicit setting during the time of the Tempo Reform of 1842, a time when the Tokugawa shogunate, feeling its ideological and political sway slipping, attempted to compensate for this by a series of edicts, of moral and ethical "reforms." Within the world of *Buraikan*, Lord Mizuno, the shogun's chief retainer, has declared that pictures of actors and fireworks are to be banned and that plays in the Kabuki and Bunraku theatres must feature filial piety and loyalty to the government. It is these themes—filial piety and governmental loyalty—which will be utilized, *played with*, in the film.

If *Double Suicide* relied on the artistic qualities of the standard aspect ratio and black-and-white cinematography, *Buraikan* revels in CinemaScope framing and gaudy colors, both put to important symbolic and formal use. The film begins on a shot of a *shoji* (paper screen) slanting back to reveal a street scene in the pleasure district. The film's final shot is simply a reversal of this, the screen tilting back up to cover the frame. This has the effect of acting like a curtain formally, but thematically it has richer associations—in one of the film's most striking images a *shoji* screen on fire slowly burns to reveal a couple making passionate love on the tatami in the midst of riot and revelry. As the dominant architectural feature of traditional Japanese homes, restaurants, and hotels, the *shoji* has strong connotations of "everydayness." Here, then, everydayness is turned into theatre, a theatre of liberation precisely from the everyday.

Role playing, or playacting, dominates the film's action. The hero, Naojiro, desires to be a Kabuki actor. He finds that becoming a *buraikan*, an outlaw, offers more interesting performance possibilities. Similarly, another of the main protagonists, Kochiyama, finds that his ordinary life as the shogun's tea-ceremony master does not satisfy his needs. At one point, he undertakes the task of rescuing a merchant's daughter from a corrupt lord. To do this, he poses as an emissary of the High Priest and hires Naojiro to impersonate a samurai-retainer. At the court of the corrupt lord, ladies-in-waiting spy on Naojiro from a room to his side (the "wings" of the stage, so to speak) and comment that "the samurai standing by the sedan is like an actor." Framing strategies typically place actors on little stages, or set off by frames within the frame to emphasize theatrical effects, while the film as a whole, like *An Actor's Revenge*, is composed mainly in horizontal planes.

In *Buraikan*, the world of theatre, of actors and acting, is specifically associated with the floating world. The rebellion against the Tempo Reform is fostered by Kochiyama who enlists a collection of outcasts and misfits— prostitutes, thieves, wastrels, a grieving father whose wife has committed suicide and whose son is missing, even a crippled, anarchistic assassin. To them, theatre is revolution and the revolution is theatre. Their aborted rebellion is inaugurated by the lighting of fireworks, a spectacle to declare their belief in theatre's liberating possibilities. It is during this riot that Shinoda offers up the image of the burning *shoji* and the lovemaking couple.

The revolution is thwarted by a combination of superior manpower (the police capture or kill the rioters) and an effort of will. Kochiyama confronts Lord Mizuno with the sight of fireworks, pulling open a *shoji* to do so (another "curtain" image). Lord Mizuno however, refuses to acknowledge the sight of the fireworks: "I have banned fireworks; therefore, there are no fireworks." It is an effective display of the power of the ruling class to write history as it happens, a display of ideological hegemony in its workings.

Another display of power is revealed in the other main plot of the film. If Lord Mizuno demonstrates the power of the government to rule the thoughts and ideas of the citizens, Naojiro's mother, Okuma, demonstrates the familial role in hegemonic rule. State and Family are thus equated, both seen as limiting, constricting forces. Naojiro wishes to marry Michitose, a glamorous courtesan of the pleasure district (Shinoda's wife Iwashita Shima again), but his mother, Okuma, forbids it. Naojiro, enraged at one point, picks his mother up out of her bath and throws her over a cliff. She does not die, however; she does not seem even to be injured. Naojiro does marry Michitose, but Okuma sleeps on the mat between them. At film's end, Naojiro again carries his mother to the cliff edge, but Okuma says that as many times as he tosses her off the cliff, she will return. This scene makes manifest the black comic tone which underlies the film, as does Ushimatsu's suicide—his wife dead, his son missing, the revolution aborted, he sits on a large barrel of lit fireworks. This black comic tone, the wild sensuality and irreverence on view, is the real Kabuki, the Kabuki of the common people, before it became the official theatre of the staid culture.

In the aborted revolution of the Tempo era, one is tempted to see a comparison to the student protests of the '60s. The humor of the film, dark though it is, offers up a vision of hope, of liberation, precisely by its outrageousness. In place of ideology, the film offers up instinct; in place of high culture it offers up popculture; in place of *giri*, it puts forth *ninjo*, but *ninjo* without guilt, without the *shinju* of the traditional culture—the *ninjo* of sex and violence, of politics, of youthful rebellion, of play.

Kawatake Mokuami and his robber plays also provided the basis for a play by Satoh Makoto, *Nezumi Kozo: The Rat* (*Nezumi kozo jirokichi*, 1969, adapted and transformed from Mokuami's play of the same name). The story concerns a real-life bandit who has literally become enshrined as a folk hero, except in Satoh's version, there are five Nezumis. The use of multiple heroes, or of a single hero with multiple aspects, links New Wave film and theatre. The *protean* nature of the hero reflects the timelessness and vitality of the popular, premodern imagination. This protean nature is reflected by the frequent device of character transformations—the confusion of identities in *Night and Fog in Japan*, the transformation of Japanese students into Koreans in *Three Resurrected Drunkards*, the roleplaying and reversal in *Diary of a Shinjuku Thief*, not to mention the dual roles taken in *Double Suicide* and the constant role playing in *Buraikan*. These film characters have their doubles in the post-Shingeki theatre through the process of metamorphosis which has been described as "none other than the mode of existence of human beings who live in multidimensional time and space. . . . And in the very midst of that multidimensionality, the waiters metamorphose into the waited."[29] Similarly, Kara Juro's plays have been described as containing "the pop-art language of cartoons." Language is stretched, sentences erupted, exaggerated, and made nonsense. "And with this, by these and all conceivable means, language goes through a bewildering transformation . . . moreover the transformation of language leads naturally to the transformation of characters."[30] We, these filmmakers and playwrights are saying, are the saviors of the world.

Oshima Nagisa and Satoh Makoto were both attracted to the Komatsugawa Incident in particular and to the Korean question in general. Li's crime in killing a high school student inspired Oshima's *Death by Hanging* in 1968. The year before Satoh produced *Atashi no biitoruzu* (*My Beatles*), which concerns a young Japanese man and his Korean wife who rehearse a play in which a Korean husband murders his Japanese wife. The Beatles appear (clearly *not* the British pop group) as potential, if ambiguous, saviors. Satoh's *Murder in Oil Hell* tells the story of a Korean woman born in Japan, repatriated to Korea, who returns illegally. She is arrested and placed in a detention camp. From here events take on various surreal qualities and imaginative episodes are played out, mostly revolving around conceiving oneself as a Hell's Angel.[31]

In terms of theme and style, we might also compare Oshima's early *Night and Fog in Japan* to Satoh's early *Ismene* (1965), a meditation on the fate of Antigone's sister revolving around the political problem of repetition. Oshima's film recurs in interesting ways in Satoh's *Chikatetsu* (*Subway*, 1966), an absurdist drama about a lightless train heading off into the night. In these two plays by Satoh, as in Oshima's film, the metaphor of night and fog, and its opposite, daylight—the waiting for the "dawn of a new day"—are the dominant images. We might note that if Yoshida Yoshishige was impelled to produce a trilogy dealing with major events of the twentieth century, so too was Satoh Makoto. His trilogy, *Kigeki showa no sekai* (*World of Showa: A Comedy*) contains within it *Buranki-goroshi, shanhai no haru* (*The*

Killing of Blanqui, Spring in Shanghai, 1979), a look at the *ni-ni-roku* (February 26) Incident as in Yoshida's *Martial Law*. Satoh's perspective on the attempted coup d'etat "reveals the philosophic presuppositions upon which such conspiracies are based that, even when those conspiracies are successful, prevent them from altering the long- term course of history."[32] We should also acknowledge another play in the trilogy, *Abe Sada no inu* (*Abe Sada's Dogs*, 1975), based on the infamous case which inspired Oshima's *In the Realm of the Senses*. Oshima's film has a specifically political dimension to it in that the very lack of politics manifested by the protagonists enabled a militaristic system to assert itself. Similarly, *Abe Sada's Dogs* reveals "the secret ritual of cultural procreation that guarantees the continuity of Japanese history."[33]

The attempt by the New Wave filmmakers and the post-Shingeki playwrights to break away from the immediate past and to engage the distant past in dialectical struggle manifested itself in the use of recurring historical figures, incidents, and issues, as we have now seen. The fact that in many instances the similarity of motifs (interest in the Korean question; use of *kuroko*) is *coincidental* indicates a remarkable degree of consistency in recognizing the major contemporary issues and the most powerful aesthetic, or formal, methods of dealing with them. Oshima Nagisa has been the filmmaker who has revealed the most significant of the many shared motifs and the most insistently radical in formalizing them. Oshima has not merely extended the radical materialism of traditional Japanese film practice, he has attempted to break with it and this may be seen at its clearest in his use of the theatrical sign. Oshima has not, like Shinoda, adapted classic plays into films, nor has he utilized specific theatrical practices identifiable as such. He has, in contrast, radically conceptualized both cinematic and theatrical signification.

Oshima's radicalism stems essentially from his refusal to acknowledge the theatrical sign, to distinguish between the cinematic and the theatrical. He does not set off his theatricalizations, does not mediate them in the way Shinoda does, for instance, by situating his films in the past. Nor does he toy with explanations for the obviously theatrical effects as Yoshida does by setting them off as imaginary, or as interior point of view. While Oshima uses flashbacks and other forms of temporal discontinuity, no clear or deliberate pattern emerges between "real" and "theatrical." In *Night and Fog in Japan* the most "real" sections are the flashbacks to 1952; the other two tenses in the film (the present and the immediate past) are highly stylized and theatricalized without benefit of mediation. In *Death by Hanging* the present tense dominates (save for a short flashback) but much of the past is *acted out* in the present. Past and present co-exist in a multidimensional experience. This multidimensionality is addressed by implication in *The Realm of the Senses* by the characters' attempts to live in a single dimension, a single realm, the realm of the senses. It is the very lack of multidimensionality that dooms the characters and, by extension, the nation. Only a multidimensional existence is capable of coming to terms with a genuine revolutionary potential.

Death by Hanging is among the most theatrical of Oshima's films and (hence?) among the most political. "*Death by Hanging* is a political film, its concern is with the politics of 'reality.' . . . it is directly about representation, identity, subject; hence its theatricality."[34] The film highlights the idea of a filmic reality, of a *diegesis*, while highlighting the reality of memory, power, and subject formation within the film. Burch brings forth this idea when he speaks of the film's "levels of reality": documentary, docudrama, fiction film, absurdist farce, moral parable, political tract.[35] McDonald, too, postulates *distinct* levels of reality: The World of Real Event, The World of Events Reenacted, The World of R's imagination.[36] This strategy on her part tries to unify the film, but in fact no unity is possible as the shift from one realm, or level, to another is progressive—we never return to an origin, a real, the real. "Involved with memory, *Death by Hanging* has no memory . . . other than the effects of that contradiction, falls outside of fiction or realism (they are one and the same), of the sure place. . . ."[37] The film proceeds to break down space, to play with and on place.

The first space, the first place, is the prison, the execution chamber, through which the camera, as if on its own, travels. (The voice-over narration is its motivation.) This is followed by the ritual of execution, the execution of R. It is only after "the body of the condemned man, R, refuses to die" that we get the first instance of diegetic sound. The space begins to shift, however, during the time "R tries to be R." Inside the prison walls, we see the playacting of R's past and the newspaper-covered "walls" of his "home." Then Oshima delivers the first exterior sequence of the film, the sequence at the riverbank taken up by Stephen Heath in this essay "Narrative Space." In terms of the treatment of the space in this scene, "simply, R is never quite there, in the place assigned. . . ."[38] R's place is then assumed by the Education officer in the rooftop reenactment of the murder. A return to the execution chamber does not return us to real space, for in the next sequence ("R is defended on the grounds that he is not Japanese") the body of the dead girl (as if the Education officer "really" strangled a schoolgirl) appears in a coffin that only R and the priest can see. Soon after, the dead girl transforms into R's older sister, although R has no older sister. In this section there are flashbacks which must themselves be put into quotation marks, so to speak, in that, while R is recalling his childhood, we see images of the "newspaper walls" from an earlier scene to R's supposed childhood. And we also see scenes we may take to be from R's real childhood, but which are, in fact, stills from Oshima's earlier *film*, "Diary of Yunbogi Boy." Oshima then presents images we understand as belonging to R's imagination, in which the young Korean conjures up crimes. He tells us that he imagined committing these crimes so often that one day they occurred in reality. Similarly, the reality of this scene, with its crosscutting, panning, and tilting camera, merges the real and the imaginary. As the woman, R's "sister," says, "Dream looks like reality and vice versa."

The problem of space, and its theatricalization, is taken up again by *The Realm of the Senses*. Here Oshima relies on a constriction of space, an interiorization, a closing-in. The architecture of traditional Japanese houses and inns is put to use to create frames within the film frame for Sada and Kichi. These are emphasized by a constant opening and closing of *shoji* screens. This recurring action serves two functions: to re-create space, open it up or close it off, and to represent the opening or closing of a (horizontal) curtain (as the curtain of Noh and Kabuki). This, in turn, relates to the idea of "looking," the fourth wall of the Western proscenium theatre, of looking at a film in which "everything can be seen."[39] Sada and Kichi often perform sexual acts for onlookers within the film. Thus the doubling of spectatorship. While such an idea of "spectatorship," of looking, inevitably brings up the issue of voyeurism and the scopophilic drive of the cinema, in this context it is worth shifting from a concern with "the apparatus of look and identification in cinema's institution of a film's view and viewer,"[40] to the idea of a ritual viewing—a participation shared between spectators, those who look at the film and those who look at *in* the film. Sada and Kichi perform sexual acts: They perform, they act, they are there to be seen. The ritual they act out is the ritual of the corrida (*Ai no corrida*, the film's Japanese title, the corrida of love), "a ritual encounter with death."[41] Sada and Kichi are sacrificial victims, are always acting out for us and in the same manner. The use of historical figures lends an air of inevitability to the film; Sada and Kichi must *perform* in a certain way, must end up in the same place.

All the films marked out by Dana Polan in his article on Oshima, "Politics as Process in Three Films by Nagisa Oshima," turn on the idea of rituals, thus establishing a link between politics and theatre. *Night and Fog in Japan* focuses on the ritual of the wedding, which is interrupted and deconstructed; *Death by Hanging* examines the ritual of execution, similarly interrupted and deconstructed. And *The Realm of the Senses* imples the ritual of the corrida and within the film establishes rituals between Sada and Kichi (sexual intercourse and strangulation). The use of ritual relates to the mystificatory function of religious ideology which naturalizes, through repetition, the status quo. The overt politicization of the content of these films simply makes clearer the link between ritual-as-religion and political rituals. The essentially theatrical nature of all rituals is the subtext of all these films.

The theatrical nature of rituals and the way in which the Japanese ruling class ropes together religious and political ideology to naturalize its existence is deconstructed in *Gishiki* (*The Ceremony*, 1971). This film is structured around a series of ceremonies which feature the gathering together of an extended family. In each successive ceremony the family becomes more and more fragmented. For Noel Burch, these ceremonies represent a "stultifying, evil theatre . . . [a] theatre of repressive fathers, a theatre of lies. . . ."[42] Oshima reveals that it is precisely the ceremonies which function to keep the family together, but when such ceremonies are revealed as hollow, meaningless (such as the famous "brideless" wedding sequence), the structures which bind the family are unraveled.

Perhaps the most completely theatricalized of Oshima's films is *Diary of a Shinjuku Thief*. While we earlier examined the film in terms of its exploration of the links between sex and politics, between revolutionary sex and political revolution, now we can also claim, along with Ian Cameron, the "the idea of performing or acting is so crucial to the film that the more one sees it, the more most of the other themes seem to be subordinate to or derived from the idea of acting."[43] As in *Death by Hanging*, the idea of a *diegesis* is thrown into relief. We might even go so far as to say that in this film there is no diegesis, save only a strong sense of place, Shinjuku. But even this requires a hesitation as Shinjuku is situated within a global context: Opening credits of the film give the time of day in New York, Paris, Moscow, Peking, Saigon. The day and time are constantly flashed on the screen (e.g., Sunday, 5:00 A.M.; Monday, 5:30 P.M, but not with a particular purpose, not with a sense of inevitability or of a mission (the digital time display in Donen-Kelly's *On the Town*, the mechanical return to the clock on the wall in *High Noon*). And while student riots break out at the film's end, they were inevitable not by the force of the plot, but by the force of history (the past, having already happened outside of the film). The film exists, as it were, in a multidimensional existence, denying us a single level, a diegesis. The lack of a diegesis, the presence of a multidimensional existence, is heightened by a breakdown between fiction and reality. Tanabe Moichi, president of the Kinokuniya Bookstore, plays himself, and a number of important sequences occur inside the famous massive bookstore in Shinjuku. Watanabe Fumio and Sato Kei, two members of Oshima's stock company, appear as themselves in clearly improvised conversational sequences, but they also appear as fictional characters (the rape of Umeko). They play themselves, they play characters, and Oshima plays with film.

Of course, the most obvious theatrical element is the presence of playwright Kara Juro and his Situation Players. The motifs of stealing and the confusion between fiction and reality in terms of playing, of acting, are both introduced in the first live-action shots. Kara Juro is being chased through Shinjuku to cries of "Stop, thief!" When caught, he is forced to strip. He does so and nothing out of the ordinary is seen. Oshima then uses an obvious jump-cut to a close-up of Kara upon whom we now see a chrysanthemum tattoo. Kara's "pursuers' then stop, unable to continue to confront this man wearing the national symbol. The pursuers stand on their heads, thus revealing that this has all been staged, that pursuer and

Shinjuku dorobo nikki
(*Diary of a Shinjuku Thief*)
Oshima Nagisa, director
Kawakita/Japan Film Library Council

pursued are players, actors. In the crowd that has gathered, we can see Birdey Hilltop standing behind Kara, seen only *after* the jump-cut, as if Birdey's existence was somehow connected to the idea of acting. Birdey's links to Kara in this fashion are supported by Cameron who claims that "the idea of theft . . . is itself 'stolen' by Birdey from Kara Juro."[44] Birdey will later steal a theatrical role from Kara, the role of Yui Shosetsu, who tried to "steal" Japan. At the same time, Umeko will steal the role of Kara's "wife," in Oshima's phrase, "stealing the act of the actor's wife."[45] The act she steals,is the act of *seppuku*, another ritual of death, but only acted out, performed, staged.

The staging of events in a confusion of cinematic and theatrical discourses is common, at moments, in other New Wave films. We mentioned earlier the works of Suzuki Seijun (*The Life of Tattoo* and *Tokyo Drifter*), and Noel Burch discusses the intriguing *Shura* (*Pandemonium*, 1971), Matsumoto Toshio's second feature which Burch mentions is "based on a recent shingeki version of a seldom performed *kabuki* text."[46] In fact, the film is derived from *Kamikaketa sango taisetsu* by Tsuruya Nanboku (1755–1829), author of the oft-filmed *Yotsuya kaidan*. Tsuruya was a specialist in the ghost story (*kaidan mono*) of which *Shura* is a variation.[47] It is beyond the scope of this study to examine very much further the intriguing and mutually revealing links between Japanese New Wave cinema and theatre, especially the post-Shingeki theatre. To do so in more depth requires more visual analysis, not only of the films but of the plays—a serious problem as plays do not exist until performed. It is important, however, to mention the deterioration of the New Wave cinema, the institutionalization of this once-radical movement, in terms of the use of theatrical conventions and of the theatrical sign.

Shinoda Masahiro's *Yashagaike* (*Demon Pond*, 1979) is a good example of a disjunctive film with a spectacular use of the theatrical sign, but whose underplayed, underdeveloped political content shows the triumph of institutionalized aesthetic radicalism at the expense of genuinely dialectical, confrontational politics. By Western standards, this fantasy-cum-disaster film is entirely unconvincing in terms of its special effects (the glory and *raison d'être* of the genre). Although the climactic tidal wave that washes away a small village is effectively done, the "demons" in the Demon Pond look exactly like what they are—actors and actresses dressed up in funny fish costumes. And these demons appear rather suddenly in the film. The film sets up an interesting enigma—Who is this beautiful woman tending a fantastic garden while all around there is drought?—and an aura of fantasy in the garish colors of the garden and surrounding forest, but it does not prepare its audience for the outlandish creatures who suddenly appear. To Japanese audiences, however, the film is very much in the manner of Kabuki. Save for the final scene of the tidal wave and subsequent transformation of the landscape into a huge waterfall (which is, in fact, a stock shot of Niagara Falls), nothing happens in the film which could not happen on the Kabuki stage.[48] Unsurprisingly, Japanese audiences tend very much to enjoy the film, while Western audiences are typically puzzled by it.

Japanese audiences respond to the film not just on the level of its overtly theatricalized spectacle. They respond to the two heroines of the film, Yuri, who tends the garden, and Shirayuki, the incarnation of the dragon-spirit who lives in Demon Pond. Both Yuri and Shirayuki are played by the same person. Shinoda thus seems to be using the same strategy he employed in *Double Suicide*. As in *Double Suicide*, the use of the same person in two roles establishes a kinship between the characters portrayed. Except in *Demon Pond* this kinship is established between a woman and a dragon, and the one who plays both roles is not a woman at all. Bando Tamasaburo, the premier *onnagata* of the Kabuki stage in the 1970s and '80s (as of this writing), plays the parts of Yuri and Shirayuki. The film is already disjunctive to the Western audience in the use of the *onnagata*. The film is also disjunctive to the Japanese, for Tamasaburo plays Yuri in realistic fashion— the elaborate costumes of Kabuki are abandoned in favor of contemporary clothing (the film is set in the early 1930s) and the dialogue is delivered in film fashion, again eschewing the stylization of Kabuki. Moreover, and quite shocking to devotees of the theatre, Yuri/Tamasaburo is shown kissing her husband. But this shock value and the realistic performance of Tamasaburo establishes an aesthetic tension between the reality of Yuri as a woman on the screen versus the knowledge that she is being portrayed by a man—precisely the same tension in the *onnagata* on the stage. Shinoda maintains that the kiss was shown to declare the decadence of Kabuki, that the romance in the theatre is portrayed exclusively by men.[49] But no such decadence comes through in the film. It functions precisely as the Kabuki tradition does, by aestheticizing the mise-en-scène and working strictly in convention (the conventional stylization of romance in Kabuki compares to the conventional stylization of romance in the cinema; in the former couples do not kiss, in the latter they do. But in neither instance is it *ultimately* disjunctive).

Demon Pond, then, save for its momentary surprise, is an instance of the Japanese cinema working within the bounds of traditional aesthetic modes. As in *Double Suicide*, the crossing of a bridge provides a source of tension, of crossing realms: cinema and theatre, reality and fiction, life and death. But unlike *Double Suicide*, once the protagonist crosses the bridge he enters completely the realm of the theatrical. The tension dissipates—even the final scene which is "cinematic" in its use of creative geography, is *obviously* cinematic, that is, theatrical, in the patent unreality of the scene. And as in *Double Suicide*, the problem of *giri* and *ninjo* is posed, this time bringing in a slightly new variation on this ingrained Japanese dilemma. Shirayuki, the dragon-spirit, is as bound by *giri* as Yuri. Shirayuki must stay in the waters of Demon Pond as long as the village bell is rung once a day, a chore which has voluntarily been taken up by Yuri and her husband. It is only when the villagers prevent Yuri from ringing the bell that Shirayuki may leave to join her lover in another pond and thus leaving unleash the tidal wave. Even dragon-spirits rebel against *giri* in favor of *ninjo*, and this one is allowed to find her true desires, albeit at the expense of the villagers.

The villagers however, have only themselves to blame for their destruction. The villagers, led by a militaristic Diet member, prevent Yuri from ringing the bell—they are jealous and frightened of her, mainly because she has water and they do not. Yuri has water precisely because of the kinship, a certain "sisterliness," that the dragon-spirit feels for her. The waters of Demon Pond tend her garden. The fact that the Diet member leads the mob against Yuri may be taken as the film's implied political dimension, that the militarist era was a rejection of genuine Japaneseness, that the village/Japan was led astray from its instinctual, folkloristic beliefs. While such a theme is in keeping with the intentions of New Wave filmmakers and post-Shingeki playwrights to seek out the essence of the Japanese folk, the power of the film to shock, to pose questions dialectically, is removed by the very institutionalization of its techniques. For if little of the film differs from traditional Kabuki (the Kabuki of the official culture), how can the mere presence of these techniques *on* film possess any revolutionary power? Far from highlighting both theatrical and cinematic techniques, *Demon Pond* merely uses cinema to film theatrical techniques. *Demon Pond* is Brechtian only in the clichéd sense, perhaps the inevitable fate of revolutionary modes.

CHAPTER SEVEN

Three Men Who Left Their Will on Film

If *Demon Pond* shows the death of the Japanese New Wave cinema in its institutionalization, the New Wave was clearly fading away much earlier than the release of Shinoda's film in 1979. Three films made at the end of the 1960s reveal the essence, the height, and the end of the New Wave. Hani Susumu's *Hatsukoi jigokuhen* (*The Inferno of First Love*, 1968; aka *Nanami*), Yoshida Yoshishige's *Eros purasu gyakusatsu* (*Eros plus Massacre*, 1969) and Oshima Nagisa's *Tokyo senso sengo hiwa* (*The Man Who Left His Will on Film*, 1970) come at the height of the New Wave, encapsulate virtually all of the themes isolated throughout this work, and portend the end of the movement. In some sense they stand as elegies not only to the New Wave of the cinema, but to the era of the '60s in Japan.

The '60s began, as we have seen, with the Ampo toso, the Anti-Security Treaty demonstrations, in 1959–60; the era ended ten years later, in 1970, with renewed protests over the renewal of the treaty once more. Yet despite the fact that demonstrations protesting the treaty's renewal were generally larger than the most massive turnouts in 1960, it was clear to almost everyone that there was "a lack of a 'feeling of urgency' (*seppakukan*) on the part of the demonstrations."[1] The treaty automatically took effect on June 22, 1970, but "even in January 1970, it was common knowledge that there would be no crisis in June."[2] Clearly something had happened between 1960 and 1970, something which greatly changed the political and social climate—something which worked its way into the New Wave cinema.

It may have been clear in early 1970 that the protests which would inevitably surround the renewal of the treaty would be little more than "merely the ritualized tenth-anniversary observance of that crucial crisis in the postwar Japanese political system,"[3] but events in the mid- and late-'60s give little evidence that this would be the case. Indeed, an increasing militancy on the part of youthful radicals might have pointed toward a crisis in 1970 equal to, if not greater than, that exacerbated in 1960. The student movement, an important part of Japanese politics since the early

'50s, was growing increasingly vocal with a large number of issues at hand, including opposition to the U.S. military occupation of Okinawa; U.S. involvement in Indochina; U.S. military financing of university projects; attendance at university courses by members of the Japan Self-Defense forces; the crash of a U.S. military jet on one college campus; and the Japan-U.S. Security Treaty. Opposition to nuclear weapons and the U.S. military combined to spark a large demonstration at Yokosuka on May 30, 1966, to protest the docking of a nuclear-powered Polaris submarine. Opposition to the Vietnam War, and Japan's implicit role in it, gave rise to the First Haneda Incident in the fall of 1967 (the subject of Ogawa's *Report from Haneda*). The Second Haneda Incident in November 1967 found many of the same students employing the same tactics to try and prevent Sato's departure to the U.S. In January 1968, the Hakata Station Incident involved students clashing with police during a demonstration in opposition to the docking of the U.S.S. *Enterprise* (an aircraft carrier) at Sasebo port. The Fukuoka District court seized news footage shot by four television stations for use as evidence—Oshima Nagisa doubtless followed this story from the start as he used the seizing of film to form an important subplot of *The Man Who Left His Will on Film*.

The year 1969 saw an increase in the amount of protest activity generally, gearing up for June 1970. October 21, 1969, was declared "International Antiwar Day." The Japan Communist party (JCP), Japan Socialist party (JSP), and Sohyo (General Council of Trade Unions of Japan) sponsored mass rallies across the nation; some 800,000 people showed up at approximately 800 sites protesting the Japan-U.S. Security Treaty and demanding an unconditional return of Okinawa to Japan. Students rioted in Tokyo (Shinjuku), Sapporo, Osaka, Nagoya, and Fukuoka. In all, 1,500 arrests were made on that day.

On November 13, Sohyo staged nationwide strikes and rallies to protest Sato's visit to the United States. In Okinawa, a protest rally sponsored by the Okinawan Prefectural Council for Reversion to the Fatherland attracted 100,000 participants. At this time, students and workers launched a five-day campaign in Tokyo to protest Sato's departure. On November 13, rocks and molotov cocktails were hurled at riot police; on November 16, twenty people were injured and two thousand arrested as students blocked entrances to several major train and subway stations. On November 17, Sato left for the United States. On December 8, the Tokyo Public Prosecutor's Office indicted 480 people who were among those arrested during the November campaign. This marked the largest number of people ever prosecuted in connection with street demonstrations. The vast majority of those prosecuted were students, part of an overall pattern of student arrests. In 1969, 70 percent of those arrested (9,747 out of 13,665) were students; of the 2,210 prosecutions made in 1969, 90 percent were students (1,916). This was an obvious response to the increase in student and youth activism. In 1969, student militants and antiwar youth workers had staged 2,460 street battles for which 740,000 persons were mobilized, of which 65 percent or so were student militants.[4]

Immediately preceding these demonstrations in the fall of 1969, a new term began to appear in Japanese newspapers and magazines: the New Left. It was the New Left, consisting of anti-JCP university students, the recently formed Beheiren (Citizen's League for Peace in Vietnam), and the Antiwar Youth Committee (*Hansen seinen iinkai*—formed by young workers from within the ranks of Sohyo) which was responsible for the new level of protest activity. The anti-JCP students and the Antiwar Youth Committee were particularly strongly linked, having coordinated the two Haneda Incidents and the Hakata Station Incident. All three groups banded together in support of the rising tide of opposition to the building of the new airport at Narita.[5] The New Left in Japan had similarities to the New Left in the United States and France, especially in their opposition to the Vietnam War and other perceived militaristic/imperialistic ventures. To Professor Yamazaki Masakazu of Yale, there was an important difference between Eastern and Western New Left: "The revolt of the students in the United States is a revolt in search of cultural principles, such as in philosophy and in world outlook; while that of the students in Japan is a self-assertion against social uniformity and similarity."[6] This is an important point to the Japanese experience of the '60s, but Professor Yamazaki fails to note that a protest against conformity was equally characteristic of American youth.

One factor in the student protests of the late '60s can explain the seeming paradox of large-scale militant activity leading up to the massive demonstrations of June 23–24, 1970, followed by the sudden decline in activity on the heels of the treaty's renewal. And this is that, just as in the United States, student activities in the late '60s "increasingly centered on campuses, in contrast to earlier periods when the bulk of student protest took place off-campus and involved primarily non-campus issues." In 1968, "116 universities experienced significant conflicts" while 1969 showed even greater disruption.[7] If the activities tended to center on campus, it was a function of the fact that protest issues tended to be sparked by campus concerns: proposed tuition raises, demands for student control over dormitories and student unions; desires for increased student role in the selection of university officials; and general complaints about inadequate teaching, equipment, and curricula.[8] At the same time that student activism increased the Japanese government instituted a series of measures aimed at clamping down on the students. In 1969, the government issued the Law of Provisional Measures Concerning University Administration, which gave the government increased authority over public institutions (typically the most prestigious institutions). Earlier in the decade, the government increased its internal police force, creating the elite 29,000-man *Kido-tai* which

> devoted its time to controlling student riots and gathering intelligence on specific student organizations; plainclothes police conducted round-the-clock surveillance of more than a hundred student activists. The national government, by the passage of special legislation, had obtained the right to intervene in university conflicts involving students. Several thousand college students acquired arrest records during the late 1960s and early 1970s, and hundreds have served time for a variety of offenses related to participation in the student movement.[9]

Perhaps no official measures or the increased police attention would have been sufficient to deter student activism. However, a change in attitude on the part of Japanese corporations might have been the death blow to mass student militantism. "Beginning in 1969, Japanese corporate employers systematically excluded ex-student activists in their recruitment, a practice upheld by a 1973 Supreme Court ruling."[10] Earlier in the decade, student activists had been perceived as desirable candidates—leadership and initiative were qualities felt to be needed in corporate Japan and student leaders were felt to possess these traits. Whatever inspired the change in attitude on the part of these companies, only the most dedicated activists dared speak out in public, dared to demonstrate in any militant manner. As in the United States, an erosion of the political base through cooptation or intimidation (not to mention the change from youth to adulthood) ended the mass protests. On this score, it is worth noting that the next generation of youth, as well as the former activists, raised hardly a fuss when the treaty came up for renewal once again in 1980—not a trace of protest could be found in Tokyo's crowded, prosperous streets.

It is not entirely clear whether Hani, Yoshida, and Oshima, beginning production on their films which stand as paradigms and elegies for the New Wave, realized that they were witnessing the last phase of mass political activism. Yet the demonstrations of the late '60s, far more violent and spectacular than those of 1960, seem to have a powerful offscreen presence. Indeed, in Oshima's *The Man Who Left His Will on Film*, the demonstrations have a powerful *onscreen* presence. This film, whose Japanese title translates as "Secret Story of the Post 'Tokyo War' Period," interpolates documentary footage of student-police clashes in two instances, footage diegetically motivated as having been taken by one of the group of student-activists/filmmakers. Similarly, documentary footage of a street demonstration appears in *Diary of A Shinjuku Thief*, as if Oshima felt compelled to acknowledge these immediate events within his fictional discourses. Such an acknowledgment on Oshima's part stems, in part, from the per-

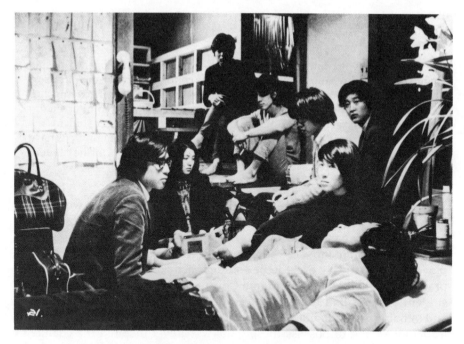

Tokyo senso sengo hiwa (The Man Who Left His Will on Film)
Oshima Nagisa, director. Kawakita/Japan Film Library Council

sonal sadness he felt comparing the generation of the late '50s to the student
activists of the late '60s. When he made *Night and Fog in Japan* in 1960, he
felt the student movement inaugurated by the Ampo demonstrations
would be better than his own generation of the early '50s. By the late '60s,
Oshima recognized the increased interest taken by the government and
the police in attempting to suppress the demonstrations, but was saddened
by the students' turn to violence. Stalinism, the very ideology that Oshima
feels destroyed his generation of student radicals, reappeared in small sects
of students activists in the late '60s. Oshima felt that this was a disastrous
move on their part, but also felt unable to communicate with the new
student activists.[11] This feeling of being unable to communicate with contemporary youth begins to explain the dissipation of the New Wave. And
it also helps explain the need Oshima, Yoshida, and Hani obviously felt
to reexamine their politics and its relationship to their cinema.

The first phase of this self-examination, then, was to pose the question
in filmic terms, to reflect on the relationship between cinema and politics;
to make, in this true sense, self-reflective films. The reflexivity of the films
assumes various forms, ranging from self-referentiality to an overt focus
on the cinematic apparatus. For instance, at one point in *The Man Who Left
His Will on Film* (hereafter referred to as *Man*), the student-militants discuss

the possibility of enlisting support for their cause to retrieve their film from the police. They decide that well-known filmmakers like Oshima Nagisa, Shinoda Masahiro, and Yoshida Yoshishige (among others) will help them. In *Eros Plus Massacre* (*Eros*), Unema, a photographer/filmmaker, is referred to an an "old good-for-nothing" (*rokudenashi*—the name of Yoshida's first film). In *The Inferno of First Love* (*Inferno*), the main characters watch a film made by a friend entitled "A Record of First Love." This film-within-the-film functions not only in an overtly reflexive manner with its similarity of title and in the way its theme reincarnates the overall theme of Hani's film, but in a humorously reflexive manner as well. This film is a virtual compendium of clichés about amateur filmmaking—overwritten narration, poor cinematography, jerky camera movements, and jump cuts. By Hollywood's standards, Hani's film itself could be accused of amateurism as *Inferno* (like *Man*) used high-speed black-and-white film, handheld camera, and jump cuts.[12] From these sorts of in-jokes, the films challengingly pose questions of cinema.

All three films focus on filmmaking as diegetic activities. *Man* begins with a series of shots seen through a handheld camera, voices off-camera comment on the shots we see. These shots draw attention to themselves as point of view, but an unknown point of view since they begin the film. The film (that is, *Man*) sets up a tension between the film being made by this unknown cameraman and the film we are seeing when the unknown cameraman's film stops and this other film begins. In *Eros*, Yoshida's alter-ego, Unema, the old good-for-nothing, is making a film about the Kanto Earthquake of 1923 and has photographic slides of the aftermath. These slides become integrated into a film about the death of the anarchist Osugi Sakaei made by Eiko, the student-heroine of the film. Her film becomes part of the film we are watching, becomes our film, the film. In *Inferno*, the heroine, Nanami, works as a nude model. Her clients, all men, photograph her and her co-workers in various staged poses. But film, that is cinema, does not stop when the camera stops. In fact, cinema may be said to begin only when film is projected, and all three films similarly focus on projecting and viewing films.

In *Man*, Motoki endlessly watches his "friend's" film (part of which we believe we saw in the opening point-of-view shots). Similarly in *Eros*, Eiko and Wada, the young male protagonist, view Unema's slides, while in *Inferno*, Nanami and Shun watch Algebra's film, "A Record of First Love." But all three films take the idea of projecting film even further. Both *Man* and *Eros* use the same startling image of a projector beaming its film not on a screen but on the nude body of a woman. In *Man*, Yasuko becomes the screen on which Motoki views the landscapes shot by his friend. In *Eros*, Wada projects slides of the earthquake onto Eiko's body. These seem all too clear representations of the place of women in narrative cinema, as *projections* of male desire. In *Inferno*, the women are *staged* as spectacle,

Tokyo senso sengo hiwa (*The Man Who Left His Will on Film*)
Oshima Nagisa, director. Kawakita/Japan Film Library Council

there to be photographed, there only for what Laura Mulvey has called
their "to be looked-at-ness." But such a reading of these projections would
be wrong, for in every instance, as we will see, the women break through
the spectacle and into the narrative, refuse to be mere projections.

Yet it is the case that the use of projectors is to be understood as a
projection of desire, not of male desire, but of the desire to create cinema,
the will to film. But this will to film leads, it seems, inevitably to death, for
in all three films a major protagonist dies. In *Man*, it is Motoki, who dies
twice, first at the start (unknown to us and to him), then at the conclusion,
in each instance jumping off a rooftop and filming his plummeting point
of view. In *Inferno*, Shun dies in a car accident, pursued by *yakuza* on his
way to meet Nanami. Shun's death on the city street, his body lying next
to a car, looks forward photographically to the way Oshima shoots Motoki's
body at the end of *Man*. In *Eros*, three central figures die, Unema and the
historical figures Osugi Sakae and Noe Ito. In each film, a protagonist who
dies is a filmmaker. Motoki and Unema kill themselves, the latter by making
a noose out of 16mm film and hanging himself; the former films himself
in 16mm up until the moment of his death. Shun, although not a filmmaker
as such, is something like a filmmaker. In one scene, he is taken to a
psychiatrist's office and hypnotized. His thoughts, his vision, suddenly

appear on a screen, projected for all to see. The deaths of filmmaking protagonists is the death of cinema, the death, at least, of a politically radical cinema. All are led to despair over the inability to film, that is, to film with certainty, to film *a* certainty. They can film only images, bits; they possess a will to film but can discover nothing, no thing, to film.

That there is nothing to film, that the will to film leads to the death of film, is a function of fading political aspirations. That there is nothing to film is also a function of the death of narrative which cannot be resurrected. The failure of political aspirations, of the '60s movement, does not permit a return to the past. The breakdown of narrative reflects the fragmentation of reality and of the individual character, now more fragmented than ever. In this regard, *Inferno* is the least complex. The film tells a story which is easily repeated—Shun, an impotent young man, a victim of child abuse, falls in love with Nanami who works as a nude model. Initially unable to make love to her, Shun is helped by Nanami to overcome his debility. On his way to consummate their relationship, he is pursued by gangsters and killed by a car. The film is complicated, fragmented, by flashbacks from Shun and Nanami's point of view. Shun remembers instances when he was molested by his stepfather. Other events seem to be memories conflated with fantasies, as Shun recalls the peace and plenitude he felt with his mother and the pain of separation when she left him. Nanami describes, narrates, for Shun her experiences, first as a factory worker and then as a nude model. In two instances, we see her at work: one in which she narrates for Shun and one in which Shun spies on her and her colleagues. In other instances, however, the film is simply *interrupted*. One entire scene, eliminated from the American release version, has no narrative relationship to Shun or Nanami whatsoever, as the camera merely watches in longshot as a street vendor sells records at a modern train station. The film is also sidetracked from this basic story, as the film-within-the-film demonstrates. Thus while preserving the basics of story, the plot is deemphasized.

The death of narrative is most overt in Oshima's *Man*. There is no story which ultimately emerges, since one of the main requisites of a story is missing: a character. The film plays with story and with character and even goes so far as to juxtapose one story alongside another, although neither is, or may be, resolved. Oshima's film is a virtual *mise-en-abîme*, a Chinese box set, a series of mirrors reflecting mirrors. It ends as it began, and seems to begin again; it is merely a film *loop*, a Mobius strip. The film is also completely self-reflexive—reflexive of the conditions of cinema, reflective upon the conditions in which meaning arises in film. The images we see are posed as problematic, and in two ways: as a problem of *who* shot the footage and the problem of *what* the footage may mean. Since the "who" of this film is in doubt, the "what" is similarly displaced. Noel Burch notes, "The character talks of himself as of another, throughout the film pursues a 'traitor' who is himself."[13] Rather than try and figure this out as if it were a mystery (whodunit), Maureen Turim and John Mowitt maintain that we should not "speak of a will *left on* film—instead, we should try to think of the radicality of a subject whose primordial cleavage is that which is staged not between man and nature, but between a subject and a representational system (a film)—especially a film whose 'signification' is generated emphatically through that subject's fragmentation and displacement."[14] Since this is the case we are literally unable to *make sense*: "[T]he representation of inconsistent and contradictory narrative structures challenges interpretations according to existing methodologies."[15]

A further breakdown in narrative, of the possibility of a narrative signified, of, in fact, a *diegesis*, arises in the comparison of, and dialectical opposition between, the documentary footage of the "Tokyo War" and the "secret story" of Motoki. The opposition between documentary and fictional modes set up by Oshima is overtly reflected in the film by the discussion the radical group holds about the proper use of film in a political context. The more overtly Marxist members of the filmmaking collective reject Motoki's personal/psychological quest for (self-)understanding through cinema in favor of a collective meaning revealed through nonfiction filmmaking. The dialectical tension that arises may be expressed as the struggle between Marx and Freud, documentary and fiction, exterior and interior, between, if you will, Lumìere and Méliès. Burch, I take it, is referring to this notion when he sees *Man* as "an ambitious attempt to develop a dialectical narrative form in that it does consider the mechanisms of the unconscious in relation to the contradictions of political filmmaking."[16] The question is not resolved in the film, nor is it resolved by the film—the best Oshima can do is posit the question in terms of struggle, in terms of the *film work*. For while Motoki commits suicide at the end, as the not-yet-known-to-be Motoki committed suicide at the start, so at the end, as at the start, a new Motoki runs into frame and steals the camera; the film loop continues, the struggle goes on.

Eros plus Massacre is similarly dialectical. Documentary is juxtaposed to fiction, Marx to Freud, history to myth, politics to sexuality. Yoshida's film alternates between two time frames, the present (1969) and the past (1916–23) and compares the political/sexual struggle of Osugi Sakae and Ito Noe to the fictional characters of Eiko and Wada (and Unema). Yet what becomes clear soon enough is that "the past" in this film is both the historical past and an imagined, or better, *re-created* past. Past and present merge, characters in the past appear in the present, until at film's end, they come forward and stand together for a portrait to end the film. Similarly, in the present, a character imagines something, plays at, pretends, all of it visualized, some of it in doubt—did it "really" happen? Thus the question, the problem of *diegesis*, mirrored in the film by the question of historical events, where, how, and by whom did they happen?

Self-referentiality, reflexivity and a dialectical narrative structure char-

Hatsukoi jigokuhen (The Inferno of First Love)
Hani Susumu, director. Kawakita/Japan Film Library Council

acterize all three films for purposes of posing the question of the nature of political filmmaking in the face of political disappointment. And they do so through a highlighting of all the major images and motifs which characterize the New Wave. All three films focus on youth; Hani's on working-class youth, as befitting the director of *Bad Boys* and *She and He*, while Oshima and Yoshida, as befitting former college activists, center on student radicals. In the death of Shun we have the death of youth caused by materialism and greed in the *deus ex machina* of the *yakuza* and the car accident. In the death of Motoki, we have the death of youth caused by the failure of political ideas, not "violence at noon" any longer, but turned inward, to suicide. The question of youth's search for identity is similarly present in all three films, posed in terms of sexuality and its links with politics. *Inferno*'s Shun is on the verge of sexual pathology. A victim of child molestation by his stepfather, he, in turn, molests a young child. Motoki and Yasuko of *Man* are reminders of Birdey and Umeko in *Diary of a Shinjuku Thief*—the two films should stand together as companion pieces, the later *Man* an inverse of the former. *Eros* juxtaposes and compares two generations of political and sexual radicals, the Taisho-era anarchists Osgui Sakae and Ito Noe and the student-radicals Wada and Eiko.

The centrality of women to questions of identity and sexuality translates

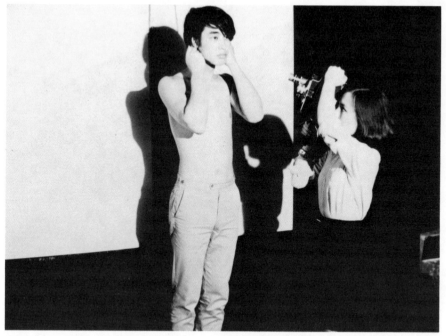

Eros purasu gyakusatsu (*Eros plus Massacre*)
Yoshida Yoshishige, director. Kawakita/Japan Film Library Council

into three films with important female characters. In *Inferno*, Shun looks
to Nanami to cure his impotence, to give him a sense that he is a man. In
Nanami's freewheeling approach to sexuality and her natural healing pow-
ers she is a throw-back to the priestess archetype of Shindo, Masumura,
and Hani's own *She and He*. And, like an Imamura heroine, she is a survivor.
In *Man*, Yasuko emerges as more than merely Motoki's projection when
she takes an active role in the refilming of the landscapes. On the other
hand, Yasuko is limited in her role by the very limitations of this film in
which there are no characters. It is in *Eros plus Massacre* that the woman's
role comes to the fore and not simply because, once again, Yoshida's wife,
Okada Mariko, is the star. For while Okada's role as Ito Noe is crucial to
the film, the true heroine, the real protagonist of *Eros*, is Eiko, the alienated
sexually active student-radical who is Unema's lover. For while Unema
possess the will to film only to commit suicide at the impossibility of filming,
Eiko, it develops, is the maker of the film, this film, a woman who leaves
her will on film. It is Eiko who possesses desire, desire for sex, desire for
politics, desire for cinema. It is her desire, her will, which eventually makes
her the central protagonist of the film, just as her desire and will make Ito
Noe the central protagonist in the complex interactions of the members of

Osugi Sakae's radical circle in the Taisho era. It is only when Eiko has come to terms with her desire, through her imagined recreations of important events in the life and death of Osugi and Ito, that the film may end.

The issue of prejudice is also addressed in the three films. Hani's *Inferno* is perhaps most centrally concerned with the problem of discrimination against working-class youths. This discrimination is both overt, as we see in Nanami's flashback to her work in a factory where she is fired for union organizing activities and in Shun's flashback to his being sent to a juvenile home when his mother abandons him, and covert, as we see when Nanami and Shun go to Algebra's school to see his film. The condescending looks and sneers the girls direct to Nanami is a clear index of the gap between the privileged classes and the working classes (memorably shown as well in Ogawa's "Sea of Youth"). The issue of prejudice is transposed to the issue of police harassment in Oshima's *Man*. The police confiscate the film of the radical group. Motoki chases the police thinking they have taken the camera of his "friend" (the not-yet-known-to-be Motoki) and he wants the footage to make sense of his friend's suicide, whereas Motoki's fellow radicals think the footage the police have confiscated is film of a student-police clash (the confiscation modeled on the January 1968 Hakata Station Incident). Motoki's belief that the police have stolen the will left on film is an interesting insight into the kinds of paranoia, possibly justified in light of the formation of the *Kido-tai*, experienced by student radicals in the late '60s. This paranoia is also present in Yoshida's *Eros* where Eiko is confronted by Hinoshiro, a policeman who claims she is a prime suspect in a prostitution investigation. Fears of persecution and harassment by the police take on increased justification in light of the fact, as Yoshida's film shows, that Osugi Sakae and Ito Noe were murdered by the military police (*kempei-tai*) in the aftermath of the Kanto Earthquake of 1923.

The dialectical/reflexive narrative structures employed by the three films, combined with the virtual compendium of the major motifs of the New Wave, gives the film the "multidimensional" expression demanded by the post-Shingeki playwrights. The theatrical sign is similarly prominent in these films. The principle of repetition is fundamental to the narratives, while the repetitions on view are increasingly theatricalized. Repetition is central to both *Inferno* and *Man* which are circular in construction: They end where they began. *Inferno* begins with Shun and Nanami going to a love hotel and then failing to make love; it ends when Shun, near the same hotel, fails, once again, to consummate their relationship (he is killed). The circular construction of *Man* is even more overt: A filmmaker commits suicide by jumping off a building; a young man wearing sneakers steals the camera and runs off. At the end, a filmmaker commits suicide by jumping off a building; a young man wearing sneakers steals the camera and runs off.

Repetition is also impacted in the films by the process of memory—the

Tokyo senso sengo hiwa (*The Man Who Left His Will on Film*)
Oshima Nagisa, director. Kawakita/Japan Film Library Council

influence of Alain Resnais seems quite clear in all the works under discussion. Oshima's *Man* seems every bit as puzzling, as *non-diegetic*, as *L'Année Dernière à Marienbad* (*Last Year at Marienbad*, 1961), which similarly relies on repetition as a narrative principle. Resnais and Oshima allow repetition-with-difference; the man, A, "reworks" his memories to try and convince the woman, X, that they met last year at Marienbad; Motoki "reshoots" the footage of his friend, he repeats it, but with variations. A shot of a mailbox in his friend's film is reshot by Motoki and Yasuko, except in the repetition, Yasuko turns the mailbox into a site of struggle as she stands in front of it and refuses to move. A shot of a public telephone repeats with Yasuko now pretending to talk on it while an office worker looks exasperatedly on. Shots of traffic on the street are repeated with Yasuko darting into a line of cars. Both films, the friend's "original" and Motoki's "repetition-with-difference" are arguably memories. Yasuko says, while watching the original footage, "That morning he embraced me. Without speaking, he simply embraced me. It was like wind blowing, water flowing, clouds racing by. The sun was shining—it was dazzling."[17] This poetic recitation is quite like that of A in Resnais's film describing the endless corridors of the luxurious spa. In *Inferno*, Shun remembers his past—pleasant images of his mother hugging him, painful images of his stepfather molesting him. Shun's memory/imagination of Momi, the five-year-old girl he apparently molests in the park, is repeated a number of times, ranging from the startling projection on the wall of his psychiatrist's office, to flashing images as he interacts with Nanami. Memory is crucial to Yoshida's *Eros*; Keiko McDonald feels the treatment of time in the film is quite "Proust-like."[18] However, the flexibility of time in this film is not a function of a single memory, nor even "cinematic memory," but rather something like the living memory of history which dialectically interacts with the present, the multidimensional existence of the modern world.

The dialectical interaction of past and present in *Eros* is seen most brilliantly through Yoshida's use of the theatrical sign. Noel Burch points to the sequence in which "a woman in old-style dress takes the ultra-modern 'bullet train,' gets off at modern Tokyo Station, but is picked up by an old-style rickshaw. . . ."[19] The "woman" Burch refers to is the character of Ito Noe and the sequence he discussses is actually a flashback-within-a-flashback, or possibly a flashback within an *imagined* (staged) sequence. The sequence begins with Eiko masturbating in a shower following her lovemaking to Unema. Yoshida then cuts to a shot of Osugi Sakae and Ito Noe walking in a park amidst flowering cherry blossoms, photographed in Yoshida's typical radically decentered compositional style—in this instance, the shot has too much headroom by Hollywood standards. From this scene of Osugi and Ito talking, there is a flashback from *Noe's point of view* to her arrival in Tokyo. We may understand this sequence in a number of ways: Eiko imagines it accurately, that Osugi and Ito walked in a park and Noe told her lover of her arrival; or it may be that both pasts (the park, the train) are Eiko's imagination. Keiko McDonald quotes Sato Tadao's comment that "Osugi and his women are not entirely the creation of Eiko's imagination . . . rather than acting as Eiko imagines, they assert the autonomy of their own imaginations and start imagining their past experience, even transcending the temporal dimension altogether and putting themselves in the present."[20] Sato perhaps has in mind a scene in front of the modern-day Odakyu Department store in which Ito Noe is interviewed by Eiko. As the two women continue their conversation in the city's outskirts, Noe sees her ex-husband, Tsuji Jun, passing by with their son. Noe inserts herself into the present and imagines herself in the past, but Eiko never imagines herself in the past, only Noe.

On the other hand, it is possible to see Ito Noe as entirely Eiko's creation, her need, her desire. We may then interpret Noe's arrival in Tokyo (which actually took place in 1910) in this highly disjunctive manner as possibly a failure of imagination on Eiko's part. She is aware of the Taisho-style kimono and of rickshaws, but cannot conceive, envision, Tokyo as other than it is now. In the same manner, Eiko conjures up Osugi's capture in a sword fight which takes place on a deserted modern-day expressway. That Osugi was killed in the aftermath of the Tokyo earthquake of 1923 is

Eros purasu gyakusatsu (*Eros plus Massacre*)
Yoshida Yoshishige, director. Kawakita/Japan Film Library Council

well known to her. Thus the expressway is littered with debris, but in the background, clearly visible, is Tokyo's modern-day high-rises. Perhaps Eiko cannot conjure up, or create, anything more than Osugi, Ito, their circle of friends and their political-sexual beliefs; or perhaps only this concerns her.

The theatricalization of *Eros* reaches an extreme when Eiko finally comes to terms with Osugi and Noe. Burch marvels at "the climactic fantasy sequence showing three successive versions of the imagined death of the martyr [Osugi] at the hands of the three women gone suddenly berserk, toppling *shoji* after *shoji* in headlong flight through a cunning labyrinth of *decoupage*. This sequence is the finest cinematic reflection I have seen on *histrionic death* . . . "[21] Unfortunately for Burch's description, only *two* of the women in his life are present in this scene, Itsuko and Noe (the third woman in his life is Osugi's wife, the least important woman to the film, that is, to Eiko). In the first version of the scene, Itsuko stabs Osugi in the neck; the two of them struggle as all around them the *shoji* collapse unaided by the fight; a metaphor. This version is the one closest to history (save for the collapsing shoji) in that Osugi was stabbed by his other mistress, in this film called Itsuko. In the second recreated/repeated version of the stabbing of Osugi, Osugi and Itsuko are in the bath and it is Osugi who forces Itsuko to stab him, as if in this instance the "actors" (Osugi and Itsuko) must live up to history, a history in which Osugi was stabbed by a mistress. The third variation finds Eiko breaking free of history and her own imagination of it, for now she envisions Ito Noe as stabbing Osugi. In a very high angle shot of the interior of the inn, Yoshida shows Noe and Itsuko arguing; the knife is sticking in the tatami. Noe seems to stab Osugi but he has no blood on him, although Noe's hands are drenched in blood. Osugi lies on his back as if mortally wounded, but converses without pain. The women help him up and walk through the corridor, the knife now sticking through Osugi's neck, although he still manages to converse without difficulty. Eventually he collapses on a shoji outside in the garden. He dies, then speaks again.

Throughout all three versions of the stabbing incident, Yoshida intercuts scenes of Eiko and Wada in Unema's film studio. Between the first and second variations on the stabbing incident, Wada films Eiko with a 16mm camera as Eiko "films" the stabbing incidents in her mind. Between the second and third variations, Eiko strips off her clothes and throws them at Wada, challenging him to make love to her. She lies nude on the floor, and he films her. She stands in front of a movie screen and grabs a cigarette lighter, challenging Wada to "set fire to me." While this is perhaps an obvious sexual metaphor, it is also a repetition-variation on an earlier scene in which Eiko tried to set fire to Unema's film of the Tokyo earthquake of 1923. She wants to set fire to the film because the man who made it is an "old good-for-nothing." Of course, it is safety film which will not burn, but, on the other hand, the filmmaker cannot "burn" Eiko, he cannot satisfy her sexually. (In an early scene, while Unema makes love to her, with Wada reading a newspaper in the next room, Eiko looks distractedly around the stark-white, Antonioni-esque room. When Unema is finished, Eiko goes into the shower to masturbate, which generates the first flashback to the Taisho-era, the scene of the cherry blossoms in the park. Eiko's sexual dissatisfaction calls up the free-love advocates Osugi and Ito.) When Eiko sets fire to her stockings, she and Wada make love. And following the third, final, variation on the stabbing incident, the most radical as it is the most "untrue" to history, Eiko and Wada argue about that interpretation. To Eiko (for it was Eiko's vision that conjured up this variation) it is a necessity that Ito Noe was the one who stabbed Osugi as an expression of passion and strength. Having come to terms with Ito, having come to the conclusion that Ito made her choices out of strength and self-will, Eiko can now end the film.

The penultimate scene of the film is a repetition-variation of another theatricalized vision of the past, this involving Osugi, Ito, and a young boy, Osugi's nephew, killed by the military police. Eiko had earlier imagined their death following a stylized trial scene. The boy, Noe, and Osugi

Eros purasu gyakusatsu (*Eros plus Massacre*)
Yoshida Yoshishige, director. Kawakita/Japan Film Library Council

sit in straight-backed chairs. Against a black background, they are each in turn strangled. We still see photographs of the courtroom, the bodies posed in various costumes. In this penultimate scene, the three bodies appear symmetrically posed on the street with nooses around their necks. Eiko kneels down next to Noe's body while, back in the film studio, Unema hangs himself with a noose of 16mm film. The motif of strangulation in the deaths is significant. McDonald claims that whereas Osugi Sakae died for his beliefs—revolution through free love—Unema "kills himself only to be free from the impoverishment of contemporary love."[22] But this is also the grim in-joke—the old good-for-nothing realizes not simply the death of love but the death of cinema. And cinema, having died, the Taisho-era characters may be called forward to pose for a picture. The magnesium flare of the flash leads to a blackout, a blackout interrupted temporarily by Eiko and Wada exiting the studio amidst another flash of bright light, the light of day, momentarily causing the screen to go white as if the projector had simply run out of film.

Noel Burch, who prizes *Eros plus Massacre* for its "freely disjunctive . . . dialectical . . . approach to narrative space-time," felt unable to deal with the film fully.[23] Keiko McDonald, in an essay from which I have already quoted, dealt with the film by presenting almost a scene-by-scene breakdown with commentary. Here, the attempt has been first to put the film in context with two other somewhat similar films which share a disjunctive, dialectical narrative strategy, a self-referentiality, an overt desire to question the nature and function of cinema, all through a focus on student radicals or alienated youth. Perhaps not yet clear from the preceding discussion is the significance of Yoshida's use of Osugi Sakae and Ito Noe. For despite the quite challenging and spectacular presentation of youthful sex and rebellion of the film's modern figures, the interest here lies in the Taisho-era figures. Yoshida is clearly using them, comparing them, to his modern-day subjects. But what, precisely, is he comparing?

Yoshida feels that the women are the major protagonists in both the modern story and the Taisho-era recreations.[24] Osugi's philosophy and political beliefs may dominate the historical record, but Ito Noe's personality and desires dominate this film. Ito Noe was born on Kyushu near the city of Fukuoka on January 21, 1895. April 1910 found her moving to Tokyo, where she entered the Ueno Girls' School from which she graduated in March 1912. Soon after, "she became the mistress of one of her teachers, Tsuji Jun, who was immediately fired. By Tsuji, Ito had a son, Makoto, on January 20, 1914, and a second, Ryuji, on August 10, 1915."[25] In November 1912, shortly after her graduation, she had begun to help with the administration of *Seito* (Bluestocking) magazine. *Seito* was formed in September 1911 by Hiratsuka Raicho. It was envisioned as a literary magazine for women, but it soon became the center of Japanese feminist ideology and controversy. The young Ito Noe thus soon found herself a member of an elite literary and political circle. Among the contributors to *Seito* were the famed Meiji poet Yosano Akiko; Mori Shigeki, the wife of Mori Ogai (one of Japan's major novelists); Koganei Kimiko, Mori Ogai's sister; Kunikida Haruko, wife of Kunikida Doppo (another important writer); and Okada Yachiyo, sister of Shingeki-founder Osanai Kaoru.[26] Also among this group of women writers and activists was Hori Yasuko, the wife of Osugi Sakae whom he had wed in September 1906. Hori contributed an essay to the January 1913 issue discussing the feudal ideology of Japan which prevented women from achieving their hoped-for status of the "New Woman."[27] Hiratsuka Raicho published an essay in that same issue which called for love as the basis for marriage and asserted that sexual fulfillment for women could only be achieved in a love relationship that Japanese social institutions militated against.[28] By the standards of that time, or any time, this was heady stuff for an eighteen-year-old girl from the country.

Through her developing interests in feminism, Ito Noe was able to turn the journal toward a greater concern with politics. In 1913, Noe had begun to read the works of Emma Goldman at the suggestion of Tsuji Jun. Noe published a partial translation by Tsuji of Goldman's "The Tragedy of Women's Liberation" in the September 1913 issue, and two more translations were published in subsequent issues under Ito's name, although Tsuji did the bulk of the translating. (Noe's English was not good enough by itself owing mostly to her relative lack of formal advanced education.)[29]

In November 1914, when Ito was not quite twenty, she became the editor and publisher of *Seito*, as well as the driving force behind the study groups formed around the journal. Throughout all of 1915 she virtually determined the contents of the journal and the tone of the discussions.[30] Among the issues she raised in the journal was contraception and abortion. "Ito argued, in the February 1915 issue, that a woman should decide to make love or not with the same freedom that a man has in choosing," but she did not favor abortion, arguing that a fetus was a child with its own destiny.[31]

Another writer connected with *Seito* was Kamichika Ichiko. It was Ichiko who provided the model for the character of Masaoka Itsuko in Yoshida's film. Her character represents the only important name change among the historical figures. This was forced upon Yoshida by Kamichika herself, who was still alive at the time. In addition to the name change, she successfully forced Yoshida into making changes in his film, including the elimination of some scenes.[32] Osugi met Ichiko in April of 1914 and began his affair with her in December 1915. In what became known as the Hayama Incident (Hikage in the film), Kamichika Ichiko stabbed Osugi. He was seriously wounded but, of course, survived. Ichiko served two years in prison, from October 3, 1917, to October 3, 1919, for her attempt on her lover's life. After World War II, she became a Diet member from Tokyo's Fifth District.[33] Meanwhile, Ito Noe had begun her affair with Osugi in February 1916; in May of that year, she left Tsuji. Coincidentally or not, February 1916 also saw the final issue of *Seito*.

In September 1917, Noe had a baby girl, Mako, with Osugi,[34] the first of five children the couple would have, all of whom were taken care of by her relatives after Osugi and Noe were murdered on September 16, 1923, by the military police in the aftermath of the Kanto earthquake.[35]

Yoshida demonstrates his belief in the centrality of the women to his film by opening with an "interview" between Eiko and a woman Eiko claims is Mako, the daughter of Ito Noe and Osugi Sakae. It is abundantly clear that this "Mako" is not Ito's daughter, played as she is by then thirty-five-year-old Okada Mariko without age makeup of any kind. (Mako would have been fifty-two in 1969.) It is also the case, as we discover retrospectively, that Ito Noe herself is played by Okada Mariko. While this Mako does not respond to Eiko's interview questions, Yoshida is able to introduce the salient facts of Ito Noe's life. Mako sits silently in a straight-backed chair, photographed in a series of off-centered angles which gradually get closer and closer. Keiko McDonald reads this strategy as revelatory of "the ambiguous nature of Eiko's imagination." The scene ends when Mako points to the camera and speaks of the absence of any memory of her mother. McDonald then notes that Mako "slowly moves her hands (and) a glittering light comes through the spaces between her fingers until the screen is completely white."[36] This leads in to the credits of the film, as McDonald notes. But she fails to note that the flaring of the white light is like a motion-picture projector, the same kind of flaring light that ends the film; that this flaring white light at the start is the beginning of the overtly reflexive stance taken by Yoshida, the clue that this is a film interrogation of Mako by Eiko and of all the daughters of Ito Noe and Osugi Sakae.

Osugi Sakae "saw society's major problem as human stagnation caused by multiple layers of habit and social sanction. Osugi theorized that, if constraints on individual activity were broken, pent-up energies would be released and these would provide the dynamism for necessary change."[37] Osugi recognized that social restraints were imposed by a variety of Japanese institutions, and so also castigated "traditional religions and art for having taught 'resignation from life and acquiescence in the power of nature.' Only in the conscious destruction of past cultural residue can man find his creativity."[38] One can already see the interest that a New Wave filmmaker like Yoshida would take in Osugi. Similarly, the anarchism favored by Osugi intersects with the images of youthful rebellion put forward especially by Oshima.

> Osugi's anarchism . . . offered a radically new personal and social ethos based on the total rejection of the traditional duty-bound ethics of altruism and self-abnegation. Osugi's own behavior demonstrated his belief in the value of bold, forceful, rebellious individualism not only to satisfy personal desires but to forge a new society in which individuals would no longer allow themselves to be docile victims of the state.[39]

Again we can see the danger of applying Western categories to Japanese revolutionary practice. The notion of individualism, retrograde to Western Marxists and other radicals, became a radical necessity juxtaposed against a culture which maintains its status quo by encouraging docility and a "transcendental" view of life.

Osugi's individualism stands, in any case, not merely opposed to neo-fedual ideology but also to Socialist thinking in the Taisho era, making strong inroads among Japanese intellectuals. Hegelian/Marxian dialectical analysis, of course, provided a strong underpinning to leftist intellectuals' views of Japanese society. Osugi was apparently influenced by Hegel; Tatsuo Arima feels that "In some respects, Osugi's view of the intellectual is close to Hegel's. Intellect can tell us only what has taken place; reality is revealed to us only when it has completed its course. But then Osugi, unlike Hegel, proceeds to argue for the destruction of reality altogether." From here, Osugi's thinking enters the realm of '60s radical notions, as Arima notes that in the destruction of reality "it is not intellect but *passion* that ought to direct man's action." And it is in this view of passion that Osugi breaks from Socialism: "the destructive potential of individual passion" refutes "the deterministic implications of socialist thinking."[40]

Osugi's anarchism encompassed not only broad social views, but also his immediate circumstances. Osugi tried to persuade his wife, Hori Yasuko, and his two mistresses, Kamichika Ichiko and Ito Noe, to allow him to continue his relationship with each of them by putting their relationship on a political, as well as sexual, basis. He used the idea, anticipating the contemporary feminist movement, that "the personal is political." Osugi made up "rules of love: Each individual was to maintain an independent, self-sufficient economic existence; . . . each was to live in his or her own apartment or house; . . . each must accord everyone else complete freedom of action, in sexual as well as other matters."[41] This can be precisely compared to what the filmic Osugi says to his mistresses and wife: "First, the three of you have to be economically independent. Second, you have to let me live separately from you instead of living with any one of you. Third, you must respect each other's freedom, including sex."[42] In Yoshida's film, at one point Osugi also compares monogamous marriage to the law of private property under capitalism—an early expression of another '60s motif.

We might also see that Osugi's anarchism, his rebellion, like that of the '60s generation, was more clearly "anti" than it was positively "pro," that his writings and beliefs stood steadfastly *against* the status quo, but did not necessarily put forward a new, coherent program in its place: "Osugi's writings were far more attractively acute and precise in describing the demise of society than in depicting the means by which social rejuvenation was to be realized."[43] Like the youthful radicals of the '60s in yet another way, "It was the very process of discord that Osugi found most beautiful. He located the roots of creation in the desire for destruction, and in his writing the terms 'creativity' and 'destruction' become uncomfortably synonymous."[44] As depicted in the rebellious youth in the films of Oshima, Wakamatsu, Suzuki, and Yoshida, Osugi's urge to rebel, to find his identity, merged with the life force of sexuality. Unfortunately, this life force was unable to sustain itself in the face of the intractability of the dominant culture. A representative of the dominant culture, indeed a virtual paradigm of it (a member of the military police), took it upon himself to murder Osugi Sakae and Ito Noe in 1923, shortly after the Great Kanto earthquake destroyed most of Tokyo.

The spirits of Ito Noe and Osugi Sakae resurfaced not to haunt the '60s generation, but to inspire it. But haunt them it did nevertheless as, like Osugi and Ito, the '60s generation passed away, killed off not by the brutality of the militarists but by the more insidious forces of economic cooptation and intimidation. Hani Susumu, Yoshida Yoshishige, and Oshima Nagisa, among the most important of the Japanese New Wave directors, found themselves, at the end of the '60s, left with nothing but ghosts save for a will to film, knowing that by then filming had become impossible.

Notes

Introduction

1. Noel Burch, "Nagisa Oshima and Japanese Cinema in the 60s," in Richard Roud, ed. *Cinema: A Critical Dictionary* (London: Martin Secker and Warburg, 1980), p. 735.

2. Joan Mellen, *Voices from the Japanese Cinema* (New York: Liveright, 1975), p. 261.

3. Renato Poggioli, *The Theory of the Avant-Garde,* trans. Gerald Fitzgerald (Cambridge, Mass.: Harvard University Press, 1968), p. 25.

4. Ibid., p. 95.

5. Ibid., p. 20.

6. Tsuno Kaitaro, "Poor European Theatre," *Concerned Theatre Japan* 2, 3&4 (Spring, 1973), p. 15.

7. Poggioli writes: ". . . the identification of artistic revolution with the social revolution is now no more that purely rhetorical, an empty commonplace. . . . The equivocal survival of the myth of a parallel artistic and political revolution has . . . been favored by the modern concept of culture as spiritual civil war. . . ." Poggioli feels, on the contrary that "the only omnipresent or recurring political ideology within the avant-garde is the least political or the most antipolitical of all: libertarianism and anarchism," pp. 96–97. I might simply suggest here that "libertarianism" is not to be taken as antipolitical within the context of traditional Japanese culture.

8. Paul Willeman, "Notes on Subjectivity: On Reading Edward Branigan's 'Subjectivity Under Seige' " *Screen* 19, 1 (Spring 1978), p. 57.

9. Dana Polan, *The Political Language of Film and the Avant-Garde* (Ann Arbor: UMI Research Press, 1985), p. 92.

10. *Sekai no eiga sakka 31: Nihon eigashi* (Film Directors of the World 31: History of Japanese Film) (Tokyo: Kinema Jumpo, 1976), p. 219.

11. Personal interview, 22 June 1984, Tokyo, Japan.

12. J.L. Anderson and Donald Richie, *The Japanese Film: Art and Industry,* expanded ed. (Princeton: Princeton University Press, 1982), p. 252.

13. Ibid., p. 253.

14. Ibid., p. 254.

15. For a discussion of what I mean by an "action picture" and an analysis of how the widescreen ratio is used see my *The Samurai Films of Akira Kurosawa* (Ann Arbor: UMI Research Press, 1983), pp. 92–97.

16. Anderson and Richie, p. 451. Although Anderson and Richie do not discuss it, television's penetration began in the major cities, precisely the same area which constituted the primary moviegoing audience, so that the numbers are a bit deceptive with regards to the *direct* competition that television posed to the movie industry.

17. Richard N. Tucker, *Japan: Film Image* (London: Studio Vista, 1973), p. 37.

18. Anderson and Richie, p. 456.

19. Tucker, p. 38.

20. Anderson and Richie, p. 456.

21. Personal interview, 26 July 1984, Tokyo, Japan.

22. From the time he became an independent producer from 1965 to 1973, when the movement was pretty much over, Wakamatsu produced at least *forty-five* films, and at least another twenty since then (with fifteen films preceding his exit from

Nikkatsu). Max Tessier, *Le cinéma japonais au présent* (Paris: Lherminier, 1984), pp. 192–93; 218.

23. The term post-Shingeki theatre, and the basic aspects of this fascinating theatrical movement are derived from the writings of David G. Goodman, whose pioneering efforts in contemporary Japanese theatre I again acknowledge.

Chapter One

1. Noel Burch, "Nagisa Oshima and Japanese Cinema in the 60s," in Richard Roud, ed., *Cinema: A Critical Dictionary* (London: Martin Secker & Warburg, 1980), p. 735.

2. Joseph L. Anderson and Donald Richie, *The Japanese Film: Art and Industry,* expanded ed. (Princeton: Princeton University Press, 1982), p. 455.

3. Audie Bock, *Japanese Film Directors* (Tokyo: Kodansha, 1978), pp. 13–14.

4. Noel Burch, *To the Distant Observer* (Berkeley: University of California Press, 1979), p. 25.

5. Ian Buruma, *Behind the Mask* (New York: Panetheon Books, 1984), p. 3.

6. David Bordwell, *Narration in the Fiction Film* (Madison: University of Wisconsin Press, 1985), p. 150.

7. Ibid., p, 150.

8. Bordwell, in this book, deals very little with the Japanese cinema and primarily with Ozu who emerges as something of a special case by virtue of his utilizing the parametric mode—"to some extent . . . this mode of narration applies to isolated filmmakers and fugitive films" (p. 274). Although proliferating terminology is something typically to be avoided, it cannot be helped in this case.

9. David Bordwell, review of *To the Distant Observer, Wide Angle* 3, 4 (1980), pp. 70–71.

10. Kristin Thompson and David Bordwell, "Space and Narrative in the Films of Ozu," *Screen* 17, 2 (Summer, 1976), p. 45.

11. Burch, *To the Distant Observer*, p. 71.

12. Masao Miyoshi, *Accomplices of Silence: The Modern Japanese Novel* (Berkeley: University of California Press, 1975), p. xiii.

13. David Bordwell and Kristin Thompson, *Film Art: An Introduction* (Reading, Mass.: Addison-Wesley, 1979), p. 258.

14. Gwenn Boardman Petersen, *The Moon in the Water: Understanding Tanizaki, Kawabata, and Mishima* (Honolulu: University of Hawaii Press, 1979), p. 186.

15. Ibid., p. 31.

16. Bordwell, *Narration in the Fiction Film*, p. 157.

17. Bock, p. 139.

18. Ibid., p. 14.

19. Tadao Sato, *Currents in Japanese Cinema*, trans. Gregory Barrett (Tokyo: Kodansha, 1982), p. 116.

20. Anderson and Richie, p. 455.

21. Bock, p. 266.

22. Burch, in Roud, pp. 735–36.

23. Dana Polan, *The Political Language of Film and the Avant-Garde* (Ann Arbor: UMI Research Press, 1985), p. 84.

24. Ibid., p. 92.

25. Quoted in David G. Goodman, "Satoh Makoto and the Post-Shingeki Movement in Japanese Contemporary Theatre," dissertation, Cornell University, 1982, p. 72.

26. Carol Jay Sorgenfrei, "Shuji Terayama: Avant Garde Dramatist of Japan," dissertation, University of California, Santa Barbara, 1978, p. 90.

27. Goodman, p. 76.

28. Burch, *To the Distant Observer*, pp. 325–26.

29. Bock, p. 318.

30. George W. Packard, *Protest in Tokyo: The Security Treaty Crisis of 1960* (Princeton: Princeton University Press, 1966), p. 321.

31. *Sekai no eiga sakka 31: Nihon eiga-shi (Film Directors of the World 31: History of Japanese Film)* (Tokyo: Kinema Jumpo, 1976), p. 219.

32. Sato, p. 220.

33. Dana Polan, "Politics as Process in Three Films by Nagisa Oshima," *Film Criticism* 8, 1 (Fall, 1983), p. 33.

34. Burch, *To the Distant Observer*, p. 329.

35. Ibid.

36. Ibid.

37. Polan, "Politics as Process," p. 36.

38. Polan, *Political Language of Film*, pp. 106–7.

39. Brian Henderson, "Toward a Non-Bourgeois Camera Style" in his *A Critique of Film Theory* (New York: E.P. Dutton, 1980), p. 65.

40. Polan, "Politics as Process," p. 36.

41. Bock, p. 318.

42. James Monaco, *Alain Resnais* (New York: Oxford University Press, 1979), p. 20.

43. For a discussion of how many Japanese intellectuals in the '60s identified with the Jewish experience, see David G. Goodman, "Preliminary Thoughts on Political Theatre," *Concerned Theatre Japan* 2, 3&4 (Spring, 1973), pp. 89–111.

44. See Noel Burch's discussion of Oshima's politics in *To the Distant Observer*, pp. 325–28. Especially relevant are Burch's points about the sense of "victimization" and the ideology of individualism.

45. Packard, p. 3.

46. Patricia Steinhoff, "Student Conflict," in Ellis S. Krauss, Thomas P. Rohlen, and Patricia G. Steinhoff, eds., *Conflict in Japan* (Honolulu: University of Hawaii Press, 1984), p. 177.

47. Steinhoff, p. 174.

48. T.J. Pempel, *Patterns of Japanese Policymaking: Experiences from Higher Education* (Boulder: Westview Press, 1978), p. 97.

49. Bock, p. 314.

50. Pempel, p. 98; Packard, p. 25.

51. Pempel, p. 98.

52. Packard, pp. 131–32.

53. Pempel, p. 98.

54. Packard, p. 82.

55. Ibid., p. 26.

56. Ibid., p. 100.

57. Ibid., pp. 157–58.

58. Ibid., pp. 165–67.

59. Ibid., p. 171.

60. Ibid., p. 177.

61. Pempel, pp. 102–3.

62. Packard, pp. 226–27.

63. Ibid., pp. 296–97.

64. Ibid., p. 302.

65. Bock, pp. 345, 356.

Chapter Two

1. Tadao Sato, *Currents in Japanese Cinema*, trans. Gregory Barrett (Tokyo: Kodansha, 1982), p. 208.
2. Donald Richie, *The Japanese Movie*, rev. ed. (Tokyo: Kodansha, 1982), p. 128.
3. Joseph L. Anderson and Donald Richie, *The Japanese Film: Art and Industry*, expanded ed. (Princeton: Princeton University Press, 1982), p. 265.
4. Quoted in Sato, p. 213.
5. Anderson and Richie, p. 384.
6. *Sekai no eiga sakka 31: Nihon eigashi* [Film Directors of the World 31: History of Japanese Film] (Tokyo: Kinema Jumpo, 1976), pp. 197–98.
7. Quoted in Sato, p. 213.
8. Anderson and Richie, p. 285.
9. Quoted in Audie Bock, *Japanese Film Directors* (Tokyo: Kodansha, 1978), p. 289.
10. Anderson and Richie, pp. 1A-E (496–500).
11. Personal interview, 26 July 1984, Tokyo, Japan.
12. *Sekai no eiga sakka 10: Shinoda Masahiro and Yoshida Yoshishige* (Tokyo: Kinema Jumpo, 1971), p. 190.
13. Quoted in Bock, p. 289.
14. Quoted in ibid., p. 315 (ellipsis in original).
15. Ibid., 344. It is worth noting that even into the 1980s, the major studios preferred to train their directors through the assistant-system as compared, for instance, to the film school training in the U.S.
16. *Sekai no eiga sakka 10*, p. 189.
17. Personal interview, 24 July 1984, Tokyo, Japan.
18. Quoted in Bock, p. 344.
19. Ibid., p. 317.
20. *Sekai no eiga sakka 10*, p. 178.
21. Ibid., pp. 190–91.
22. Bock, p. 316.
23. Ibid., p. 318.
24. Sato, p. 217.
25. Ibid., p. 216.
26. Ian Cameron, "Nagisa Oshima Interview," *Movie* 17 (Winter 1969–70), p. 8.
27. Sato, p. 216.
28. Max Tessier, *Images du cinéma japonais* (Paris: Henri Veyrier, 1981), p. 234.
29. Cameron, "Nagisa Oshima Interview," p. 9.
30. Ibid.
31. Sato, p. 51.
32. Ibid., p. 52.
33. Quoted in Keiko I. McDonald, *Cinema East:. A Critical Study of Major Japanese Films* (East Brunswick, N.J.: Associated University Presses, 1983), p. 146.
34. Ibid., p. 344.
35. *Sekai no eiga sakka 10*, p.73.
36. Bock, p. 345.
37. *Sekai no eiga sakka 10*, p. 78.
38. Personal interview, 24 July 1984, Tokyo, Japan.
39. *Sekai no eiga sakka 10*, p. 204.
40. Bock, p. 303.
41. Dave Kehr, "The Last Rising Sun," *Film Comment* 19, 5 (Sept.-Oct., 1983), p. 33.
42. Bock, p. 303.

43. Ibid.
44. Kehr, p. 33.
45. Bock, p. 303.
46. Joan Mellen, *Voices from the Japanese Cinema* (New York: Liveright, 1975), p. 180.
47. Ibid., p. 188.
48. Ibid., p. 180.
49. Ibid., p. 181.
50. Joan Mellen, *The Waves at Genji's Door: Japan Through Its Cinema* (New York: Pantheon, 1976), p. 346. A weakness of Mellen's criticism in this book is her willingness to take the directors at their own words.
51. Bock, p. 359.
52. Ian Cameron, *Second Wave* (New York: Praeger, 1970), p. 67.
53. Cameron, "Nagisa Oshima Interview," p. 10.
54. Mellen, *Waves*, p. 357.
55. Noel Burch, *To the Distant Observer* (Berkeley: University of California Press, 1979), p. 362.
56. J. Hoberman, in a typically eccentrically perceptive review of Oshima's *Cruel Story of Youth* (*Village Voice*, July 24, 1984, p.53), likens the Oshima film to Fuller's works. But Oshima is far too overtly intellectual to be reminiscent of the instinctual brilliance of Fuller.
57. Burch, p. 363.
58. *Sekai no eiga sakka 31*, p. 224.
59. Sato, p. 35. The *tateyaku* is the hero of the period drama, strong, fearless, and full of pride; the *nimaime* are the pathetic, weak, but sexually attractive heroes of contemporary plays and films.
60. Sato, p. 226.
61. Tessier, p. 126.
62. This is one of only two films by Suzuki included in Kinema Jumpo's *Eiga shijo besto 200 shirizu: Nihon eiga* (*The Great Films of the World: Japan*) (1982).
63. Sato, p. 228.
64. *The Great Films of the World: Japan*, p. 331.
65. Sato, p. 228.
66. Kazuko Tsurumi, "Student Movements in 1960 and 1969: Continuity and Change," in Shunichi Takayanagi and Kimitada Miwa, eds., *Postwar Trends in Japan* (Tokyo: University of Tokyo Press, 1975), p. 203.
67. Ben-Ami Shillony, *Revolt in Japan: The Young Officers and the February 26, 1936, Incident* (Princeton: Princeton University Press, 1973), pp. 72–73.
68. Ibid., p. 5.
69. Ibid., p. 10.
70. Ibid., pp. 80, ix.
71. The concept of these three films as a Taisho-Showa trilogy was expressed in a personal interview with Yoshida on 22 June 1984, Tokyo, Japan.

Chapter Three
1. Keiko I. McDonald, *Cinema East: A Critical Study of Major Japanese Films* (East Brunswick, N.J.: Associated University Presses, 1983), p. 36.
2. Noel Burch, *To the Distant Observer* (Berkeley: University of California Press, 1979), pp. 347–48.
3. McDonald, p. 47.
4. Ibid., p. 46.
5. Arthur G. Kimball, *Crisis in Identity and Contemporary Japanese Novels* (Rutland,

V.: Charles E. Tuttle, 1973), p. 77. Kimball maintains, too, the Mishima Yukio is similarly concerned with identity.

6. Ibid., p. 133.

7. Ibid., p. 136.

8. McDonald, p. 38.

9. Ibid., p. 42.

10. Joan Mellen, *Voices from the Japanese Cinema* (New York: Liveright, 1975), p. 171.

11. Allan Casebier, "Images of Irrationality in Modern Japan: The Films of Shohei Imamura," *Film Criticism* 8, 1 (Fall, 1983), p. 43.

12. Ibid., p. 42.

13. Ibid., p. 45.

14. Joan Mellen, *The Waves at Genji's Door: Japan Through Its Cinema* (New York: Pantheon, 1976), p. 371.

15. Ibid., *Waves*, p. 374.

16. Ibid., *Waves*, p. 371.

17. Ibid., *Waves*, p. 374.

18. Raymond Durgnat, *Sexual Alienation in the Cinema* (London: Studio Vista, 1972), pp. 144–46.

19. Mellen, *Waves*, p. 371.

20. Ibid., *Waves*, p. 372.

21. Ian Buruma, *Behind the Mask* (New York: Pantheon, 1984), p. 102. On p. 104 of this book, Buruma quotes a paragraph from Nosaka Akiyuki's source novel for Imamura's film describing a visit to a *toruko*.

22. Mellen, Waves, p. 384.

23. This point is noted by Audie Bock, *Japanese Film Directors* (Tokyo: Kodansha, 1978), p. 299. I wonder if Imamura was inspired by the statue of Hachiko which stands in front of Shibuya Station, a tribute to a faithful dog who awaited his master's return and which has become a handy landmark and meeting place in the street-nameless Tokyo.

24. Mellen, *Waves*, p. 13.

25. *Eiga shijo besto 200 shirizu: Nihon eiga* (The Great Films of the World/Japan) (Tokyo: Kinema Jumpo, 1982), p. 345.

26. Ibid.

27. Mellen, *Waves*, p. 13.

28. Bock, p. 300.

29. Burch, p. 330.

30. Ibid., pp. 330–31.

31. Ibid., p. 331.

32. Ibid., pp. 330–31.

33. Ibid., p. 339.

34. *Mainichi Daily News*, July 23, 1984, p. 9.

35. Ian Cameron, "Nagisa Oshima Interview" *Movie* 17 (Winter 1969–70), p. 13.

36. Ian Cameron, *Second Wave* (New York: Praeger, 1970), p. 81.

37. Cameron, "Nagisa Oshima Interview," p. 12.

38. Mellen, *Voices*, p. 270.

39. Mellen, *Waves*, pp. 367–68.

40. Durgnat, pp. 305–7.

41. Quoted in Cameron, *Second Wave*, p. 90.

42. For a discussion of the origins and aims of the Takarazuka Theatre, see Buruma, pp. 113–15.

43. Ibid., p. 117.

44. Fukusaku may be said to have a tangential connection to the New Wave. He

directed his first film for Toei in 1961 and, like Suzuki Seijun, used genre films to make personal statements. For an overview of Fukasaku's career, see Keiko McDonald, "Kinji Fukasaku: An Introduction," *Film Criticism* 8, 1 (Fall, 1983), pp. 20–32.

45. Elliott Stein, "Lizards and Snails and Puppy Dogs' Tails," *Village Voice*, Dec. 4, 1984, p. 57.

46. Buruma, p. 117.

47. Burch, p. 356.

48. Donald Richie, *The Japanese Movie*, rev. ed. (Tokyo: Kodansha, 1982), p. 192.

49. *Great Films of the World/Japan*, p. 381.

50. Personal interview, 7 July 1984, Tokyo, Japan. Considering that the producer of the film is French, and that post-production was done in France, there is no reason to doubt Oshima, especially since Barthes' book was published in France in 1970.

51. Peter B. High, "Oshima: A Vita Sexualis on Film," *Wide Angle* 2, 4 (1978), p. 71.

52. Dana Polan, "Politics as Process in Three Films by Nagisa Oshima," *Film Criticism* 8, 1 (Fall, 1983), p. 40.

53. Ibid., p. 39.

54. Quoted in ibid., p. 39.

55. Joseph L. Anderson and Donald Richie, *The Japanese Film: Art and Industry*, expanded ed. (Princeton: Princeton University Press, 1982), p. 454.

56. Quoted in Buruma, p. 57.

57. See also Richard Tucker, *Japan: Film Image* (London: Studio Vista, 1973), p. 127.

58. Burch, p. 351.

59. Sato Tadao, "*Wakamatsu Koji no eiga*" (Wakamatsu Koji's Films), *Ato Shiata* 93 (Art Theatre 93), p. 11.

60. Burch, p. 351.

61. Buruma, p. 59.

62. Ibid., p. 58.

63. Ibid., p. 59.

64. Ibid., p. 61.

65. Burch, pp. 352–53.

66. Ibid., p. 354. As David Bordwell points out in his review of *To the Distant Observer*, Burch has a "habit of putting a claim in italics as a substitute for suporting it." *Wide Angle* 3, 4 (1980), p. 70.

67. Burch, p. 354.

68. Ibid., p. 353.

69. Ibid.

70. Ibid., pp. 353–54.

71. A black and white still of this scene is reproduced in ibid., p. 355.

72. Ibid., p. 352.

73. Ibid.

74. Sato Shigeomi, "*Pinku eiga ni okeru Wakamatsu Koji no ichi*" (Wakamatsu Koji's Position in Pink Films), *Art Theatre* 93, p. 35.

75. That Adachi Masao could be so perceptive about the left-wing radical fringe is belied by his own actions later in the '60s when the filmmaker left Japan to join a Palestinian terrorist organization.

76. Shinada Yukichi, "*Wakamatsu Koji jiko a kataru*" (Wakamatsu Koji Talks About Himself), *Art Theatre* 93, p. 20.

77. Tucker, p. 125.

Chapter Four

1. Joan Mellen, *Voices from the Japanese Cinema*, (New York: Liveright, 1975), p. 201.

2. Richard N. Tucker, *Japan: Film Image* (London: Studio Vista, 1973), 65.

3. Joseph L. Anderson and Donald Richie, *Japanese Film: Art and Industry*, expanded ed. (Princeton: Princeton University Press, 1982), p. 36.

4. Noel Burch, *To the Distant Observer: Form and Meaning in the Japanese Cinema* (Berkeley: University of California Press, 1979), p. 95.

5. Anderson and Richie, p. 64.

6. Tadao Sato, *Currents in Japanese Cinema*, trans. Gregory Barrett (Tokyo: Kodansha, 1982), p. 78.

7. Audie Bock, *Japanese Film Directors* (Tokyo: Kodansha, 1978), p. 40.

8. Sato, p. 78.

9. Keiko McDonald, *Mizoguchi* (Boston: Twayne, 1984), p. 104.

10. Tucker, p. 59.

11. Bock, p. 36.

12. J. Dudley Andrew and Paul Andrew, *Kenji Mizoguchi: A Guide to References and Resources* (Boston: G.K. Hall, 1981), p. 27.

13. Bock, p. 51.

14. Joan Mellen, *The Waves at Genji's Door: Japan Through Its Cinema* (New York: Pantheon, 1976), p. 309.

15. Bock, pp. 41, 43.

16. Andrew and Andrew, p. 28.

17. Bock, p. 43.

18. Ibid., p. 41.

19. Sato, p. 76.

20. Ian Buruma, *Behind the Mask* (New York: Pantheon, 1984), p. 33.

21. Andrew and Andrew, p. 28.

22. Ibid.

23. Buruma, p. 34. Buruma makes no distinctions in Mizoguchi's cinema as we are here setting forth.

24. Anderson and Richie, pp. 176–177.

25. Buruma, p. 24.

26. Bock, pp. 197–198.

27. Anderson and Richie, p. 192.

28. The English title of Imai's film often appears as *Muddy Waters*, as in Anderson and Richie. However, *Troubled Waters* is preferable now in light of the success of Oguri Kohei's *Doro no kawa* (1981) called *Muddy Water* in English (*doro* means "mud"). "Troubled Waters" is also the translation preferred by Robert Lyons Danly.

29. Robert Lyons Danly, *In the Shade of Spring Leaves* (New Haven: Yale University Press, 1981), p. 140.

30. Ibid., p. 133.

31. The Japanese title is also translated as *Irezumi*, and Masumura's film adaptation is sometimes listed as *Spider Girl*.

32. Sato, p. 90.

33. Ibid., p. 231.

34. Mellen, *Voices*, p. 82.

35. Buruma, p. 36.

36. Sato, pp. 81–82.

37. Quoted in Bock, p. 292.

38. Ibid.

39. Mellen, *Waves*, p. 301.

40. Bock, p. 287.

41. Mellen, *Waves*, p. 241.

42. Sato, pp. 86–87.

43. Dave Kehr, "The Last Rising Sun," *Film Comment* 19, 5 (Sept.-Oct. 1983), pp. 34–35.

44. Buruma, p. 37. Buruma certainly overstates the case of a direct continuity between the ancient mythology and the contemporary psyche in general. It is safer to say that Imamura is overtly bringing the Shinto mythos to the fore.

45. Mellen, *Waves*, p. 295.

46. Ibid., p. 300.

47. Ibid., p. 297.

48. Ibid.

49. Ibid., p. 299.

50. Tucker, pp. 69–70.

51. Mellen, *Waves*, p. 300.

52. Donald Richie, *Japanese Cinema: Film Style and National Character* (Garden City, N.Y.: Anchor Books, 1971), pp. 158–59.

53. Sato, p. 231.

54. Buruma, p. 61.

55. Burch, p. 350.

56. Bock, p. 348.

57. Ibid., p. 347.

58. Anderson and Richie, p. 467.

59. Gwen Boardman Petersen, *The Moon in the Water: Understanding Tanizaki, Kawabata, and Mishima* (Honolulu: University of Hawaii Press, 1979), p. 186, note 32.

60. Mellen, *Waves*, p. 393.

61. Ibid., p. 392.

62. David G. Goodman, "Satoh Makoto and the Post-Shingeki Movement in Japanese Contemporary Theatre," dissertation, Cornell University, 1982, p. 226.

63. Bock, p. 312.

Chapter Five

1. Mikiso Hane, *Peasants, Rebels, and Outcastes: The Underside of Modern Japan* (New York: Pantheon, 1982), p. 225.

2. Ibid., p. 255.

3. Quoted in Joan Mellen, *The Waves at Genji's Door: Japan Through Its Cinema* (New York: Pantheon, 1976), p. 237.

4. Ibid., p. 241.

5. Ibid., p. 242.

6. Ibid., p. 405.

7. Kobe Abe, *The Face of Another*, trans. E. Dale Saunders (New York: Alfred A. Knopf, 1966), p. 112.

8. Ibid., p. 218.

9. Ian Cameron, "Nagisa Oshima Interview," *Movie* 17 (Winter 1969–70), p. 9.

10. Ian Cameron, *Second Wave* (New York: Praeger, 1970), p. 67.

11. Dana Polan, "Politics as Process in Three Films by Nagisa Oshima," *Film Criticism* 8, 1 (Fall 1983), p. 34.

12. Mellen, p. 422.

13. Stephen Heath, "Anata mo," *Screen* 17, 4 (Winter 1976/7) pp. 49–66.

14. Tsuno Kaitaro, "Biwa and Beatles: An Invitation to Modern Japanese Theatre," *Concerned Theatre Japan*, Special Introductory Issue (Oct. 1969), p. 25.

15. Quoted in David G. Goodman, "Preliminary Thoughts on Political Theatre," *Concerned Theatre Japan* 2, 3&4 (Spring 1973), p. 103.

16. Kazuko Fujimoto Goodman, "Discrimination and the Perception of Difference," *Concerned Theatre Japan* 2, 3&4 (Spring 1973), p. 150.

17. Tsuno, p. 26.

18. Dana Polan, *The Political Language of Film and the Avant-Garde* (Ann Arbor: UMI Research Press, 1985), p. 32.

19. Noel Burch, *To the Distant Observer* (Berkeley: University of California Press, 1979), p. 334; Burch's italics.

20. Tadoa Sato, *Currents in Japanese Cinema*, trans. Gregory Barrett (Tokyo: Kodansha, 1982), p. 238.

21. Mellen, p. 432.

22. T.J. Pempel, *Patterns of Japanese Policymaking: Experiences from Higher Education* (Boulder: Westview Press, 1978), p. 115.

23. David E. Apter and Nagayo Sawa, *Against the State: Politics and Social Protest in Japan* (Cambridge, Mass.: Harvard University Press, 1984), p. 121.

24. Ibid., p. 123.

25. Ibid., p. 124.

26. Burch, p. 360.

27. "A 60s Movement in the 80s: Interview with David Apter," in Sohnya Sayres et al., eds., *The Sixties, Without Apology* (Minneapolis: University of Minnesota Press, 1984), p. 89.

28. Burch, p. 361.

29. Personal interview with Ogawa Shinsuke, 23 June 1984, Tokyo, Japan.

30. Imai Tadashi is a favorite of the Japanese critical establishment, but Westerners, even and especially those of a leftist slant, are typically critical of his work. This seems rather perverse in light of his admirable record as a precursor and contemporary of the New Wave. The attitude toward Imai taken by leftists seems to recall Woody Allen's comment about intellectuals in *Stardust Memories*: "Intellectuals are like the Mafia—they only kill their own."

31. Personal interview with Tsuchimoto Noriaki, 9 July 1984, Tokyo.

32. Burch, p. 362.

33. This young boy struck me as the most memborable and moving of the victims. Joan Mellen comments upon him and others in her discussion of the film, p. 442.

34. Ibid., p. 439–40.

35. Burch, p. 362.

36. Personal interview with Ogawa.

37. Mellen, p. 433.

38. Sylvia Harvey, *May '68 and Film Culture* (London: BFI, 1980), p.25.

39. Personal interview with Ogawa.

40. Burch, p. 334; Burch's italics.

Chapter Six

1. Noel Burch, *To the Distant Observer* (Berkeley: University of California Press, 1979), p. 336.

2. Ibid., p. 338.

3. David G. Goodman, "Satoh Makoto and the Post-Shingeki Movement in Japanese Contemporary Theatre," dissertation, Cornell University, 1982, p. 18.

4. Ibid., p. 17.

5. Ibid., p. 20.

6. Tsuno Kaitaro, "Biwa and Beatles: An Invitation to Modern Japanese Theatre," *Concerned Theatre Japan*, Special Introductory Issue (October 1969), p. 17.

7. Tsuno Kaitaro, "The Tradition of Modern Theatre in Japan," quoted in Goodman, p. 68.

8. Hirosue Tamotsu, "The Secret Ritual of the Place of Evil," *Concerned Theatre Japan* 2, 1&2 (1971), p. 14.

9. Tsuno, "Biwa and Beatles," p. 17.

10. Audie Bock, *Japanese Film Directors* (Tokyo: Kodansha, 1978), p. 343.

11. Goodman, p. 27.

12. Tsuno, "Biwa and Beatles," p. 8.

13. Personal interview with Shinoda Masahiro, 24 July 1984, Tokyo.

14. In Tokyo in 1984, I saw a Kabuki production of *Natsu matsuri naniwa kagami*, in which Kanzaburo, an *onnagata* actor, played Otatsu, a "young beauty," and Giheiji, "an unscrupulous old man."

15. Keiko McDonald, *Cinema East* (East Brunswick, N.J.: Associated University Presses, 1983), p. 52.

16. Ibid., p. 61.

17. Burch, p. 230.

18. Ibid., p. 235.

19. Don Kirihara, "Kabuki, Cinema and Mizoguchi Kenji" in *Cinema and Language*, Stephen Heath and Patricia Mellencamp, eds. (Frederick, Md.: University Publications of America, 1983), p. 100.

20. Burch, p. 290.

21. Personal interview.

22. Carol Jay Sorgenfrei, "Shuji Terayama: Avant-Garde Dramatist of Japan," dissertation, University of California, Santa Barbara, 1978, p. 149.

23. Ibid., p. 252.

24. The English title for Chikamatsu's play is given as *The Woman Killer in the Hell of Oil* in *Major Plays of Chikamatsu*, trans. Donald Keene (New York: Columbia University Press, 1961).

25. Goodman, p. 189.

26. Ibid., p. 191.

27. Ibid., p. 187–88.

28. *Naozamurai* is the short, or English, title given to the play by Samuel L. Leiter, *Kabuki Encyclopedia* (Westport, Conn.: Greenwood Press, 1979), p. 210.

29. Tsuno Kaitaro qtd. in Goodman, p. 74.

30. Yamamoto Kiyokazu, "The World as Public Toilet," *Concerned Theatre Japan* 1, 2 (Summer 1970), p. 216.

31. Goodman, pp. 168–73.

32. Ibid., p. 280.

33. Ibid.

34. Stephen Heath, "Anata mo," *Screen* 17, 4 (Winter 1976/7), pp. 56–57.

35. Burch, p. 334.

36. McDonald, 127–28. Emphasis added.

37. Heath, pp. 59–60.

38. Stephen Heath, "Narrative Space" in his *Questions of Cinema*, (Bloomington: Indiana University Press, 1981), p. 65.

39. Stephen Heath, "The Question Oshima," in *Questions of Cinema*, p. 150. This quote is also put to use by Dana Polan, "Politics as Process in Three Films by Nagisa Oshima," *Film Criticism* 8, 1 (Fall 1983), p. 38.

40. Heath, p. 150.

41. Polan, p. 39.

42. Burch, p. 342.

43. Ian Cameron, *Second Wave* (New York: Praeger, 1970), p. 81.

44. Ibid., p. 85.

45. Ian Cameron, "Nagisa Oshima Interview," *Movie* 17 (Winter 1969–70), p. 13.

46. Burch, p. 356.

47. I have unfortunately been unable to see this film. This information is taken from *Ato Shiata (Art Theatre)* 84: *Shura*. Also see Leiter, p. 413.

48. In the very same *Natsu matsuri naniwa kagami* referred to above (note 14), a real pool of water was used in the climactic murder scene at the end, with which the audience was much impressed.

49. Personal interview.

Chapter Seven

1. Ellis S. Krauss, *Japanese Radicals Revisited: Student Protest in Postwar Japan* (Berkeley: University of California Press, 1974), p. 2.

2. Omori Shigeo, "June 1970," *Japan Quarterly* 17, 4 (Oct.-Dec. 1970), p. 385.

3. Krauss, p. 3.

4. Omori, p. 389.

5. Fukashiro Junro, "The New Left," *Japan Quarterly* 17, 1 (Jan.-Mar. 1970), p. 31. See also the discussion of Ogawa's Sanrizuka series in Ch. 5.

6. Quoted in Fukashiro, p. 33.

7. T.J. Pempel, *Patterns of Japanese Policymaking: Experiences from Higher Education* (Boulder: Westview Press, 1978), p. 115.

8. Ibid., p. 116.

9. Patricia G. Steinhoff, "Student Conflict," in *Conflict in Japan*, Ellis S. Krauss, Thomas P. Rohlen, and Patricia G. Steinhoff, eds. (Honolulu: University of Hawaii Press, 1984), p. 175.

10. Steinhoff, p. 176.

11. Personal interview with Oshima Nagisa, 7 July 1984, Tokyo.

12. The American release print overemphasizes some of these traits in that, shortened by some thirty minutes, the choppiness of the film is more apparent than real.

13. Noel Burch, *To the Distant Observer* (Berkeley: University of California Press, 1979), p. 341.

14. Maureen Turim and John Mowitt, "Thrity Seconds Over . . . Oshima's The War of Tokyo or The Young Man Who Left His Will on Film," *Wide Angle* 1, 4 (1977), p. 38.

15. Ibid., p. 36.

16. Burch, p. 341.

17. Quoted in Keiko McDonald, "How to Read Oshima's *The Man Who Left His Will on Film*," Paper presented at the Association for Asian Studies Convention, Washington, D.C., March 23–25, 1984.

18. Keiko McDonald, *Cinema East* (East Brunswick, N.J.: Associated University Presses, 1983), p. 171.

19. Burch, p. 348.

20. McDonald, *Cinema East*, p. 173.

21. Burch, p. 349.

22. McDonald, *Cinema East*, p. 195.

23. Burch, p. 348.

24. Personal interview with Yoshida Yoshishige, 22 June 1984, Tokyo.

25. Thomas A. Stanley, *Osugi Sakae, Anarchist in Taisho Japan: The Creativity of the Ego* (Cambridge Mass.: Harvard University Press, 1982), pp. 92–93.

26. Sharon L. Sievers, *Flowers in Salt: The Beginnings of Feminist Consciousness in Modern Japan* (Stanford: Stanford University Press, 1983), p. 168.

27. Ibid., p. 177.

28. Ibid., p. 180.

29. Ibid., p. 181–82.
30. Stanley, p. 93.
31. Ibid., p. 189, note 14. See also Sievers, pp. 183–84.
32. McDonald, *Cinema East*, p. 198.
33. Sievers, p. 172, note 2.
34. Stanley, p. 110.
35. Sievers, p. 186.
36. McDonald, *Cinema East*, p. 175.
37. Stanley, p. 169.
38. Tatsuo Arima, *The Failure of Freedom: A Portrait of Modern Japanese Intellectuals* (Cambridge, Mass.: Harvard University Press, 1969), p. 62.
39. Stanley, p. 170.
40. Arima, pp. 63–64.
41. Stanley, p. 96.
42. Quoted in McDonald, *Cinema East*, p. 182. A slight variation on this speech of Osugi's delivered to Itsuko may be found in Tadao Sato, *Currents in Japanese Cinema*, trans. Gregory Barrett (Tokyo: Kodansha, 1982), p. 95.
43. Arima, p. 60.
44. Ibid., p. 65.

New Wave Filmography

The Japanese title is followed by the release date in Japan, followed by either the release title (RT) or the translation title (TT); where a release title has not entered into general knowledge, both titles are given. This information is followed by black and white (b&w) or color; if the film was originally shot in CinemaScope, I have so indicated; if there is no indication, then no anamorphic process was used.

This filmography was compiled from a variety of sources (and is not necessarily complete; it reflects titles mentioned in the preceding chapters). Among the sources used to secure Japanese titles, release titles, and information on cinematography and aspect ratio were: Audie Bock, *Japanese Film Directors* and Max Tessier, *Le cinéma japonais au present* (complete citations for these sources may be found in the bibliography).

Adachi Masao
Seiyugi (1968) TT: *Sexual Play*, b&w, CinemaScope

Hani Susumu
"Kyoshitsu no Kodomotachi" (1954) TT: "Children in the Classroom"
"E o kaku kodomotachi" (1956) TT: "Children Who Draw"
Furyo shonen (1960) RT: *Bad Boys*, b&w
Mitasareta seikatsu (1962) RT: *A Full Life*, b&w, CinemaScope
Kanojo to kare (1963) RT: *She and He*, b&w
Bwana Toshi no uta (1965) *The Song of Bwana Toshi*
Andes no hanayome (1966) *Bride of the Andes*
Hatsukoi jigokuhen (1968) RT: *Nanami*; TT: *The Inferno of First Love*, b&w

Imamura Shohei
Nusumareta yokujo (1958) TT: *Stolen Desire*, b&w, CinemaScope
Nishi ginza eki-mae (1958) TT: *Nishi Ginza Station*, b&w, CinemaScope
Hateshi naki yokubo (1958) TT: *Endless Desire*, b&w, CinemaScope
Nianchan (1959) RT: *The Diary of Sueko*; TT: *My Second Brother*, b&w, CinemaScope
Buta to gunkan (1961) RT: *Pigs and Battleships*, b&w, CinemaScope
Nippon konchuki (1963) RT: *The Insect Woman*, b&w, CinemaScope
Akai satsui (1964) RT: *Unholy Desire*; TT: *Intensions of Murder*, b&w, scope
Jinruigaku nyumon (1966) RT: *The Pornographers*, b&w, CinemaScope
Ningen johatsu (1967) RT: *A Man Vanishes*, b&w
Kamigami no fukaki yokubo (1968) RT: *Kuragejima: Tales from a Southern Island*; TT: *The Profound Desire of the Gods*, color, CinemaScope
Nihon sengo-shi: Madamu onboro no seikatsu (1971) RT: *History of Postwar Japan as Told by a Bar Hostess*, b&w
Karayuki-san (1975), color
Fukushu suru wa ware ni ari (1979): RT: *Vengeance is Mine*, color
Eijanaika (1980), color
Narayama bushi-ko (1983): RT: *The Ballad of Narayama*, color

Kurahara Koreyoshi
Kyonetsu no kisetsu (1960) TT: *Crazy Season*

Masumura Yasuzo
Kuchizuke (1957) TT: *Kisses*, black and white

Donryu (1957) TT: *Warm Current*, black and white
Kyojin to gangu (1958) TT: *Giants and Toys*, black and white
Shisei (1966) RT: *Tattoo*
Akai tenshi (1966) TT: *Red Angel*, b&w, CinemaScope

Matsumoto Toshio
Bara no soretsu (1969) RT: *Funeral of Roses*
Shura (1971) RT: *Pandemonium*

Ogawa Shinsuke
"Seinen no umi" (1966) "Sea of Youth"
Assatsu no mori (1967) RT: *The Oppressed Students*; TT: *Forest of Pressure*
Gennin hokokusho (1967) RT: *Report from Hanedan*; TT: *Eyewitness Report*
"The Sanrizuka Series":
   Nihon kaiho sensen—Sanrizuka (1968; 1970) RT: *Japan Liberation Front—Summer in Sanrizuka; Winter in Sanrizuka*
   Daisanji kyosei sokuryo soshi toso (1970) RT: *The Three-Day War in Narita*; TT: *The Third Struggle Against Forced Surveying*
   Daini toride no hitobito (1971) RT: *Peasants of the Second Fortress*
   Iwayama ni tetsuto ga dekita (1972) RT: *The Building of Iwayama Tower*
   Heta Buraku (1973) RT: *Heta Village*
Dokkoi ningen bushi (1974) RT: *A Song of Common Humanity*, b&w
Nippon-koku: Furuyashiki-mura (1982) RT: *A Japanese Village: Furuyashiki-mura*, color

Oshima Nagisa
Ai to kibo no machi (1959) TT: *A Town of Love and Hope*, b&w, CinemaScope
Seishun zankoku monogatari (1960) RT: *Cruel Story of Youth*, color, CinemaScope
Taiyo no hakaba (1960) RT: *The Sun's Burial*, color, CinemaScope
Nihon no yoru to kiri (1960) RT: *Night and Fog in Japan*, color, CinemaScope
Shiiku (1961) RT: *The Catch*, b&w, CinemaScope
"Yunbogi no nikki" (1965) "Diary of Yunbogi Boy," b&w
Etsuraku (1965) RT: *Pleasures of the Flesh*, color, CinemaScope
Hakuchu no torima (1966) RT: *Violence at Noon*, color, CinemaScope
Muri shinju nihon no natsu (1967) TT: *Japanese Summer: Double Suicide*, color, Cinema-Scope
Nihon shunka-ko (1967) RT: *A Treatise on Japanese Bawdy Song*, color, CinemaScope
Kaette kita yoppari (1968) RT: *Three Resurrected Drunkards*, color, CinemaScope
Koshikei (1968) RT: *Death by Hanging*, b&w
Shinjuku dorobo nikki (1969) RT: *Diary of a Shinjuku Thief*, b&w
Shonen (1969) RT: *Boy*, color
Tokyo senso sengo hiwa (1970) RT: *The Man Who Left His Will on Film*, b&w
Gishiki (1971) RT: *The Ceremony*, b&w, CinemaScope
Natsu no imoto (1972) RT: *Dear Summer Sister*, color
Ai no koriida (1976) RT: *The Realm of the Senses*, color

Shindo Kaneto
Onibaba (1966) b&w, CinemaScope
Honno (1966) RT: *Lost Sex*, b&w, CinemaScope
Kuroneko (1968), b&w, CinemaScope

Shinoda Masahiro
Koi no katamichi kippu (1960) TT: *One-Way Ticket for Love*
Kawaita mizuumi (1960) RT: *Youth in Fury*; TT: *Dry Lake*, color, CinemaScope

Yuhi ni akai ore no kao (1961) TT: *My Face Red in the Sunset,* color, CinemaScope
Shamisen to otobai (1961) TT: *Shamisen and Motorcycle*
Namida o shishi no tategami ni (1962) TT: *Tears on the Lion's Mane*
Watakushi-tachi no kekkon (1962) TT: *Our Marriage*
Kawaita hana (1963) RT: *Pale Flower,* b&w, CinemaScope
Ansatsu (1964) RT: *Assassination,* b&w, CinemaScope
Utsukushisa to kanashimi to (1965) RT: *With Beauty and Sorrow,* color, CinemaScope
Shokei no shima (1966) RT: *Captive's Island,* TT: *Punishment Island,* color, CinemaScope
Sarutobi (1967) RT: *Samurai Spy,* b&w
Akanegumo (1967) RT: *Clouds at Sunset,* color, CinemaScope
Shinju ten no Amijima (1969) RT: *Double Suicide,* b&w
Buraikan (1970) RT: *The Scandalous Adventures of Buraikan,* color, CinemaScope
Chinmoku (1971) RT: *Silence,* color
Himiko (1974), b&w
Sakura no mori no mankai no shita (1975) RT: *Under the Cherry Blossoms,* color
Hanare goze orin (1977) RT: *Melody in Grey,* TT: *Blind Orin,* color
Yashagaike (1979) RT: *Demon Pond,* color
Setouchi shonen Yakudan (1984) RT: *MacArthur's Children,* color

Suzuki Seijun
Kanto mushuku (1963) TT: *Kanto Wanderer,* color, CinemaScope
Nikutai no mon (1964) RT: *Gate of Flesh,* color, CinemaScope
Shunpu den (1965) RT: *Joy Girls,* b&w, CinemaScope
Irezumi ichidai (1965) TT: *The Life of Tattoo,* color, CinemaScope
Kenka ereji (1966) RT: *The Born Fighter;* TT: *Elegy to Violence,* b&w, CinemaScope
Tokyo nagaremono (1966) TT: *Tokyo Drifter,* color, CinemaScope

Takahashi Osamu
Kanojo dake ga shitte iru (1960) TT: *Only She Knows*
Shisha to no kekkon (1960) TT: *Marriage with the Dead*

Tamura Tsutomu
Akunin shigan (1960) TT: *Volunteering for Villainy*

Teshigahari Hiroshi
Otoshiana (1962) RT: *Pitfall,* b&w
Suna no onna (1963) RT: *Woman in the Dunes,* b&w
Tanin no kao (1966) RT: *The Face of Another,* b&w
Moetsukita chizu (1968) RT: *The Ruined Map,* b&w
Summer Soldiers (1972)

Tsuchimoto Noriaki
Paruchizan Zenshi (1969) TT: *Pre-history of the Partisan Party,* b&w
Minamata: kanja-sans to sono sekai (1972) RT: *Minamata: The Victims and Their World,*
    b&w

Wakamatsu Koji
Kabe no naka no himegoto (1965) RT: *Secret Act Inside Walls,* b&w, CinemaScope
Taiji ga mitsuryo suru toki (1966) RT: *The Embryo Hunts in Secret,* b&w, CinemaScope
Okasareta byakui (1967) RT: *Violated Angels;* TT: *Violated Women in White,* b&w,
    CinemaScope
Yuke, yuke nidome no shojo (1969) TT: *Go, Go You Who Are A Virgin for the Second Time,*
    b&w, CinemaScope

Sekusu-Jakku (1970): RT: *Sex-Jack*
Tenshi no kokotsu (1970) RT: *Angelic Orgasm*, b&w, CinemaScope

Yoshida Yoshishinge
Rokudenashi (1960) TT: *Good-for-Nothing*, color, CinemaScope
Chi wa kawaite iru (1960) TT: *Blood is Dry*, color, CinemaScope
Amai yoru no hate (1962) TT: *Bitter End of a Sweet Night*, color, CinemaScope
Akitsu onsen (1962) TT: *Akitsu Springs*, color, CinemaScope
Arashi o yobu juhachinin (1963) RT: *18 Roughs*; TT: *18 Who Stir Up a Storm*, b&w,
   CinemaScope
Nihon dasshutsu (1964) TT: *Escape from Japan*, b&w, CinemaScope
Mizu de kakareta monogatari (1965) TT: *A Story Written with Water*, b&w, CinemaScope
Onna no mizuumi (1966) RT: *Woman of the Lake*, b&w
Joen (1967) RT: The Affair, TT: *Flame of Feelings*, b&w, CinemaScope
Honoo to onna (1967) RT: *Impasse*, TT: *Flame and Women*, b&w, CinemaScope
Juhyo no yorumeki (1968) RT: *Affair in the Snow*, b&w, CinemaScope
Saraba natsu no hikari (1968) TT: *Farewell to the Summer Light*, b&w, CinemaScope
Eros purasu gyakusatsu (1969) RT: *Eros plus Massacre*, b&w, CinemaScope
Rengoku eroica (1970) TT: *Heroic Purgatory*
Kokuhakuteki joyu-ron (1971) TT: *Confessions among Actresses*, b&w, CinemaScope
Kaigenrei (1973) RT: *Coup d'etat*, TT: *Martial Law*, b&w

Bibliography

Abe Kobo. *The Face of Another*. Trans. E. Dale Saunders. New York: Alfred A. Knopf, 1966.

——. *The Ruined Map*. Trans. E. Dale Saunders. New York: Alfred A. Knopf, 1969.

Anderson, Jospeh L., and Donald Richie. *The Japanese Film: Art and Industry*. Expanded edition. Princeton: Princeton University Press, 1982.

Andrew, J. Dudley, and Paul Andrew. *Kenji Mizoguchi: A Guide to References and Resources*. Boston: G.K. Hall, 1981.

Apter, David E., and Nagayo Sawa. *Against the State: Politics and Social Protest in Japan*. Cambridge, Mass.: Harvard University Press, 1984.

Arima, Tatsuo. *The Failure of Freedom: A Portrait of Modern Japanese Intellectuals*. Cambridge, Mass.: Harvard University Press, 1969.

Armes, Roy. *The Ambiguous Image: Narrative Style in Modern European Cinema*. Bloomington. Ind.: Indiana University Press, 1976.

Arnott, Peter. *The Theatres of Japan*. New York: St. Martin's Press, 1969.

Ato Shiata [Art Theatre] 84: Shura.

Ato Shiata 93: Tenshi no kokotsu.

Bock, Audie. *Japanese Film Directors*. Tokyo: Kodansha, 1978.

Bordwell, David. *Narrative in the Fiction Film*. Madison: University of Wisconsin Press, 1985.

——. Rev. of *To the Distant Observer* by Noel Burch. *Wide Angle* 3. 4(1980): 70–73.

——and Kristin Thompson. *Film Art: An Introduction*. Reading, Mass.: Addison-Wesley, 1979.

Branigan, Edward. "Subjectivity under Seige—From Fellini's *8 1/2* to Oshima's *The Story of a Man Who Left His Will on Film*." *Screen* 19. 1 (Spring 1978): 7–40.

Burch, Noel. "Nagisa Oshima and Japanese Cinema in the 60s." *Cinema: A Critical Dictionary*. Ed. Richard Roud. 2 vols. London: Martin Secker and Warburg, 1980. 735–741.

——. *To the Distant Observer: Form and Meaning in the Japanese Cinema*. Berkeley: University of California Press, 1979.

Buruma, Ian. *Behind the Mask: On Sexual Demons, Sacred Mothers, Transvestites, Gangsters, Drifters and Other Japanese Cultural Heroes*. New York: Pantheon, 1984.

Cameron, Ian. "Nagisa Oshima Interview." *Movie* 17 (Winter 1969–70): 7–15.

——. *Second Wave*. New York: Praeger, 1970.

Casebier, Allan. "Images of Irrationality in Modern Japan: The Films of Shohei Imamura." *Film Criticism* 8. 1 (Fall 1983): 42–49.

Danly, Robert Lyons. *In the Shade of Spring Leaves: The Life and Writings of Higuchi Ichiyo, A Woman of Letters in Meiji Japan*. New Haven: Yale University Press, 1981.

Desser, David. *The Samurai Films of Akira Kurosawa*. Ann Arbor: UMI Research Press, 1983.

Durgnat, Raymond. *Sexual Alienation in the Cinema*. London: Studio Vista, 1972.

Eiga shijo besto 200 shirizu: Nihon eiga (Great Films of the World/Japan) Tokyo: Kinema Jumpo, 1982.

Fukashiro, Junro. "The New Left." *Japan Quarterly* 17. 1 (Jan.-Mar. 1970): 27–36.

Goodman, David G. "Preliminary Thoughts on Political Theatre." *Concerned Theatre Japan* 2. 3&4 (Spring 1973): 26–111.

——. "Satoh Makoto and the Post-Shingeki Movement in Japanese Contemporary Theatre." Dissertation, Cornell University, 1982.

Goodman, Kazuko Fujimoto. "Discrimination and the Perception of Difference." *Concerned Theatre Japan* 2. 3&4. (Spring 1973): 112–151.

Hane, Mikiso. *Peasants, Rebels, and Outcastes: The Underside of Modern Japan.* New York: Pantheon, 1982.

Harvey, Sylvia. *May '68 and Film Culture.* London: BFI, 1980.

Heath, Stephen. "Anato mo." *Screen* 17. 4 (Winter 1976/7): 49–66.

———. *Questions of Cinema.* Bloomington, Ind.: Indiana University Press, 1981.

Henderson, Brian. *A Critique of Film Theory.* New York: E.P. Dutton, 1980.

Hibbett, Howard S., ed. *Contemporary Japanese Literature: An Anthology of Fiction, Film, and Other Writings Since 1945.* New York: Knopf, 1977.

High, Peter B. "Oshima: A Vita Sexualis on Film." *Wide Angle* 2. 4 (1978): 62–71.

Hirosue, Tamotsu. "The Secret Place of Evil." *Concerned Theatre Japan* 2. 1&2 (1971): 14–21.

Imamura Shohei no eiga. [The Films of Imamura Shohei]. Tokyo: Koga Shoten, 1971.

Kawabata Yasunari. *Beauty and Sadness.* Trans. Howard Hibbett. New York: Alfred A. Knopf, 1975.

Kehr, Dave. "The Last Rising Sun." *Film Comment* 19. 5 (Sept.-Oct. 1983): 32–40.

Kimball, Arthur G. *Crisis and Identity in Contemporary Japanese Novels.* Rutland, Vermont: Charles E. Tuttle, 1973.

Kirihara, Don. "Kabuki, Cinema and Mizoguchi Kenji." *Cinema and Language.* Eds. Stephen Heath and Patricia Mellencamp. Frederick, Md.: University Publications of America, 1983: 97–106.

Krauss, Ellis S. *Japanese Radicals Revisited: Student Protest in Postwar Japan.* Berkeley: University of California Press, 1974.

———. Thomas P. Rohlen and Patricia G. Steinhoff, eds. *Conflict in Japan.* Honolulu: University of Hawaii Press, 1984.

Kreidl, John Francis. *Alain Resnais.* Boston: Twayne, 1977.

Leiter, Samuel L. *Kabuki Encyclopedia.* Westport, Conn.: Greenwood Press, 1979.

Major Plays of Chikamatsu. Trans. Donald Keene. New York: Columbia University Press, 1961.

Malcomson, Scott L. "The Pure Land Beyond the Sea—Barthes, Burch and the Uses of Japan. *Screen* 26. 3–4 (May-August 1985): 23–33.

McDonald, Keiko I. *Cinema East: A Critical Study of Major Japanese Films.* East Brunswick, N.J.: Associated University Presses, 1983.

———. "How to Read Oshima's *The Man Who Left His Will on Film.*" Association for Asian Studies Convention. Washington, D.C., Mar. 23–25, 1984.

———. "Kinji Fukasaku: An Introduction." *Film Criticism* 8. 1 (Fall 1983): 20–32.

———. *Mizoguchi.* Boston: Twayne, 1984.

Mellen, Joan. *Voices from the Japanese Cinema.* New York: Liveright, 1975.

———. *The Waves at Genji's Door: Japan Through Its Cinema.* New York: Pantheon, 1976.

Miyoshi, Masao. *Accomplices of Silence: The Modern Japanese Novel.* Berkeley: University of California Press, 1975.

Monaco, James. *Alain Resnais.* New York: Oxford University Press, 1979.

Omori, Shigeo. "June 1970." *Japan Quarterly* 17. 4 (Oct.-Dec. 1970): 383–392.

Packard, George W., III. *Protest in Tokyo: The Security Treaty Crisis of 1960.* Princeton: Princeton University Press, 1966.

Pempel, T.J. *Patterns of Japanese Policymaking: Experiences from Higher Education.* Boulder: Westview Press, 1978.

Petersen, Gwenn Boardman. *The Moon in the Water: Understanding Tanizaki, Kawabata, and Mishima.* Honolulu: University of Hawaii Press, 1979.

Poggioli, Renato. *The Theory of the Avant-Garde.* Trans. Gerald Fitzgerald. Cambridge, Mass.: Harvard University Press, 1968.

Polan, Dana B. *The Political Language of Film and the Avant-Garde.* Ann Arbor: UMI Research Press, 1985.
———. "Politics as Process in Three Films by Nagisa Oshima." *Film Criticism* 8. 1 (Fall 1983): 33–41.
Richie, Donald. *Japanese Cinema: Film Style and National Character.* Garden City, N.Y.: Anchor Books, 1971.
———. *The Japanese Movie.* Rev. ed. Tokyo: Kodansha, 1982.
Sato, Tadao. *Currents in Japanese Cinema.* Trans. Gregory Barrett. Tokyo: Kodansha, 1982.
———. *Nuberu bagu igo: jiyu o mezasu eiga* [*After the nouvelle vague: Films for Freedom*]. Tokyo: Chuo Koron, 1976.
———. *Oshima Nagisa no sekai* [*The World of Oshima Nagisa*]. Tokyo: Tsukuma Shobo, 1973.
Sekai no eiga sakka 6: Oshima Nagisa [*Film Directors of the World*]. Tokyo: Kinema Jumpo, 1970.
Sekai no eiga sakka 10: Shinoda Masahiro, Yoshida Yoshishige. Tokyo: Kinema Jumpo, 1971.
Sekai no eiga sakka 31: Nihon eiga-shi [*Film Directors of the World: History of Japanese Film*]. Tokyo: Kinema Jumpo, 1976.
Shillony, Ben-Ami. *Revolt in Japan: The Young Officers and the February 26, 1936 Incident.* Princeton: Princeton University Press, 1973.
Sievers, Sharon L. *Flowers in Salt: The Beginnings of Feminist Consciousness in Modern Japan.* Stanford: Stanford University Press, 1983.
The 60s Without Apology. Ed. Sonnya Sayres, et al. Minneapolis: University of Minnesota Press, 1984.
Smith, Henry DeWitt, II. *Japan's First Student Radicals.* Cambridge, Mass.: Harvard University Press, 1972.
Sorgenfrei, Carol Jay. "Shuji Terayama: Avant Garde Dramatist of Japan." Dissertation, University of California, Santa Barbara, 1978.
Stam, Robert. *Reflexivity in Film and Literature: From Don Quixote to Jean-Luc Godard.* Ann Arbor: University Microfilms International Research Press, 1985.
Stanley, Thomas A. *Osugi Sakae Anarchist in Taisho Japan: The Creativity of the Ego.* Cambridge, Mass.: Harvard University Press, 1982.
Sweet, Freddy. *The Film Narratives of Alain Resnais.* Ann Arbor: UMI Research Press, 1981.
Tessier, Max, ed. *Le cinema japonais au present.* Paris: Lherminier, 1984.
———. *Images du cinema japonais.* Paris: Henri Veyrier, 1981.
Thompson, Kristin, and David Bordwell. "Space and Narrative in the Films of Ozu." *Screen* 17. 2 (Summer 1976): 41–73.
Tsuno Kaitaro. "Biwa and Beatles: An Invitation to Modern Japanese Theatre." *Concerned Theatre Japan* Special Introductory Issue (Oct. 1969): 6–32.
———. "Poor European Theatre." *Concerned Theatre Japan* 2. 3&4. (Spring 1973): 1–25.
Tsurumi, Kazuko. "Student Movements in 1960 and 1969: Continuity and Change." *Postwar Trends in Japan.* Ed. Shunichi Takayanagi and Kimitada Miwa. Tokyo: University of Tokyo Press, 1975.
Tucker, Richard N. *Japan: Film Image.* London: Studio Vista, 1973.
Turim, Maureen, and John Mowitt. "Thirty Seconds Over . . . Oshima's The War of Tokyo or The Young Man Who Left His Will on Film." *Wide Angle* 1. 4 (1977): 34–43.
Willemen, Paul. "Notes on Subjectivity: On Reading Edward Branigan's 'Subjectivity Under Siege.' " *Screen* 19. 1 (Spring 1978): 41–69.

Yamamoto Kiyokazu. "The World as Public Toilet." *Concerned Theatre Japan* 1. 2 (Summer 1970): 214–219.

Yamanouchi, Hisaaki. "Abe Kobo and Oe Kenzaburo: The Search for Identity in Contemporary Japanese Literature." *Modern Japan: Aspects of History, Literature and Society.* Ed. W.G. Beasley. Berkeley: University of California Press, 1975: 166–184.

Yoshida, Sanroku. "Kenzaburo Oe: A New World of Imagination." *Comparative Literature Studies* 22. 1 (Spring 1985): 80–96.

Personal Interviews in Tokyo, Japan, 1984:
Yoshida Yoshishige, 22 June.
Ogawa Shinsuke, 23 June.
Oshima Nagisa, 7 July.
Tsuchimoto Noriaki, 9 July.
Shinoda Masahiro, 24 July.
Kinoshita Keisuke, 26 July.

Index